DOWN FROM LONDON
By
Alison Dilnutt

With special thanks to: Victoria Falkoner, Sarah Horner, Neil Lawson, Steve Allen, Julia Clark, Bekka Kill, Nick Copland, Richard Waller, Elizabeth Waller, Victoria Falconer, Mark Field, Philippa Sarll, Julia Sewell, Emma Epton, Chris Conway, Em Peasgood, Tony Rix, Chris Stone, Michelle Newbold, Kate and Ricky Neame, Sharon Tucker Rogers, Charlotte Raymond-Barker, Nick Stroud, Diana Lewis, Sam Orrell-Scott, Ian Harris, Sam Jones, Alex Jackson, Helen Mills, Sheline Gledhill, Natasha Andrews, Liz Dilnutt and Andy Capon for helping with research, beta reading, editing, misbehaving in the blog, insulting C.K. Blaine and supporting me through the whole process. Huge thank you to Peter at Bespoke Book Covers http://bespokebookcovers.com/ for totally nailing it and giving me the iconic cover that perfectly fitted my story. Extra special thanks to my parents, John and Pam King for their continued encouragement. Lastly, heartfelt thanks to Marc, for telling me all along I could get away with it, but mainly for wearing the beard.

Chapter 1

Flood

Easter 2014

A more talented writer, or perhaps a better man wouldn't have needed to do it, but I had. Back then, two decades ago, the temptation had seemed too much to resist. I needed an idea for a script and I didn't care where it came from - so I stole it. Now, as I sat alone, staring glumly at the semi-circle of empty chairs before me, I was acutely aware that I might finally be made to admit my dishonesty.

As I waited for the first horribly eager adult learners to arrive, my apprehension was growing and I began to perspire slightly. I tugged at the stiff shirt collar I was unused to wearing and wished I could grab my coat and make a run for it. Instead, I stayed put, nervously grinding my teeth.

The grim, florescent light of the local Community Arts Centre gave the location a depressing Church Hall pallor, rendering it akin to the gritty *mise-en-scène* of a social-realist drama. If this were a film, it would have been an ideal setting for scene featuring an emotional Alcoholics Anonymous meeting, or, maybe, a tense prison group-therapy session.

I sipped a tepid cup of coffee, needing the caffeine and indulged myself a deep sigh. This new reality couldn't be further from my exciting old life in London. I sorely regretted that I had programmed the screenwriting course at all and felt the pull of a local pub.

If this *had* been some sort of addicts' meeting, I was ready to come clean; to admit I was powerless to resist my pathological aversion to the truth. That I, C.K.Blaine was a compulsive liar and a fraud. But even if my ideal support group, 'Mythomanics Anon' had existed, I'd probably even lie when it was my turn to 'share' as well.

Tonight, after twenty years, I was likely to finally get caught out. And I'd brought it all upon myself.

I could recall the crucial conversation that I had overheard; the idle chitchat that presented a tantalising solution to my problem, just like it was yesterday. It was the summer solstice 1995 and I had come to Whitstable, under mounting pressure to produce a screenplay about rave culture, hoping the sea air would shift my thinking.

All that shifted was my backside from one bar stool to another.

In one particularly salubrious boozer, two ruddy cheeked, rough women next to me had begun to gossip about the short, ferret faced young chef who had emerged from the kitchen and darted through the pub to the front exit.

'Jason Jenkins,' said the first woman hoarsely, curling her lip.

'Murderer,' growled her friend.

'Burned his old mum alive in her own home,' said the first.

My ears had pricked up.

'Too out of his head to even realise,' her friend said. 'Never been proved, mind. But he did it.'

Now, part of me wished I had just finished my pint and that would have been that. I'd have skulked back to London, to my boring job as a copywriter for a Soho advertising agency, where I would have idled my years away, day dreaming about writing a script that would become a cult film to make me rich and famous. But instead, hungry for a story, I'd abandoned my beer and ran out of the pub, catching a glimpse of the puny young man as he scurried along in a peculiar gait, disappearing towards the park.

From there, I followed him until dawn, going from gaudy pub to decrepit club, to filthy squat to drug fuelled party, to the apocalyptic sunrise on the beach. That night, I was taken on the most debauched and horrifically warped adventure of my life and all the while I was observing him, weighing up whether he could have burned his own mother alive.

From what I saw that night, what I witnessed, I was convinced he was capable.

I had my story.

Jason's alleged matricide and his nihilistic antics that night turned into a script and I took it to market. To my shock and delight, it attracted a producer who said it had legs. My screenplay, *Burn*, got handed back and forth from editor, to producer, to the broadcaster financing the project, who all inevitably wanted changes. Gradually, the original morphed into something different, unrecognisable and the real Jason Jenkins on that night in '95 seemed to disintegrate. His anonymity, and with it, the concealment of my dishonesty, I hoped, was assured. The film got made, but I carried the personal shame of knowing the provenance of the story.

I'd won a Bafta and rode the wave of instant fame and recognition and ended up here in 'Islington by the Sea', literally, beached. Five years ago, I'd moved the family out of London in the hope that Whitstable would once again provide inspiration, but so far, nothing. In the intervening years, I had barely written a shopping list. As a result, I talked a lot about writing instead of actually doing it, earning what my wife called 'irony money' as a painter and decorator. But the dream persisted. The day job provided me with ample time to ruminate and fantasise about a second bite of the cherry.

What was missing, rather crucially, was an idea.

A year ago, I'd got drunk and alluded to my wife about my writer's block. Pippa was terse. Write a blog, she said. But a blog about what? How I libellously hijacked an unsubstantiated rumour and turned it into a bad script that got altered out of all recognition for which I took the credit? No.

Now, time had run out. I had less than no money. It had all gone and I'd lied so Pippa didn't know. Thankfully, her job at a regional marketing company had sustained us, but she'd starting to make ultimatums about me finally getting a

3

'proper grown up job' and use the degree I got all those years ago.

I'd started to avoid going home. I drifted from pub to pub and had unwittingly become a local 'character'. I sat swaying, inebriated at the bar, hour after hour with other disillusioned ex-Londoners. The vitriolic locals had named us 'down from London's' or D.F.L.'s for short, once the exodus had started. I let the cheeky builders, nut cases and local faces have the craic at my expense, hoping they would be accepting, all the while avoiding the reality that was me.

To dodge confronting my immediate situation, I'd created elaborate fantasies about the future, where again I achieved international acclaim and unimaginable riches, where I was famous, desired by beautiful women and respected. But all too often, the fantasies turned sour. My underlying anxiety, like the background hum of a dysfunctional fridge freezer, started to throw in questions: 'But what if you never have another idea?', 'But what if you have an idea, but you can't write anymore?' and the most terrifying, 'But what if you write another screenplay and *nobody wants it*?'

I was back right where I was in '95 but worse. Skint, desperate for creative vision, for recognition and financial reward, but now saddled with a house, two teenage daughters and a wife that liked shoes a little too much.

So, there I sat in the dismal room at the Arts Centre, the deep anxiety tightening in my chest, reminding me that I had no business running a screenwriting course, despite being the Bafta award-winning screenwriter of *Burn*, the UK's most successful home-grown film of 1997.

The course had come together as another tactic to delay getting a proper job and to get Pippa off my back. To be fair, she had put up with a lot. I'd misled her about our wealth, what work I'd had as a result of *Burn* and my lack of application. She had been supportive for longer than any reasonable person could have been expected. I suspected she

4

was too ashamed to let any cracks show in our outwardly perfect life by the seaside.

As the enthusiastic, naïve looking students nervously filtered in, I drained the cold coffee and began my performance. I reflected soberly, that tonight, it might be me actually learning something from them.

****

Relieved the first session was over and I hadn't been exposed as a fraud, I began slowly stacking chairs. I needn't have worried after all. Nice enough as the students were, there was no one there who might have uncovered my blatant lack of expertise. None of them suspected that I'd based my film on a local boy some might even have known or been related to.

Just then, as my thoughts returned to that pint, I noticed Joanne, the only female student, lingering at the door. I felt a sudden petulant fury and took it out on the seating, ramming each chair into the stack with unnecessary but satisfying force. I was not in the mood to give any more of my night to personal mentoring.

Joanne Kemp's was the only notable piece of writing. She was a rather flat, middle aged drudge who seemed totally out of place on the course – better suited to a night at the Bingo, quite frankly. But miraculously, she had invented a colourful letter writer called Minerva Frend. Just sixteen when she wrote her first letter in 1940, we found out immediately that Minerva, or Minnie as she was known, was in love with a roguish local fisherman called Robert Rowden. It was bold, sexy, toe curlingly honest. Joanne's historical detail was immaculate, as was the language for that era. Yet there was something not right about it that I struggled to identify beyond my ability to be convinced that Joanne had actually written it.

During our one-to-one feedback, Joanne had become quickly defensive when I questioned what she planned to happen in the narrative arc of the story, but by that point in the evening, I couldn't be bothered. The pub beckoned again.

I'd wrapped the session up after that and thanked everyone for coming, handing out assignments for the following week. I'd felt slightly depressed that I'd quite enjoyed it.

I ignored Joanne's lurking presence for as long as possible. Eventually she started to tiptoe into the room.

'Hi, forgotten something?' I said with as little animosity as I could manage. Joanne approached and handed me the tatty sack she'd had been clutching all night. 'What's this?' I said, peering inside. There were dozens of envelopes tied up into batches secured with faded ribbons, each with a musty yellow bulge and curiously perfect italic copperplate in the inconsistent blue-black ink of a fountain pen.

Joanne took a ragged deep breath. I could smell the cigarette smoke on her words. 'I want you to have these. I should never have taken them.'

'Ok, Joanne, that's pretty cryptic. What are they, and where did you take them from?' I was now feeling really irritable and could not get the anticipation of tasting a hoppy, golden beer out of my head.

'I took them today from the lady I work for. *Worked* for actually, because she's dead.'

She had got my attention.

'It's Minnie, Minerva from that letter I read out. I looked after her for the Council, her and three others. I've been doing her for two years.' I impatiently nodded at her to continue, no longer caring if my imaginary pint went flat. 'I arrived at tea time and found her dead with a note and this bag laying on her chest.'

Joanne was gabbling fast. I had forgotten how much I loved hearing about other people's moral failures.

6

'In the note, she told me to hand deliver all her old letters to her solicitor and another sealed letter to the local newspaper. She did herself in, the poor cow.' Joanne began to pant, so I pulled out two chairs and sat her down. 'She told me not to read the letters, but I'd already found them at the back of her wardrobe last night and, well, curiosity got the better. I took half of them home and read them, then snuck them back in there this morning.'

'Why would you do that?' I knew exactly why she would do that, because that was exactly what I'd have done.

She dipped her head. 'Minnie, well - there's been rumours about her for years. Everyone knew I was her carer. People are always asking me about her, about what I know. I suppose it made me feel important.' She rubbed her eyes and looked at me. 'I just wondered if the letters would shed any more light on what people said she had done.'

I nodded for her to go on, rubbing her shoulder in what I hoped she wouldn't think was a sexual way.

'You never heard of her? About what happened the night of the flood?' Joanne smiled, unpleasantly.

'Nope. Are the letters enlightening?' I wondered what it was Minnie was meant to have done. My gut instinct told me to avoid asking.

'Yes and no. They're confusing.'

'How come you didn't just take them to the solicitor on the way here?'

'The ambulance took forty-five minute to arrive. By the time they'd taken her away, the solicitor's was already shut. I remembered your course and I came straight here. I wasn't rational.' She was visibly still in shock. 'I'm ashamed to say, I read the other half of the letters on her front door step while I waited for the paramedics. The last one was written on the night before the great flood, in 1953. Just before she -' Joanne looked sheepishly up at me, like I could absolve her guilt. The look of a long lapsed Catholic. What on earth could have given Minnie such notoriety?

'Alright then, did you read the letter for the newspaper? If not, why not just take it there tomorrow? Only you and I know you've seen any of this.' I was now acutely curious about the archive and suspected there were some delicious revelations in the letter to the press, but didn't want to seem too keen.

'It's all very well reading letters that are open, but opening a sealed letter, it just seems wrong – and probably illegal.' Joanne picked up the candy striped pillowcase and dropped it onto my lap.

'Why do *I* have to have them?'

'Because it's *your* fault,' she said and looked at me with the familiar hostility that I seemed to bring out in the locals. 'I want nothing more to do with them. It seemed like a bit of harmless fun reading them when she was alive. You know, something to tell the girls at my slimming club on Friday. A bit of gossip. Now she's dead it's different. They're – dirty.'

'I don't get it, why my fault for God's sake?' I whined, hoping she wouldn't change her mind and take the letters to the lawyer herself.

'You made us bring three-hundred words of original writing. Well I hadn't done it, had I? I panicked. I copied Minnie's first letter and pretended it was mine. That was wrong. It was disrespectful. I'm only here because my best mate Jane made me sign up. She's always fancied herself as a writer but didn't want to come alone. She's a *divorcee*. She bloody bailed out on me and left me here by myself though, didn't she. She's probably off on a date.' She rolled her eyes then fixed me with a hard look. 'Those letters will only bring bad luck. I reckon Minnie knew I'd read some of them. For all I know, she cursed them. Now, I won't speak ill of the dead and I can't very well bin them, but I won't give them house room.' She stood and zipped up her jacket. 'They're your problem now. Just promise me you'll take her unopened letter to the paper tomorrow?'

8

I gave her an enthusiastic nod. 'Sure, of course. No problem, Joanne.'

'Right. I'm off home.'

She quickly walked out, visibly less tense, unburdened, seemingly relieved to be heading back to her ordinary life.

I dived into the bag and located the thick letter addressed to the local paper. I knew if I opened it, I could always anonymously deliver it and the much older, sepia letters to the lawyer, yet I still felt an unexpected and rare throb of shame. I enjoyed it for a moment; an unusual reminder that I wasn't completely devoid of ethics. Then it was dissolved by my impatience and I tore at the envelope with child-like expectation.

****

I let out a luxurious sigh of satisfaction as I folded the letter back up. I sat for a while and absorbed the facts. A slow smile crept across my face. From a separate part of the Community Arts Centre I could hear the distant voices of another evening class, the knitters perhaps, or Rachel, the pretty, but disappointed looking centre manager, preparing to lock up and go home.

My mind was racing. I had just read the truth about a murder. It had to be Whitstable's best kept secret and I was the only living person who knew.

No wonder Joanne found the letters confusing. They were only half the story. A fabrication. I wondered, for a moment, if anyone would care if I used Minnie's story. Joanne was an inconsequential woman who probably wouldn't know who to talk to, save her immediate family or the fatties at her slimming class. It could be done. The names wouldn't even have to be changed - it could legitimately be 'based on a true story'. Besides, who would question the creative licence of an established, international award-winning screenwriter?

I was the only one who knew what was in that letter intended for the local newspaper. What really happened in 1953 when the water broke the defences and crept into the town. My screenplay would be just another version of the truth, based on a fallacy, derived from a lie. Albeit a lie Minerva Rowden created to do good rather than harm. Dear Minnie, I thought, what a marvellously and devilishly cunning old bird you were!

I stuffed the letters into my Superdry bag, dragged on my Parka and headed out into the chilly dusk. Finally, it was time for that pint.

I headed to a back street pub near my fisherman's cottage. It was a locals' place; tiny and garishly decorated. There were florescent cards cut into awkward star shapes, blu-tacked to the bar advertising cheap food. A couple of women at the far end were enjoying a game of darts. As I well knew, locals didn't put up with crap beer, so I ordered a pint of bitter.

After a cursory scan of the local paper, in which I featured as a 'Whitstable Pearl' with my screenwriting class, I surreptitiously studied the men around the bar.

No one had taken any notice of me save for glancing over when I first came in. I recognised several of them and I knew they recognised me, but tonight, they were deliberately ignoring me. I felt uncomfortable, agitated. I regretted coming in, wanting instead to be at home reading Minnie's letters. I picked up the paper again and flicked impatiently through the property section, noting with uneasy pleasure that my cottage was now worth considerably more than I paid for it, despite the recession.

As I scanned the prices, I became aware of another presence emerging from the Gents, joining the men. I felt apprehensive about looking up. The hairs stood up on my arms. From my peripheral vision, I could see he was small, bald and looking my way. I turned to gaze out of the window catching a glimpse of the famous sunset lingering in the spring sky and in a panic, I sank the remainder of my pint in one.

Before I slipped out of the door, I couldn't resist the compulsion to glance momentarily at the man.

It was him.

I half ran to our cottage, convinced Jason Jenkins was following. Once inside, I found my heart was pounding. I hadn't seen him since I followed him all those years ago. I had assumed he was dead or in prison. But the compact, fierce man at the bar was very much alive and the stinging look I registered when our eyes met was one of recognition. And hatred.

I calmed down. The familiarity of my home soothed my panic. I felt the usual reluctance to find Pippa. Lately, I never knew what I was going to find, despite my new efforts to generate work.

I quietly entered the kitchen where she was drinking wine with her friend Julia. Our daughters and their friends were upstairs, thumping about and playing loud music. No wonder our neighbours despised us.

'Your turn,' she said, motioning towards the pandemonium above, barely acknowledging me.

'Nope, sorry,' I said, smiling broadly. 'I'm writing tonight.' She looked up, her face flushed and astonished. I wondered how much she'd had this time.

'I must go,' slurred Julia and left to drag her princesses away from their boy band karaoke.

'What are you writing?' Pippa asked, all sly eyes.

'A thriller,' I improvised, 'set in the town, leading up to the 1953 flood. Told you this place would inspire me.'

As I left, almost inaudibly, I heard her say, 'Only took twenty fucking years.' My face twisted because she knew I'd been a little lost, stuck. I felt I should fight back, but I couldn't wait to start reading Minnie's story. I ignored her.

As I bounded up to the tiny converted loft, I allowed myself to fantasise about it reaching the big screen, imagining Emma Watson playing young Minnie. I flicked on my computer and emptied out the packs of letters onto my desk.

It was then that Jason Jenkins' face flared up in my mind. Not his bloated, battered middle aged face, but the narrow, weasel face of Jason Jenkins then, that night. Wild, mad, furious. His eyes afire with the rush of insurgency. I knew seeing him again to be a portent - I hadn't yet paid the price for my first scam. Now I wondered if his re-emergence was a warning not to pull the same trick twice.

Then I thought of Emma again, wading through 1953 flood water, moist-eyed and pouted mouth and decided it was worth the risk.

I typed:

The Memory Floods (working title)

By C. K. Blaine.

Boom Shakalak! I was back.

Chapter 2

Jack

May 2014

Jason Jenkins leaned heavily into the buggy as the crowd came to a halting stumble on the steep slope to Whitstable Castle. Crushed in by other families following the May Day procession, with his two-year old granddaughter Aleisha asleep, he was hoping he could find a shady spot and have a nip from his hip flask, before she woke up. The procession had faltered and he was trapped, grateful he had the buggy to rest on like a Zimmer frame, shaking, sweat breaking out on his brow. Around him were other grandparents, but few he recognised. He thought about his town and how alien it was now. There had been a time when he couldn't walk from one end of the high street to the other without bumping into several members of his family, or more often, without having to duck into a convenient alley to avoid a tasty geezer he'd upset. Now he just saw a sea of strange faces. He looked at the elderly people dressed elegantly in white on the bowling green and almost laughed. He knew he'd be dead before he was old enough to want to join up. And he'd only do that if they had a cheap bar.

Aleisha stirred, awakened by the lack of motion and the cacophony of the Morris Men's bells and clacking sticks. Scores of other grumpy, hot children awoke unhappily from their naps, nearby. Jason felt conflicted. He loved the bones of her, but he needed a sup. He was beginning to really shake. He pushed ahead. Before him were just a bunch of D.F.L.s with their posh buggies and polka dot skirts. He was proper Whitstable, born and bred.

He pushed on, calling 'S'cuse, s'cuse me' as he nudged Aleisha's buggy at their ankles, through the crowd. Finally, at the top of the slope, the Morris Men were performing and Jack in the Green was stalking around the edge of the show. Jason thrust Aleisha through the perimeter of the audience just as Jack loomed, and she let out an ear-splitting scream. It had never occurred to Jason that a man dressed as a hedge would frighten her. He bared his crooked teeth at the hedge and unclipped the terrified infant from her seat. She clung to him like a baby monkey, burying her head in his collar and crying 'gone, gone Gandad'.

That's when Jason saw him again. The writer who called himself C.K. Blaine. Jason swerved deftly away from the scary man dressed as a tree and walked towards the writer. He was dressed in rolled up chinos, a Breton top and had tilted his straw trilby upwards. He stood, looking bored and distracted, next to a pretty girl who looked a young thirteen. Jason stopped directly in front of the man. If he'd been taller, he'd have blocked his view of the Morris dancers, blocked his view of anything else much, he was so close. It didn't matter, his presence had been acknowledged. Jason wasn't sure what he wanted this confrontation to achieve, but he knew they had shared a night that had changed both their lives. Blaine's had led to success and wealth, his to a life-sentence of failure, guilt and shame. He barely went an hour without replaying it. The catalogue of mistakes were on mental loop and only the heaviest drinking could assuage it.

Aleisha helped him with his quandary. 'Wee wee, Gandad,' she called into his ear. He locked eyes with Blaine. There was so much he wanted to know. But Aleisha was squeezing his sides with her heels like a brat on a piebald pony, so he walked swiftly away.

Jason Jenkins needed answers. Answers he'd waited twenty years to get. He'd seen, with deep satisfaction, the fear in the writer's eyes. He smiled and knew it could keep for now.

Jason abandoned the worn out buggy and pulled Aleisha into the dark interior of the Castle. It wasn't a real castle, but an old Manor house that had been owned and run by the local council for decades until it got a multi-million pound make-over just a few years before. Everything seemed so new and fresh, it made Jason uncomfortable.

He hurriedly helped Aleisha onto the toilet, trying not to think of the last time he had been in the building. That time he had hidden in there, on that night, back when it was a dusty rabbit warren of oppressive wooden panelling and threadbare municipal carpets. He looked at his hand, the scarring still clear, but now white. He couldn't remember how he'd got in, then he'd gone to sleep for a while, recovering, sobering, coming down. When he'd awoken, his hand was sliced, throbbing and covered in blood. As he had cleaned up his injury, the strong morning light had flooded the gloomy interior. He knew immediately, he had to get out. He'd wrapped his damaged limb in some rough green paper towels from the Gents and made a run for it. Then he'd headed for the one house where he knew he would be safe. To Tracy's house.

Jason took his granddaughter out into the light and strapped her back into the buggy. There was no sign of Blaine. He felt the usual sensation of sickness, the feeling of dread as the script of that night – with all the missing scenes that he had attempted to imagine over the years – re-ran for the millionth time in his head. And with it he felt the familiar, nauseating need to escape his thoughts, his mind, his lunacy and pretend none of it had ever happened.

****

His ex-wife, Tracy, was already at his home when he returned. She'd let herself in and had made a cup of tea. Jason hated that. He felt even more trapped now than he had when he had been married to her and that had been a long time ago.

'Did you have a nice time?' Tracy hugged Aleisha tight and smiled kindly at Jason. He looked away. Her inherent goodness always wounded him.

'She was scared of the Jack. It was too hot, she's tired. Too many D.F.L.s. It did my bloody head in.'

Tracy frowned, looking disappointed. She had told him to take the baby to the Castle. She still told him what to do. She would always have power over him and she'd never let him forget that without her alibi, he'd probably have gone down. He remembered Blaine and became aware of a queasy suspicion that his antics that night, a lifetime ago, might now come back to bite him. He might finally be punished. And yet he still had an overriding compulsion to know.

'Well my darling, shall we go home to Nanna's house now and get some tea? Granddad looks very tired.' Aleisha stumbled with her thumb stuck in her mouth towards the door. 'Granddad will need to look after your Daddy tonight, won't he sweetheart?'

Tracy gave him a sad smile, then took the baby to her Escort and left Jason alone. He poured a vodka and put the football on. He knew his son, Joe, had picked up his methadone from the chemist that weekend. He was supposed to stay at home for a few days, but it was now 4pm and there was no sign. Jason knew he'd have to go looking. Once the vodka settled his nerves, he didn't feel like eating and headed out.

Jason ducked into the pub on the edge of town and ordered a Hurlimann. None of the staff had seen Joe. He'd been banned for a year, but most of them lived around the estate and knew where Joe hung out.

It was turning into one of those early May, Whitstable evenings that made Jason wistful. He imagined, if he got hammered enough, he might believe he was still young. That he could be transported back to before his Mum died and before he lost *Her*, the only girl he had ever really loved.

He wandered into the garden and settled at an empty bench as far away from the band playing pub rock classics, as he could. He watched the pub staff tending a hog roast and the young people drinking, the sentimental lurch turning into a feeling of regret and of time wasted.

The bench suddenly sprang up on one side as a tall man settled opposite him. Fran lit up a huge spliff. They were far enough away from the other customers and notorious enough for the young glass collectors to leave well alone. They sat parallel, facing ahead, hand around a pint, staring grim faced at the people enjoying themselves.

'Fran.'

'Jace.' Fran passed him the joint. 'I saw your boy earlier.'

Jason wasn't sure whether to believe him. Fran liked to play games. He wasn't right in the head these days and that possibly made him even more dangerous. They shared a secret. They also shared guilt, although for different transgressions, but they were linked inextricably. If one went down, so did the other. And it all came back to that night. Jason was always conscious of that, especially now Fran was increasingly becoming an unknown quantity.

Jason looked at his acquaintance. Whereas twenty years before, he'd have passed for a young Frank Zappa, now Fran was emaciated and leathery. His trademark long hair and pirate tash and beard were not white but yellow and dreadlocked with food and filth and his hair was always worn down, to conceal his missing ear. He wore wrap-around iridescent yellow snowboarding shades from the nineties because they made him 'feel happier'. With the absence of an ear, he had to ram them in to his matted hair to keep them up and they rarely came off. He always smelled of urine and patchouli oil.

'Where?' Jason handed the spliff back.

'By the pub on the beach.' Fran turned, lowered his shades and looked at Jason over the top. His eyes were veiny, red pits. He smiled and his crusty face creased like mud on a parched river bed.

'Sound.'

Jason didn't really want to leave but he wanted to get away from Fran, from the truth that had linked them for two decades. The truth he thought would get easier to bear with time.

He knew he had to find Joe. The chances were if he didn't get him home by dark, he'd get wasted and that meant he might lose him. There had been enough near misses for this to be a real possibility.

Jason arrived at the pub on the beach as the wind dropped and the Bank Holiday weekend really turned into a crowd pleaser. It was packed, rammed. The beach leading up to the pub was full of families. Alien families. It made Jason mad. The sound of children laughing, of seagulls cawing, was like a personal insult. When he looked at outsiders enjoying *his* beach with their little kids in a way he hadn't with his own blood, it made him furious. And now, in his forties, he had to look after his adult son, be more responsible for him than he ever had been when he had been little.

Jason shouldered his way bullishly through the punters who were four deep at the bar. The staff all knew him and knew better than to keep him waiting. He had a lager set down before he'd even put his elbow on the sodden beer towel. A couple of women he'd barged aside, now crushed behind him, were tutting. He revolved one hundred and eighty degrees, turned his back on the bar and leaned nonchalantly towards them. Just inches away from the women, Jason noisily sank his pint and belched into their faces. He turned his head and slammed the glass on the bar, then shouted 'Please!' smiling to himself as the women reversed through the waiting crowd, looking violated. 'Go fucking home…' he mouthed at them, smiling malevolently.

'Nicely done, son,' said a voice to his right. Jason looked around and saw Mack. He was reading an unnecessarily large newspaper and had a pint of ale and a nip of single lined up before him. He did not look at Jason. They had history. Jason didn't know how to respond, but he knew it wasn't a compliment.

'You seen Joe?' Jason's second pint arrived. More thirsty Londoners moaned and rolled their eyes around the bar.

'Yeah. He just left.' Mack lowered the newspaper and looked over the top of his reading glasses. He had mischief in his eyes. 'You're looking well, Jason.'

Mack's Scottish accent ebbed and flowed. It depended on many things, mainly his mood, also who he was interacting with, sometimes what he was drinking. With Jason Jenkins, Mack couldn't help be anything but the broad Glasgow of his youth.

Jason drank half his pint before responding. Mack had slowly folded up the newspaper and put it on the bar, all the while, gazing at Jason. A puckish smile playing around the corners of his mouth.

'How did he look? Seem, I mean?' Jason didn't want to sound worried, but he was. He didn't like Mack fucking him about.

Mack slid off the stool, knocked back the scotch and picked up his pint.

'He looked, and seemed a fuck load better than you do, pal,' he said. He sauntered off, purposelessly slowly, hips swinging, smile lopsided. Although they hated each other, what Mack had told Jason was that Joe was ok. It was the truth. He could relax.

He walked out of the pub and there was something about the air, the smell that made him think about his dad. Jason walked right along the beach to the end of Island Wall. The evening air was filled with the scent of barbecues and salt. He hurried passed Wavecrest Terrace, deliberately not looking at the house where part of that tragic night had happened, and scurried on. He turned off the beach, sorry to leave the low sunshine, knowing he'd miss the sunset, and headed across the golf course – the old Salt Pans, to where John Jenkins was being nursed. On the way across the golf course, the start of old Salt Road, the ancient Stony Way, Jason's phone buzzed. A text message from Joe. Simply, 'I'm home'. As Jason continued across the raised path, he remembered a story his dad had told him: A big man, a fisherman, had been found drowned, murdered it turned out, floating across the salt marsh when the flood water receded in 1953. The details eluded him and he knew, with sadness, his dad would never be able to tell him the story again. He wondered momentarily if John Jenkins had known the poor soul.

John was sitting in the communal room bolt upright in his chair, with his eyes shut. He was one of only two men in the home. Once, the others would have loved him for his convoluted tales, but now he was mute; shut down. Isolated in his own world that seemed, by his facial expressions and his reactions to the outside world, to be one of pain. Jason hated visiting him, but could barely stay away for more than a few days. Dad was still his dad. All the while he was alive, Jason still felt like just a boy. Never a grown up and never would be until he was finally orphaned. And even then it seemed unlikely.

Jason sat next to John and stared out of the window at the beautiful spring time garden. The cherry bows heavy with drunk bumble bees, now heading home, beyond that to the deadly level crossing that Jason had lingered upon many a time. He'd stood in an altered state, mesmerised by the converging metal tracks, like an iconic shot in a road movie, wondering if obliteration would be better than the monotony and suffering of going on.

John stirred. Jason suspected he'd been awake the whole time.

'Alright boi,' he said, eyes closed still, voice rich and playful.

'Alright, Dad. Been lovely today.' Jason stroked his dad's dry, white hair. 'Your favourite time of year. Do you remember?' John looked up and out of the double doors at the garden abundant with blossom, tulips and birds. 'It's when you met Mum.' Jason knew what topics to stick to and the version of the truth to adhere to. The safe, sanitised version of a marriage that was in reality unpredictable and often violent. Jason, like his Dad, preferred not to remember his mother's unhappiness.

The nurse came around and offered Jason's dad a sherry. All the dears had a quaff after dinner, before bed. He knew the girl and he knew her Mum, and her Aunt, who he vaguely remembered shagging on Reeves' beach in his teens. She always left the bottle behind the sliding door between the lounge and the kitchen, along with a separate glass for Jason. After their sherry, and their evening medications, the dears started peeling away. Shuffling off with their frames, another day conquered. They felt mildly uncomfortable about men now, more familiar with the supportive world of female camaraderie.

Finally they were alone and as the sky turned crimson, Jason reached round and poured himself a generous nip of sherry and topped up his dad's glass.

'She was so pretty. I'd known her since I was a child. She was the prettiest girl in the town, I swear it. It wasn't until May Day I knew I loved her.' John wiped away a tear. 'We walked out that night. From down our way, all the way up to Tankerton and along The Street, just as the tide turned and sun went down. I'll never forget it. That night we became engaged.' John's eyes, rheumy and opaque with cataracts, yet still pale blue, remained unblinking. For a moment, his face was still, free of the familiar ticks and judders. He looked contented, kindly. Then the cloud returned and his brow lowered. His jaw started to chump up and down and his eyes darted. Jason thought of the shouting, her black eyes, and his dad's protracted absences. Jason knew he'd lost him to the same distant reality and not the sugar coated one they liked to imagine.

Normally, Jason would call a nurse and slip away when his Dad blanked out, but today, wrong footed by his

21

encounters with both C.K. Blaine and Fran and feeling the panic of nearly losing Joe, he was reluctant to leave. He hoped it would pass. He was too pissed to remember what happened when he'd stayed beyond this point before, but he seemed to think it wouldn't end well.

John suddenly became alert and sat forwards, gripping the arms of the chair. His look was intense, his memory suddenly alive and activating his feelings. He fixed on his son with some dismay.

'You,' he said, his voice quaking, a shaky gnarled finger raised in an accusatory wobble. 'You were – always a wrong 'un.' Jason swigged at his sherry and looked about, he remembered why he'd stopped staying for too long. His dad started rocking, 'She's burning!' John shouted. His fists were in tight balls and he was bouncing back and forth against the back of the chair 'Burned…' John said, his voice trailing off.

Jason left him, called a nurse and told her John needed the toilet.

He lingered on the deadly crossing, looking up the railway line. Re-imagining old westerns and silent movies. Cowboys riding up the tracks and damsels tied to them as the steam train tore along. His vision blurring as the lines glinted ahead.

He hurried on, too cowardly to even conjure how the impact might feel. He stumbled home. The pianola of old memories started up again, the same old songs playing their gaudy, disturbing melodies of the things that bothered him every single day: Of *Her*, his one and only love, and his mum. The tunes becoming disharmonious, warped, unreliable as he struggled to make sense of them through the fug of alcohol and the decades of trying to forget.

Back in the house, he searched for evidence Joe was home. There was none. Eventually, he crept into his son's room. After a few seconds his eyes adjusted and he made out the pale shape of his supine boy. Tucked up, vulnerable, as though he were an infant, his face smooth and youthful, gently snoring and ignorant, once again, of the distress he had caused.

Jason looked down at his only child and felt relief, love, but beyond that, he felt resentment. If only he hadn't been born, been conceived that night, the night that went on to define who he was and who he would become, Jason Jenkins might have escaped.

He might have had something like a life.

Chapter 3

Ear

July 2014

It was early July and Pippa's birthday weekend. This event had increasingly become an excuse for her to showcase her perfect life to those still stuck in London. Typically, it was hot, which meant the town was jam-packed. Keeping her happy necessitated that our family shuffled about, cheek to jowl behind processions full of beer-soaked men with beards, bells and kerchiefs, participating in the boring, publically funded arts events and struggling through the hell that was the harbour. She said being in town was what we did to show we were part of the community. I wasn't sure what community she was talking about. The vast majority of people enduring the crowds weren't from anywhere near the CT5 postcode.

No one understood that this took me away from my writing. I was temptingly close to finishing it, my dark and mysterious historical thriller. I'd managed to practically lift the letters wholesale into script form, I was just struggling with how to portray Minnie as an elderly woman, having always made a point of avoiding old people. I was working again with Douglas, my producer on *Burn* and we had interest from another broadcaster with a new fund for film. I'd even started writing a blog about life in the town and was gaining quite a following, principally with people who aspired to live in Whistable. Any negative vibes from locals who actually knew how to use social media, I just brushed aside. But despite these modest achievements, the background drone of discontent, of worry about what might happen, or rather, what might *not* happen, was always present. None of this Pippa knew.

Shortly after my screenwriting course, Pippa had got herself a full-time job back in London as Director of

Something Important in Marketing. We barely saw her from Monday to Friday and she was angling to stay there in the week, 'maybe buy a small place in town'. All because I forced the family to move to this 'shithole'. Actually, it had been her that had pushed us to move, along with several other families with primary aged children, all with aspirations to avoid Independent School fees and take advantage of the Kent Grammar School system.

I had resented it, knowing that my opportunities to network and get future projects off the ground had been massively reduced, but I was still basking in the limelight and still glowing with the success of my film. Sitting on the beach watching the sunset with a beer seemed like a good alternative to working. All the same, now the tables had turned, the balance of power had shifted and I had effectively become *her* wife. I liked to complain, because that was what she expected, but really, I had now come to resent her when she *was* there.

She had invited three families down for the weekend. Back when we lived in town, they used to be our friends, before kids, before Whitstable. Now my interactions with them felt forced, fake even. Pippa knew I couldn't slink off on my own if we had guests, so the whole weekend was arranged without my knowledge. Apparently, earning a hundred and fifty grand a year meant she could decide what happened with my time. Fuck off it did.

They'd all rented a large house in Seasalter. That meant three humiliating days of domestic servitude and agonising small talk. Add to that, babysitting children I disliked, tolerating the continual boasting and one-up-manship of the adults who were all successful creatives, while watching the women deface our bit of beach with Cath Kidston bunting and having to cook what was most probably horse meat on a crap barbecue. All on a heaving fake beach made of painful 'pebbles' dredged from the sea floor off the coast of Belgium, surrounded by other people from London. When I could have been writing!

One of the other dads, Guy I think, had organised the kids to collect as many oyster shells as they could to make a sculpture on the pebbles.

'What does an oyster shell look like, Daddy?' asked Sheridan, his five-year old.

'It looks a bit like an ear, darling,' he said, finding two nearby and holding them up beside his head to comic effect. 'Why don't you all go and collect as many as possible and we'll make a sculpture!'

The kids all scattered and were soon lost in the heat-haze among burning English bodies. Our women were either whippet thin, vein-riddled yogis, or porridge-thighed, cupcake fatties; the men in our party, without exception, sucking their stomachs in until they'd had enough Prosecco to not care.

I was quietly impressed. Guy's superior male parenting had effectively got rid of them for the best part of an hour. Only my contemptuous fifteen-year old daughter stayed, thunderous behind her giant shades as she stared at her mother who was getting steadily drunk with the three other, almost identical women. Isobel, my eldest, hadn't turned on me yet. I'd been spared so far and I did everything I could to stay in her favour. It was expensive. She reclined, long legged, in her tiny floral playsuit, plugged into her iPod, ignoring the young and old men staring at her. It made me uncomfortably proud.

I reluctantly left my seat on a breakwater, after observing the refreshingly louche locals drinking lager on the roof terrace of the nearby speedboat club and joined my people, the other D.F.L.s. There was an awkward pause and I sensed I had been the topic of conversation.

'So Conrad,' said Andrea, Guy's wife and slightly less annoying than my own, 'I heard you are writing again.'

'Again?' I asked, defensively. 'I haven't stopped.' I thought, with shame, about the freelance work I'd had to scavenge about for in those wilderness years before moving here. Writing DVD box blurb and crafting synopses for appalling chick-lit dust covers.

'Oh,' she said. 'But you haven't got anything onto screen for a while.'

I cringed behind my shades. The others shuffled and kicked pebbles about, sipping drinks.

'No,' I said, feeling trapped. 'But these things take as long as they take.' They all nodded, except Pippa.

'Well, at least you've had a chance to bond with your girls and it's given Pip the opportunity to re-establish her career.'

Pippa was staring at the ground and twisted her mouth in a secret smile I didn't like. There was going to be trouble later.

The first of the brats came back with their arms full of shells. They each had a pile and began hotly debating what they would design as a sculpture. Gerard, one of the other dads who was in graphics, volunteered to help mark out the initial shape.

I disengaged from the throng, sat back on a breakwater and basked in the heat, listening listlessly to Pippa's jaunty shrill about fashion, work and children. The sun was getting lower and the sea was disappearing into the sky in a dusty blue haze. The sounds of the jet skis and speed boats bumping along made me feel sleepy. I was broken from my tipsy trance by Sheridan leaning on my leg.

'Uncle Con,' she said. 'This one looks like an ear, doesn't it?' She laid the object on my sunburnt, bare thigh and I pushed my sunglasses up onto my head to get a look at it. The children had the giant seahorse half completed and a puce faced Pippa was overtly mouthing the word '*barbecue*' at me over and over from twelve feet away. As my eyes accustomised, I felt an unpleasant tickle on my leg. I lifted the object up between a pincered thumb and finger and held it to the sun.

It was, without mistake, an ear. An actual human, probably male, ear. Or, at least, the bottom part of an ear. I looked about and realised no one but me knew. I looked at it again. It was a smoky burgundy colour, like a dried pig's ear you'd find in a pet shop box, somewhat like a giant pork scratching, except there was a stud through the crusty lobe. I realised what tickled was a clump of human hair stuck at the back in a gristly gnarl. I laughed. Sheridan laughed. I told her to put it on the seahorse as an actual ear. She smiled and ran off.

I sipped my beer and stared at my wife. She bared her teeth at me and pointed to the inadequate throwaway barbecue I had bought and, slowly, slowly I mouthed the words 'Fuck You'.

I tipped my sunglasses back onto my nose and returned to watching the sea, ignoring the ugly aggregate works looming up over the beach, blighting the view, churning out lung clogging smog. I thought about how I had actually nearly finished the script. How much I owed to Minerva Rowden. I felt a pinch of trepidation, uncertain if I should go through with it, then it passed and I thought of the premiere, the praise and the pay check.

As my eyes drifted across the beach towards the prom and the huts, I felt a creeping sense of discomfort. Between the low sea wall and the indoor bowls alley, there stood a solid, compact figure; gripping a can of lager, stripped to the waist, his saggy gut shining and burnished pink in the rich sunset. He was motionless. Brow low, jaw jutting, scowling at the horizon in my direction.

Jason Jenkins elevated his arm in a large arc and without thinking, I involuntarily waved back. Too late, I realised he had been swiping a wasp away from his beer. He'd seen me - seen my mistake. He bowed forward, shielding his eyes from the glare. I wanted to turn away and pretend I hadn't seen him; that it wasn't really me. But we'd connected.

He clambered onto the sea wall and thankfully, just at that moment, one of the other children let out a piercing scream. The ear had been discovered and in the ensuing commotion and chaos, Jason Jenkins slipped away.

****

'I just don't get why you had to call the bloody police,' I shouted down from my study as Pippa furiously stamped about in the girls' bedrooms, attempting to placate the youngest and failing due to her own fury.

'Oh shut up!' she shouted back.

We were both drunk. The gloves were off. I was just warming up. I felt my rage was justified and I was pissed off that she had assumed the moral high ground. Once the sobbing from the bedroom below subsided, Pippa's negative presence deadened the air at the foot of the steep attic stairs.

'Come down here, Conrad,' she said with barely controlled exasperation. I left it exactly seven minutes just to annoy her.

In the kitchen she was sipping a large glass of white wine and staring at nothing somewhere just above the floor. She did not raise her eyes when I came in, whisky tumbler nestled to my chest. I was smiling. I was feeling a fuck-it moment approaching.

She shut her eyes in the overly-dramatic way she did when she was about to tell me what I'd done wrong. I used the opportunity to study her and realised, at that moment at least, I found her repellent. There was no trace of the pretty, admittedly slightly bolshie, girl I had married. Instead, in my kitchen, was a ruddy faced, hostile woman with back fat bulging over her expensive bra, saggy jowled and stout about the ankles. If I had met her now, I wouldn't want to fuck her. I doubted anyone would, actually. This cheered me up, until I remembered that I was married to her.

She opened her eyes and resumed her soft gaze above the floor.

'Are you really as stupid as you sound?' she said. A rhetorical question? I sipped my whisky. 'If you really don't understand why we called the police then you must be.' She looked at me and her eyes were red. Not from crying, from the wine. 'You are stupid,' she stated flatly. 'I've always known it, but somehow I've managed to ignore it. You used to have other things about you that compensated, but I'm at a loss to remember what those were. Why exactly are you so angry that I called the police?'

I thought back to the boredom of waiting for them at the beach and the discomfort of knowing Jason Jenkins was there, quite possibly watching as the crowd gathered, hidden from view. The long, convoluted circus that ensued as they cordoned off the area where the ear came to rest was embarrassing. The hours passed as they interviewed every family member, even the kids. I'd started to sober up; get a hangover. We had booze frustratingly close by, but I couldn't exactly neck a beer while the constable was interrogating me. It was infuriating and I blamed Pippa and her stupid morals for ruining my day.

'We found a human ear, Conrad!' she shouted. 'I'm so sorry it interrupted your day, but I had no option. I can't bloody believe you were just happy to leave it there! I can't believe that police officer knew who it belonged to either. It's been there for six months! It's gross. I mean, what kind of town is this where some idiot gets his ear bitten off on a night out?' Pippa drained the glass and clapped it down by the sink. 'Do you know what that officer told me? Hmm?' She was staring at me with wild eyes. Now it was me gazing at the air above the ground. She resumed. 'He told me, Conrad, this is the second time in twenty years that someone has had their ear bitten off here. Some hippie activist had the top of his ear bitten of in the 90s. That's one per decade! That must make Whitstable the ear biting-off capital of Europe, for Christ's sake.'

'Oh, I don't know,' I interrupted. 'I'm sure it's probably worse in, er, Serbia.'

'Shut up!' she bellowed and threw her wine glass at me, missing.

The turning point.

'Shut up, shut up!' she screamed, sucking air in and out of her nostrils so fast they had gone white at the edges. 'I hate it here!' she screeched. 'I'll tell you who that ear belonged to. A drug dealer. An arrogant, lager drinking div-head, who sponges off the state, is barely literate and uses violence so casually it's a form of communication. He drives a white BMW, lifts weights, but only works on his "guns" and got his girlfriend pregnant when she was 17, after which he had a scary tattoo of the baby's face immortalised on his calf,' she spitted, 'and then left her for her sister!'

I was baffled. 'Do you know him then?' I asked, wondering why the police would divulge so many details about the victim.

'No! I work in *marketing,* Conrad! You are so spectacularly stupid, it's beyond belief!' she shouted back. 'He's a Whitstable everyman, Mr. No-Ear - he's just like all the other idiots in this shithole. And yet you love it! Well I don't and I never have. Do you remember when we came down back in the 90s when the fish restaurant first re-opened? Our bed and breakfast room was burgled that night, remember? I've hated it here since then. I'm sure that was an inside job. Our Whitstable was a fantasy. It never existed. I should never have agreed to move here. And that's why I'm off.'

'But *you* made *me* move here!' I whined, but she was no longer listening. I looked at her to see if she was bluffing. Her face was hard but her eyes were sparkling with triumph.

'I told the girls tonight,' she said, her breathing almost normal. 'Isobel won't come. She says she'd rather live with you. It's a lie of course. She's shagging someone. You can keep her, Conrad, I don't need the trouble. I'm taking Miranda before she is corrupted by the underclass in this town. I plan to spend the rest of the summer in London. I don't see any point in staying down here at all now.' She started rubbing her forehead hard as she yawned. We stood in silence for a minute as I began to sway. She sighed. 'Look, let's see where we are in late August, and work out what to do then.' Her tone had softened. 'It doesn't have to be permanent. It's really up to you. Have you got anything to say, Conrad?' she asked.

I thought for a really long time.

'I've nearly finished my screenplay,' I offered. She threw her head back and laughed with the hunch shouldered venom of a hyena. Then stopped abruptly and moved toward the cleaning cupboard where she reached in and retrieved a dustpan and brush. As she slowly walked past to leave, she thrust them into my ribcage

'Too late, mate.' she said. 'Good night.' She stopped in the doorway, her face shadowed in the half light. I thought she was going to change her mind, but instead she said, 'Oh. And thanks for ruining my birthday.'

Then she was gone.

She left a gaping silence that was occupied quickly by my vexation that I didn't have the last word. Three or four unwanted memories of us visiting Whitstable in our youth emerged, serving only to fan my self-pity and leaving me vaguely sad.

Then I thought of my film script and the snapshots vanished. I thought of Emma Watson wading through the floods, her dress clinging to her perfect breasts and I felt hope. I brightened when I realised that this meant I got to enjoy fame a second time, potentially as a single man. And the first thing I was going to do - an action that sent clear signal that I was no longer to be dictated to, that I was my own man - was to grow a really big *beard*.

Chapter 4

Score

August 2014

Jason Jenkins picked his way through the hordes of people seated on coats and blankets across Tankerton slopes, waiting for the fireworks to start bursting across the mud flats from a barge anchored out in the bay. His progress was hampered by the weight of his sleeping granddaughter in this arms and his slight inebriation. Joe followed behind him; glum, mute, carrying the folded up buggy.

All three were exhausted and sunburnt, shattered from a day at the Regatta, cruising the stalls, ignoring Aleisha's demands to go on every ride until her belligerent screams forced Jason to put his hand in his pocket. Jason had searched in earnest for the beer tent, but there still wasn't one. Years and years had lapsed since the mammoth riot between locals and the pigs - started, if he remembered rightly by his tasty mate Keith - but still no tent. So instead, he bought eight cans from the Indian's at Tankerton Circus and they settled on the beach in the blistering heat for the afternoon. Aleisha toddled about, chatting to other children, eating crisps and paddling with her skirt tucked into her pull-ups. Joe sat silently texting a mystery woman and Jason sat and drank. He'd done what Tracy had suggested – a nice day at the Regatta for Aleisha, now he just had to bide his time until she met them at the fireworks to take the little girl home to bed.

As they approached the tennis courts, the first barrage of fireworks lit up the sky and woke Aleisha up with a start. She immediately began to scream, utterly terrified and leapt from Jason straight into Tracy's robust arms. Tracy smiled and squeezed her eyes at Jason, covering her granddaughter's ears, then promptly turned and headed for her Escort parked across the pavement. Joe nodded goodbye to his dad, then swaggered along behind his mum, hood up, stained trackies slung low, carrying the buggy on his shoulder like an African boy soldier with a rifle.

At last Jason was free to please himself. He headed away from the fireworks and over the hill. When he reached the cannons that pointed out across the Thames Estuary, he looked down towards the large, solid building that had once been the pub that did the best after-hours lock-ins. Jason's pace slowed as he approached the building. It was no longer a pub surrounded with tiny bedsits and flats. Now it was a smart residential address, remodelled into large, gentrified apartments.

Twenty or so years before, Jason had been among the exodus of thirsty punters coming over the slope after the fireworks had finished, heading as fast as possible to the pub before the bar got so packed it took forever to get served.

On such a night, he had first lost *Her*. It had been 1992 and he'd come to the pub with his cousin, Theresa Gann, who lived in flat 14 with her boyfriend Freddie Hook. Fireworks finished, they'd come over the hill, drunk, whizzed up, wanting another drink. In the bar, it was already standing room only. Bodies pressed chest to back, sweating and swaying, arms lifted high, passing dripping pints in plastics overhead, the floor sticky and beer soaked. It was a tinder box of potential menace as such a disparate group gathered, not used to sharing the same space. The air was thick with old grievances rubbing shoulders with fatigue and testosterone. Jason felt like he was having a panic attack and dragged Theresa out before they'd even got past the fruit machine at the door.

'What's up with you?' she said, looking irritated.

'I think I over-did the billy. I can't breathe.'

She giggled and patted his shoulder as Freddie appeared.

'Let's go up the flat and have a smoke. That'll sort you out.' They re-entered the pub and pushed past the crowds into the back of the bar, trudged through the kitchen laughing at the bar staff struggling to cope with the baying customers and deeper into the dark guts of the building. Barely anyone who lived there used the front door. Mack, the landlord, wasn't fussed that the regulars that inhabited the myriad dwellings used his kitchen to enter the pub. Most of them had some shifts there anyway.

Up in the flat, Jason yanked open the sash window as high as it would go and looked out at the crowds continuing to flow over the hill and down toward the pub and the Castle beyond. His heart began to regulate as Theresa set about putting a fat one together.

'We scored a cushdy one tonight.' Freddie joined him at the window. 'That bed and breakfast at the end of the High Street. We bagged £300 and we found this.' Freddie held up a wrap between his fingers.

'Sound! What is it?' Jason reached forward to take it, but Freddie snatched it away.

'Allow me to introduce you to your Aunty Nora. This is the bollocks man!' Freddie and Theresa laughed conspiratorially as she passed Jason the elegant spliff. 'I've never done cocaine before, and now we can, courtesy of our London friends going by the name of Blaine.'

'Table for two, 8pm thank you very much! You should have seen them, Jace. They were loaded. The bloke who booked was dressed like a pirate. No shit. He had a goatee and a stripy top on. Maybe he thinks just because it's by the sea, everyone here is a sailor.'

'Cunt,' Jason said, before taking a long, deep drag on the spliff.

His cousin and her boyfriend had a tasty little scam going for a while. Theresa waitressed full-time at the new fish restaurant that had just opened in town. No one could have predicted it would have such an impact on Whitstable, but by early summer, train loads of moneyed customers were drawn to the town to sit in the converted store house, guzzling the simple grilled fish and drinking Sancerre. The phone did not stop ringing with bookings and the diary was always full. Getting a table for Sunday lunch had proved an art and as the covers became more and more sought after, so the prices soared higher and Theresa's tips got ever more generous. The phrase that guaranteed her the best gratuity was always, 'Oh and we don't charge for the sunsets!' It was so easy, it was nauseating.

The scam was simple but they knew it was short-term. It couldn't be sustained, but while there were rich pickings, they took the opportunity when they could. Freddie argued that it was just the top earners putting cash back into the economy.

Here was how it worked: Any customer that booked on a Friday or Saturday night, Theresa would ask for a contact telephone number. Provided it didn't have a local code and was a London number, she would simply ask, 'Are you staying down for the weekend?' It didn't work every time, but with astonishing regularity, in the name of polite small talk, the customer would reply something along the lines of, 'Yes, were staying at the X'. Despite the town's recent surge in popularity, there were still very few places people could stay. A smattering of low grade bed and breakfasts, the brewery's big hotel up in Tankerton and the pub where everyone had their wedding reception in, down in town. Theresa had friends or relatives working as chamber maids, receptionists and bar staff in most of these places. She would tell them the surname and they would tell her which room and take 20% of whatever they got. For the three or four smaller guesthouses, Freddie had acquainted himself with the layout of the rooms. He didn't even have to be quiet, the landladies were used to people coming and going. He suspected they didn't care much either way.

As the couple arrived at the fish restaurant for their meal at their pre-chosen booked time, Freddie and any number of his accomplices would be helping themselves to their belongings. Theresa had honed the technique over the weeks and months. The D.F.L.s that yielded the best results were young couples. So far, the police had been extremely disinterested. The managers of the hotels just apologised and recommended the customer's request the safe for their valuables in future or berated them for not having travel insurance. On especially good nights like that one, there was a huge chance the victims wouldn't even bother to report it. Who was likely to own up to losing two grams of high-quality cocaine? It was sweet.

Knowing the pub would have settled down, Jason and his friends each snorted a fat line of the free coke and headed downstairs just as they started to come up. By the time Jason re-entered the kitchen, he couldn't feel his face. He was dancing as he walked, arms held out as though he was flying or balancing on a high rope. They slipped through the bar door and ordered pints and chasers. Jason could barely drink. His lips as fat and immobile as if he'd had an injection at the dentist. It was really, really good shit.

Jason gave his cousin a hug and shook Freddie's hand, then went off to play. The music blaring out was some old jazz that Jason didn't like. He was right up for a party and looked about for people he knew. Then he saw *Her*. Sasha Reeves.

She was standing in the next room, holding a pool cue, playing Winner Stays On. She was lit from above by the low pool table lights and as she dipped forward to take her shot, her face shadowed like a classic Hollywood beauty. Every bloke in the room was watching her. She was perfect. She missed the shot, stood back and laughed and her opponent squeezed her arm. Jason felt an electric bolt go right through his body, his head was buzzing and he was chewing the insides of his cheeks.

Her opponent was his cousin, Theresa's brother, Robbie. It took him a moment to survey the scene. She was there with Tracy Shilling, her best friend. Robbie was there with Mildew, Dipper and Bungle. Everyone, it seemed was steamed except the two players, circling each other with caution around the table. Theirs was a careful dance, as though engaged in a ceremonial martial art, the sticks just ornamental, all just an excuse to be near, touch, look. Jason, in one moment, could see she liked Robbie. The way she slinked around the edge of the baize, the way she flicked her long, wavy, ash brown hair as he slammed each ball into a pocket. She stared at him doe eyed, a little smile twisting shyly on her lips.

Tracy came bounding over and flung her arms around Jason's neck just as Mack rang the bell for last orders.

'Want a drink, Jace? You look mullered.' Tracy's face had two bright red circles on each cheek like she'd been slapped hard. Her pale ginger hair had been bleached a straw coloured blonde. Wearing a white boob tube and cut off denim shorts, Jason could see her freckly, burnt shoulders were already beginning to peel.

'Yeah alright. Pint please. I'm so caned, I feel sober. You should find Theresa, she's got some banging stuff.' Tracy grinned and staggered off to the bar along with everyone else. Every week it was the same. Everyone drank as much as possible before the last bell, then hoped it would be their turn, that Mack would smile down on them and make them special by letting them stay for a lock in. Jason was still waiting to be invited.

As Tracy stumbled through the door spilling their pints, Robbie dropped the black in on a double. Sasha gave him a big smile and then approached to rack up the cue right by Jason's arm. She leaned so close to Jason as she clipped the cue into place, that her hair, which smelled of apples, swung over her shoulder and brushed his face. He'd never been this close before. She was at least six inches taller than him and it gave him unprecedented visual access to her breasts. He was staring at them and Tracy was staring at him. She nudged him hard with her elbow and passed him his pint, breaking his gaze.

'Alright Jace.' Robbie strode towards his younger cousin. Straight-faced, he nodded curtly then stood next to Sasha, gripping his cue, waiting for the next contestant. Jason could tell by her proximity to Robbie that they were going to be together, that they had crossed that line, whether they knew it or not. She couldn't take her eyes off him. Jason looked at his cousin. He was just a fraction taller than her, and whippet fit. A scaffolder by trade, he was lithe and muscular. He always had money and unlike a lot of his friends, he didn't drink much, preferring to play football. Jason thought about it. He'd never seen Rob drunk. And now he realised he'd never seen Sasha drunk either.

Mack, the Governor strolled casually around the corner, put the money in the table and let out the rumble of coloured balls. As he racked them up, Jason saw he had an opportunity to get a lock in, if only he could hang around with Robbie for long enough. Mack tended to favour and respect the people he found it difficult to beat. Jason wanted to stay as long as he could so he could be near *Her*. Tracy leaned on his arm and he managed to prevent himself from shrugging her off. Sasha smiled at her friend with encouragement and Jason's heart sank as he realised that shagging her might be necessary if he was to get an after-hours beer.

The pub gradually began to empty as the glasses got cleared and the tired bar staff urged people to go away. Jason was still buzzing nicely and had found the perfect equilibrium between being coked off his tits and pissed out of his skull. Robbie and Mack didn't speak, apart from to praise one another, or mutter over a particularly tricky snooker or enviable score. Jason was impressed with how cool Robbie was. That he was even able to play pool, to look at the balls, care where they went, what time of day it was, whether he breathed another breath, when right behind him was the most exquisite and deliciously compelling being the Universe had seen fit to create. *Her*.

Finally, Robbie had the edge and the black plopped into the pocket without touching the sides. Mack paced towards him with his hand out and spoke a confidence in his ear, nodding towards Sasha, as they shook on his defeat.

As Mack replaced his cue next to Jason, he tipped his head towards the flat dregs of his beer and said, 'Finish it, pal or I'll take it off you. Now off you go home to your mum.' Mack looked at Tracy who had her eyes closed and was leaning her face on the wall. 'And you can take that with you an'all.' Jason felt like he'd been punched in the guts. He knew the insult was about his height, the fact that he looked younger than his twenty-two years, that he was puny. He could see Robbie and Sasha resting on some bar stools, settling in for the night. Cosying up and getting intimate. Jason felt his heart pounding again. He felt the walls tipping towards him, his vision pulsing in and out with his breathing. He was stinging with anger and needed to get out, to somehow let it out.

He left Tracy where she was and silently walked to the bar where he slammed the glass down, looking at Mack, hard.

'Well thank you, sonny,'

Mack said in sarcastic sing-song Celtic, then snatched the glass and rammed it in the washer.

Jason was furious. All the while Sasha was single, he stood a chance. But now she was loved up, with his cousin of all people, his hopes were shattered. He took a long piss against the pub wall, then slunk around the front by the hedges. He peered in through the window and watched Mack suggest to the chosen elite that they play Killer. Jason's heart was thumping in his chest as he strained against the shrubs to get a last look at *Her*. Then, just as he wiggled his way forwards, Mack swooped towards the windows, banged the glass right in front of his face and shut the curtains to block him out. He heard laughter erupt from within.

Jason was not ready to go home to his mum. He was wide awake, the alcohol wearing off fast as the powerful stimulant won through and the cool summer breeze blew around him. He took off up the slopes and then wound his way down through the beach huts to the sea front. He sat on the wall, his legs dangling and made a spliff. It was difficult to light it with the wind coming in off the sea as the tide turned. He was near a bin and dropped down onto the prom to bend behind it and get some shelter. Sparking it up, he tossed the match into the rubbish.

As he sat smoking, thinking solemnly about how he could win Sasha back, about what might impress her, he noticed a flickering light in the bin. A chip wrapper had caught on the discarded match. At first it was just an orange fray around the edge of the greasy paper, then the glow spread until the paper ignited and little licks of fire played around it.

Jason watched, mesmerised as he drew deeply on the delicious squidgy black hash.

The flame was beautiful. It grew and grew, until he could hear it crackling at the rubbish. He heard objects shifting downward as the flames became strong, eating up the spaces, devouring the trash. Jason felt the fire burning in his heart, his anger at being passed over, his love for Sasha, ever since he could remember, since childhood, just gaining momentum. He smiled at the flames and urged them on. They released something in him that gave him peace, made him still.

The heat coming off the bin forced him to edge up the sea wall. The fire was curling and crackling two feet above the parameter, letting out a low rumble. Jason knew he really ought to put it out, but he couldn't bring himself to. He smiled in the heat as he understood that what he really wanted was to see what would happen if it were left to go completely out of control. As out of control as he felt.

Slowly the sides of the bin began to warp and bulge. With excitement, Jason could see that the whole structure was melting onto the concrete. A putrid smell of polycarbonates filled his lungs and he moved upwind. As the heat intensified, the bin sank faster. Jason was reminded of the Wicked Witch of the East melting into the puddle as the bin was conquered by the fire, consumed and defeated. The form collapsed and spread out across the path in a wide, molten circle. Its uneven perimeter still bulged as the fire subsided and the sea air cooled the material.

The shrill sound of distant sirens snapped Jason from his reverie. That night, he had felt elated, exalted as he bid farewell to the friendly fire. He had walked away, sedated and soothed towards the harbour, ready finally to go home to his mum.

A new fire had been ignited in him and he knew it needed nurturing. He had found his ideal drug, more potent and effective than anything he had taken before. He also knew that as long as he was alive, whether she would ever be his or not, he would always love Sasha Reeves. He was prepared to wait as long as it took for another chance.

****

Jason was still staring up at the old building when he was bumped out of his memories by the jostling crowds. The fireworks had finished and the powerful wave of happy, tired families streamed past him. He stood solid, buffeted by their careless collective forward motion and realised that tears were streaming down his face. Jason felt the lost years burning like that first fire he had innocently lit, his life extinguished and reduced to ash and dust, blowing away to nothing on the sea air.

He slowly let his weight fall forwards and allowed his body to be swept along in the darkness with the power of the crowd, giving up any plans for the night, helplessly drifting downwards, homeward bound. Yearning for oblivion again.

Chapter 5

Boost

September 2014

The first couple of weeks after Pippa left, I hardly noticed. I was engaged in intensive talks with producers, directors and finance people and my mind was totally consumed by the film which was due to go into production in mid-autumn. Miranda's absence, however, took my breath away. I felt my guts flip over every time I passed her empty bedroom. It felt more like a bereavement than a temporary separation.

In my downtime, I'd taken up kite surfing, taking lessons from a guy called Wade and I bought myself a VW T4 to carry the kit. It made me feel vital, like I was twenty-five again. It helped take my mind off the dubious sources I'd exploited to write my material and my ever increasing anxiety about whether the film would be a success.

I'd sacrificed my boarding every weekend that Miranda had visited in order to spend time with her. I could see she was changing rapidly and I realised it was Miranda the child I was mourning, the real girl fast becoming a woman. I felt her slipping further away each time. She missed her friends and didn't want to talk to me much or go to the usual Whitstable events she would have enjoyed the year before. When Isobel was around, which was rare, they argued. By the time I put her back on the train, I felt drained and relieved, but torn apart with the guilt. I missed her terribly when she wasn't there and I found her impossible when she was.

The publicity people for the film's distributers leaked a story about it heading for production to the trade journals which got picked up by the culture departments of some of the broadsheets. A broadsheet did an interview with me – a kind of 'back from the dead' piece which I thought lent me a certain bad-boy notoriety. My beard was coming along nicely and my hair was now touching my shoulders and I'd taken to wearing it in a top-knot. I had blonde highlights to blend in my grey hair and used a tanning bed before the photo-shoot. They photographed me with my kite near The Street – a spit of beach where two tides meet, and took interior shots of me at Beacon House, which over looked it. That weekend I got more than 500 new followers to my blog, blainelivingthedream.

I was feeling so good, so wired that I'd managed to ignore my debt to Minnie and my paranoia about Jason Jenkins. The last time I'd seen him was at the Regatta and mercifully, he hadn't seen me. I had run about the tacky stalls, trying to engender a sense of fun to the day, but Miranda just followed reluctantly at a distance, morose and acutely embarrassed. We'd had a bite at the big hotel, then found a patch of grass to watch the fireworks. Miranda was fuming. Her mobile battery had run out and was in a monumental strop that I wouldn't let her go home to charge it. I knew it was my last family fireworks with her and we were going to ride it out, whether we enjoyed it or not. I wanted people to see me out, with my daughter, being a dad.

As she was berating me for not understanding and being cruel, I spotted Jason and a scrawny young man unsteadily making their way across the crowd. Jason had the same small girl with him that I'd seen at the Castle. I'd heard her call him Granddad and I wondered if the boy, who looked barely out of his teens, was his son. I reclined back onto my elbows and pulled my beany down a little lower. He looked so wasted that I doubted he could have seen what was in front of him. They passed and I went unnoticed. It felt like another mini triumph, but it left a strange void. I became fixated by the very same beach huts just a few hundred yards away, where we had ended up that night. The feeling of time-lapse became even more salient as the explosions began. I was back there again, watching fireworks of a more sinister and deadly nature.

I couldn't stay.

I tugged Miranda's sleeve to get her up and let her think we were going home to charge her phone. She linked arms with me in a rare show of affection and I clung on.

Coming down the hill I saw Jason again, standing motionless, staring up at the Victorian building that used to be a pub, murmuring to himself. We were able to pass in the darkness unnoticed and we hurried through the Castle grounds and down into the town.

Now my public profile had been raised again, there was a low level but ever-present worry that he would find me and set about ruining my success. My schedule kept me from dwelling on it too much, but it was always there, eating away at my nerves.

I had also put off thinking about Pippa. The week after the article came out in August, Pippa came to visit. Suddenly she was in our tiny house, filling it up with her red lips, her perfume and her vivacity. Neither of us were the same people we'd been the day we found the ear. I felt strong, newly purposeful and bursting with refreshed positivity. She had lost weight, had her hair cut short and seemed self-possessed and calm.

We went out and ate at the fish restaurant for old time's sake. She was impressed that people were pointing and staring at me. A customer asked for my autograph and the owner came to chat about locations for the film. Throughout the meal, a pretty young waitress was coyly smiling and I felt like I'd proved a point. Pippa sat quietly taking it all in, then when the last wine was poured, she broached the subject we'd been at pains to avoid.

'It isn't really over for us, is it?' She was smiling with gentle, drowsy eyes.

'I don't know. I've not had time to think.' It was true, but it sounded like a brush off.

'I thought that was what we'd agreed to do. *Think*.' She rubbed her forehead, the old Pippa making an appearance, albeit in a less stressed-out shell. She began again, in a quiet voice. 'Things have happened for you. We aren't in the same place we were six months ago. You've had a boost, your career is lifting off again. Maybe we should make a renewed effort to make it work, now there's less pressure.'

The waitress smiled again, I smiled back making her blush and look away. I knew I had to make a decision, but Pippa's pushiness had irritated me. I felt cornered. 'I don't want it to go back to how it was before,' I said, trying to open up my position, but she jumped in.

'It won't!' She took my hands. 'We won't let it – it'll be just how it was when you wrote *Burn*, I promise darling.'

I slowly withdrew my hands and put them on my lap. My throat was tight and I couldn't look at her. 'Pip, I kind of like my life now, without you. I'm having fun.'

She took a sharp inhalation of breath. I knew this was not what she was expecting. But it was true. I liked my freedom, the kite, the pubs, the business meetings and the writing. It was selfish, but I didn't want to have to make room for her at that moment. I didn't want to have to consider her.

'Have you met someone?' Her voice was strained, deliberately quiet. Her eyes were darting about at other tables, judging their hearing range. I was genuinely surprised, I'd been too wrapped up in the film and my life to think about other women.

'No, I haven't.'

'In that case, you are just being selfish.' She bent forward across the table. 'I supported you for *years*. I did everything. I cleaned the house and cooked the meals, paid the bills and the mortgage. Yes, you did the school run and helped with the children, but we shared that. You owe me a second chance, *Conrad*.'

I saw a hardness in her face I didn't like. And I saw that sharpness only getting more set in and more determined as the years went by. There, in her face was a future where there was no fun to be had and no remittance from the burden of my responsibility.

'Funny how you came back just as I got successful again, isn't it?' My words came out in a sarcastic drawl, the wine and the late hour taking its toll. The couple at the next table had stopped talking and were leaning towards us slightly.

'Funny how you don't want me around now you don't need my money!' she countered, now unworried about her volume.

'That's not it at all! I didn't stay with you because I needed your money, I was struggling. I was – depressed.'

She blinked at me and we both took a sip of water.

'Ok, look, I don't want to fight. That's not why I came down here. The fact is, Miranda is back at school on Tuesday - we have to make a decision.'

I nodded. I knew I was going to hurt her, but I wasn't ready to go back. 'I think you'll be going back to London Pip, for now at least. I need more time.'

She discretely wiped away a tear and nodded. My insides felt raw. She gestured for the waitress.

'Look,' I said, 'this film, the script, it happened by accident. Of course I've wanted to work, to continue to work after *Burn*, but it didn't happen, no matter how hard I tried. If I hadn't been lucky enough to come by that old girl's letters, my source material, I would probably be looking for a normal job right now.' Pippa looked up.

'What letters?' I realised my mistake. I'd offered her something real to take the sting out of my decision, but I'd misjudged it. I'd always wondered how she might react if I told her about Jason Jenkins and the origins of *Burn*. Now I was about to find out. The bill arrived and Pippa snapped her card on the plate. 'I said, *what* letters, Conrad?'

I squirmed in the uncomfortable wooden seat. I knew I should try and bullshit my way out of it, but there was a strange release in sharing my wrongdoing. A relief in finally confessing.

47

'I was given some really old letters to take to a lawyer. I stole them instead. I turned it into a script. That's it.'

'And this person who wrote them, is this person alive? Still around?'

'No, she's dead. She killed herself.'

Pippa snorted out an incredulous laugh.

'Jesus, Conrad. And that's what turned into *Flood*?' Her lips were pursed and her eyes were narrow.

'Yes. I did make up the crucial twist at the end. That's all mine.'

'Well, I don't know how you can live with yourself. You're right. This is too soon. I'll sleep on the sofa tonight. Miranda can come up this weekend and get her stuff. She'll have to live with you in the week for school and she can come to me Friday nights until we work out what we can do long term.' She ran her hand through her short spiky hair. 'Listen Conrad, don't you dare try and blame your iffy moral decisions on me. Whatever drove you to use those letters, it's your call. It's down to you and you're going to have to live with the consequences. Any other skeletons in the cupboard while we're here?'

I thought about telling her everything. Jason, his crazy, wreckless behaviour that night and how now, it was haunting me, contaminating a future I had dreamed of. There were elements of my culpability that I could barely admit to myself. That I'd seen someone get hurt, possibly die and I did nothing about it. I had returned to London in shock and ignored the TV pleas from police for witnesses. I'd told no one. I was so excited about the material, that I actually had a real drama to draw upon, I didn't stop to think about what was the right thing. I just carried on writing. I just put the real history out of my mind.

The story had continued in the national news for weeks afterwards. When I pitched *Burn* at the panel, they just assumed I'd taken the news story and embellished it, fictionalised it and made it a tale that could have happened in

48

any town. They felt I'd caught the zeitgeist. But there was still only one other person who knew that wasn't true and I knew it was only a matter of time before he found me. Jenkins.

'No,' I said, 'no skeletons.' I remained tight lipped and got up to leave. We walked silently side by side down the Horsebridge towards the back streets. Pubs were kicking out and there were playful male voices bellowing and girls shrieking further up the High Street.

'I won't miss *that*,' said Pippa in a wry voice, walking with her arms crossed to keep out the cold.

As we turned down an alleyway, we saw a figure slumped against the wall at the other end, silhouetted by the orange glow of the street light. It appeared to be a young lady rather worse for wear. Her skirt had risen up to her waist and she was violently throwing up through her long hair, onto her own shoes.

'Christ. Look at the state of her!' said Pippa as we approached warily.

As we neared and the girl straightened, panting, wiping the long rope of saliva from her slack mouth, her shape became sickeningly familiar. With alarm, I realised the girl was my own daughter. Pippa rushed to her, putting an arm around her waist and pulling her hair away from her pale, sweaty face.

'Darling, are you alright?' The girl collapsed onto her mother.

'Mum, take me home,' Isobel slurred.

'What the bloody hell happened?' I heard myself saying.

'Shh! Not now Conrad, look at her! Let's get her to bed.'

We each took one of her arms and hooked them around our shoulders, then dragged her home. She smelled of puke, fags, weed and sickly-sweet alcohol. Her head lolled about and she continued to drool onto her chest, whimpering and moaning.

Back in the fisherman's cottage, Miranda, to my relief, was asleep. We stripped Isobel and gave her a quick wash with a flannel before putting her to bed in her pyjamas. We worked silently together, whispering lifting instructions, items to be fetched, clothes to be adjusted. We were a team unified by our shock and concern. United in a rare moment where the present demanded our total attention. Isobel had passed out by the time we tucked her in. We made sure her airway was clear and we left her bedroom door open.

Downstairs, we sat side by side on the sofa, staring ahead. I took Pippa's hand. It was all I could think of to do. She turned to me and I knew if I wanted, I could have taken her to bed. We were both wounded and it would have been a salve. Throughout the evening, I had registered with confusion that I still desired her, probably more than I had in years. She looked fitter and younger, her career success had spilled over into new a confident sexiness. But it still wasn't enough. To come together now would have sent a mixed message that I might never have untangled. I set her hand on her lap and rose. She turned away.

'I'm going to bed, Pip. We can talk in the morning.'

Without looking up, almost inaudibly, she said, 'Sleep well.'

****

I got up early on Sunday and left a note each for Pippa and Miranda. The tide was coming in and there was a strong cross-shore wind developing. I texted Wade and we arranged to meet at Long Rock for a dawn patrol. I knew being out on the board would blow the detritus of the night before away. I couldn't face Pippa and resolved to call her in a few days.

After a month of lessons, I finally got my first boost and racked up at least ten seconds of airtime. The rush was incredible, but Wade called time as the wind was nuking us. Some experienced Charlie Browners were performing some shit hot moves and were getting some seriously big air. Once we'd packed up, we sat in my VW, drinking coffee and watching them in awe, the faint outline of Holland in the distance beyond Sheppey Island.

By the time I got back, as I'd hoped, Pippa and Miranda had left for London. I felt unsettled, like I'd made a mistake, or missed a crucial opportunity, but I shrugged it off and opened my email. Sitting in my in-box was a message from the editor of a prominent Sunday paper, asking if I'd like to turn my blog into a regular Sunday column called D.F.L. He loved the angle that I was completely assimilated, accepted by the locals and was a fully functioning and beloved member of the community.

I felt uneasy. I'd certainly given that impression in my blog posts. I made sure they were smattered with Instagram images of me sharing a pint, shopping, on the beach, eating out, all with locals, albeit framed uncomfortably in the background, scowling. I thought of Jason Jenkins. I thought of the men around the bar the first night I'd seen him again and I knew it wasn't true. There was a hide of resistance so tough it was impenetrable by anyone who wasn't related to a Whitstable family. Even marrying in made little difference. I would always be an outsider.

By the time I'd had a shower I'd decided to accept the offer. I wrote fiction, so it didn't really matter, I argued to myself. I'd been planning on getting myself out and about a bit more, and now Pippa was out of the picture, I felt ready to be more sociable. Besides, who actually cared if the locals liked me or not? There were enough people like me, the evil D.F.L.s to talk to.

I was replying with an acceptance and writing a blog about my successful boarding that morning, when I heard the front door slam. I ran down the attic stairs, into the front bedroom and over to the window in time to see Isobel striding up the road, apparently recovered, with freshly washed hair and clean clothes on. I pulled the window open and leaned out.

'Hey! Where are you going? Don't you think we ought to talk about last night?' Without even looking over her shoulder, she gave me the middle finger and walked on, disappearing down the same alleyway she had decorated just a few hours before. I texted her and told her to come home, knowing I wouldn't receive a response and decided to leave her to stew.

Feeling buoyant about my new status and job title, I decided to have a nap then head out to the pub to catch some live music and find some material for my first column.

I got to the big pub in the middle of town by 3pm, when a band playing Cajun music were just starting up. The pub was full of families, the ratio of D.F.L.s to locals was about eighty to twenty. I met Giles by the bar and we ordered double gin and tonics and talked at length about my daughter's state of inebriation the previous night and Pippa's departure. I asked him what he thought I ought to write about in my column.

'How about, "When does a D.F.L become a Local" as a starter?' he asked. Giles had only moved down the previous summer. Not having children meant he had no need to interact with locals on a daily basis bar from those working in service industries. He worked in London and from home and had a group of gay friends who'd all moved to the area over the last decade.

'God knows. Maybe I should be asking them. How about I try it this afternoon?'

'Alright,' he said, chinking his glass against mine. 'We can conduct an informal, completely unscientific survey for your column. What fun!'

As we sipped our drinks and our chatter was drowned out by the trumpets, I noticed a woman at the end of the bar. She was in profile but I recognised her fragile features, blue eyes and freckles. I thought back to the few times we had met at the Community Arts Centre when I conceived the screenwriter's course and came to her to plan it and book it in. She looked just like a young Jodie Foster; delicate nose, pale shoulder length hair, wide, intelligent eyes. I couldn't remember her smiling once, yet here she was with some friends, happy and looking relaxed - not the disappointed, tired woman I had encountered at all. I remembered how intensely she'd looked at me in our meetings, like she was trying to fathom me out or like she thought she'd met me before, but was too shy to ask.

As I stood and watched her at the bar, willing her to turn and see me, I realised it was possible that she was attracted to me. And why wouldn't she be?

She was so different from Pippa. She was petite, fair and lithe, like a ballet dancer. She had a seriousness and composure about her I hadn't encountered before. Everything about her seemed so English somehow, even her name, Rachel. I suspected she was much cleverer than me, but I knew that I wouldn't let it get in the way. She took a tiny sip from her wine, then turned and put the glass on the bar and looked up. I remained cool, raised my glass and nodded. The half-smile on her face vanished and she stood staring at me for a few moments, which I could only interpret as her wrestling with her feelings. Then she smiled rather coldly, tilted her head to one side and beckoned me over.

'Would you excuse me Giles, I think I have my first survey respondent.' Giles grinned and winked at me.

'She looks like an expert Con, make sure you get a full statement out of her.'

I patted Giles on the shoulder and set off, for the first time in twenty-five years as a single man, to talk to the most intriguing woman in the building. As I walked along, I ignored the other women at the tables, their fawning eyes following me as I picked my way through the customers at the bar. I knew I was recognised, that I looked good these days. I felt a surge of confidence and strode taller.

I moved forward, smiling broadly, imagining the possibilities. Then, from nowhere, a little negative voice began whispering a short mantra of discouragement: 'Conrad, you're going fuck it up,' it said. 'Conrad, you're going to *really* fuck it up.'

Chapter 6

Sealegs

October 2014

It was already seventeen degrees when Jason got dressed, despite being 6am and mid-autumn. He pulled on the stiff, filthy combats previously encrusted with mortar and brick dust and yesterday's scabby old tee-shirt that smelt slightly of sour perspiration and old deodorant. He crept out to the kitchen, mindful not to wake his son, when he heard the squeak and click of the warped front door pulling-to.

He scurried to the front window just in time to see a young woman in school uniform walking away. She flicked her long, brown hair over her shoulder and turned back towards the house, biting her lip and making a love heart shape with both hands at his son's window upstairs.

Jason stood watching her as she disappeared down the road to the town. She was beautiful. He felt a strange yearning, a finger-poke of sadness, yet he also felt pride that his son could have pulled such a stunner. Grammar bird too, by the look of the uniform. He made a mental note to find out her age. Not that it mattered much. He watched her swinging her hips, her waist length hair swaying as she walked and all he could see and feel was *Her*. Sasha.

Knowing Joe was up, he put the radio on and had a loud sing along to Kasabian while he made his tea and toast. He had been lucky enough to bump into his mate Bungle's son Emo in the pub. He wasn't actually an Emo. He'd got the name because he'd accidently caught his arm in some barbed wire on a building site and ripped it to shreds. The nickname had started as a piss-take about him self-harming and it had stuck.

Emo had got him some work labouring for Dave Boswell. He could finally leave Joe now, there was no need to stay nearby. Jason was a working man and had missed the routine, the graft, the kinship. Only a year ago, it would have been impossible to work. Joe had been so very ill, Jason had been forced to take matters into his own hands. He and Tracy had barricaded Joe into his room and fed him milk; the only thing he could stomach, until the worst of the withdrawal had been overcome. Joe had tried to kill himself once he'd got over the physical withdrawal. Then he'd tried to kill Jason. They'd had to restrain him, Jason and Tracy. They knew it wasn't the way a doctor might do it, that it was probably illegal, but they couldn't afford to get Social Services sniffing around after Aleisha's mother had passed away. So Joe was a prisoner and slowly, incrementally, he got over the worst of it until he was sane enough to appreciate that they'd saved this life. When he was clear headed enough, he'd taken himself to the doctor for some professional help. Jason could barely believe that only a year on, the boy was fit enough to have a girlfriend.

Jason heard the rumble of the Transit and yanked on his high-vis vest, pulled on his rigger boots and snatched his hard hat. Emo was holding the door of the idling van open for Jason. 'You're in the middle,' he said flatly. Jason sensed an atmosphere. He jumped into the middle seat and nodded at Dave who sat stiff and recalcitrant. As soon as Emo had clambered in Dave tore away, throwing the van in a great arc in the quiet road, clipping the wing mirror of a parked car and nearly catapulting Emo out as he struggled to slam the door.

'We're fucking late. That twat decided to get wasted last night.' Dave offered Jason a cigarette which he gladly took. He chuckled as he lit it and looked at Emo who had bundled his hoody into a pillow on the window and was settling in for a restorative kip on the way to the site.

'Fuck off Dave. I'm young. That's what we do. Just coz you're too old to handle it anymore,' Emo said lazily with his eyes shut, his lip still prone to a slight chemical gurn. Dave raised his eyebrows at Jason and they sniggered conspiratorially.

They waited until they were twenty minutes into the journey, then, when Emo was snoring softly, his mouth hanging open with a thread of dribble webbed to his chest, Jason pushed the button and opened the electric window. Emo's hoody flew onto the motorway and his head crashed onto the top of the door. Dave and Jason boomed with laughter. The van snaked in the road as they fought to control their mirth. Emo, holding his wounded ear bellowed, '*Bastards!*' as hot air blasted them through the gaping window and they sped on towards Ashford.

On site, it was the usual chaos. Jason sipped coffee from his flask and overheard the site manager, Alan, telling Dave the job was a total clusterfuck already and they were only three weeks in. He pointed a finger at the Head Engineer. 'He's from South Africa. He asked someone for some lead for his pencil on the first day. Totally green. They won't let him forget it.' Jason noticed Emo pulling a face that suggested he didn't get it either, but he let it go.

Alan introduced them to the rest of the gang. There was Nibs, the digger driver with the prosthetic nose. Badger the labourer for the ground workers who had a badger tattooed on his forehead and called everyone 'beauty'. Horse, the dumper driver, who allegedly had an enormous cock and promptly offered to show them. Finally Veronica, the other engineer, fresh out of college, haughty and aloof. Jason instantly disliked her and mused that it really ought to be her they called Horse.

Jason hadn't realised how unfit he was. The weather was oppressively hot and the lads had discarded their tee-shirts and just wore their hi-vis vests. Jason staggered back and forth, grunting, panting under the weight he was carrying, his loose belly swaying over his low slung trousers. He looked at Emo with unabashed envy as he deftly created the curved exterior wall. He was slim, sculpted and seemed to have completely recovered from his mash up the night before. Jason could smell the alcohol in his own sweat as it coursed down his back and dripped from the tight plastic of his hard hat into his eyes. It was only 11am and he was already fantasising about a nice cold can of Stella.

They stopped for a break and Jason could barely unscrew his flask, the pain in his back was so intense. He let out a groan and twisted stiffly. 'I can get you something for that Granddad,' Emo perked up.

'Like *what*?' Jason quite liked the lad, but he didn't want him to know it. There had to be some respect.

'I get tablets for all the old silverbacks, don't I, Dave?' Dave punched Emo so hard on the shoulder he fell backwards off the pipe he was sitting on, his sandwich falling into the dried mud. 'Ooh, touchy!' Emo mocked, good-humouredly.

Nibs jumped down from the digger in front of them and as he landed with an awkward jolt, his nose came away from his face, landing by the sandwich. Emo grimaced, picked it up as he retrieved his lunch and passed it back to him. They stared at Nibs, who stood smiling, the hole where his nose used to be was surrounded by tatters of papery looking adhesive that ruffled softly in the hot breeze. 'Not to worry,' he said with a nasal twang, 'I've got a whole box of them in the motor.' Emo stuffed the filthy sandwich into his mouth as a gag.

'Poor bastard,' said Dave. And they laughed as Nibs made his way across the site, leaving a succession of faces both disturbed and amused, in his wake.

The afternoon dragged until someone dug into a fibre optic cable and the whole site ground to a halt. The cable had provided internet to several big firms including Ashford International Station. The digger driver that severed the cable effectively stopped the Channel Tunnel and caused the biggest tailback of lorries in Operation Stack on the M20 that Kent had ever seen.

When it became obvious that absolutely no more work was going to happen that day Dave got the lads to pack up. 'Pub!' he announced and they set off for home. When they hit heavy traffic, Dave snapped the beacon on the roof of the Transit and they coasted right down the hard shoulder past a seven mile jam on the A2. 'What's the Story, Morning Glory' by Oasis started playing on the local radio station and as Jason and Dave sang along loudly, Emo, sighed heavily, rolled his eyes and stared out at the orchards on the outskirts of Faversham as they rushed past.

The first sip of ice cold lager slid down Jason's gullet like nectar. The three filthy, stinking men sat at the bar as the pub bristled with sun seekers taking advantage of the Indian summer. They sank their first pint without speaking, merely quenching their severe thirst and promptly ordered another. Jason bought some cigarettes and they moved to the benches on the beach outside. He put a cigarette in his mouth and pulled out his matches. Emo snatched them from his hand and held them childishly in the air.

'Didn't think you were allowed matches,' he teased.

'Fuck off.' Jason grabbed the matches back and lit the fag. His gaze drifted towards the elegant towering houses of Wavecrest. He could hear the sound of drills and hammers floating across the beach. Nearly all the houses had been completely refurbished. Gone were the pokey bedsits thrown up by greedy landlords, the buildings full of cell like rooms of stud walls and dark corridors. Jason shuddered when he spotted a familiar figure sitting on the next breakwater. He knew Fran wouldn't come over. Dave couldn't stand him. Fran gave him a slow salute and Jason reluctantly nodded back.

'I don't know why you bother with him,' Dave said, blowing smoke sideways out of his mouth. 'Fucking hippy. He hasn't done a day's work in his life. That's if you don't count sellotaping yourself to a tree to protest about a road being built as work, anyway. Fucking waster. He's a nasty

59

bastard as well. We all remember right? What we all know what he did. People don't change.'

'Well, let's just say we have a common problem.' Jason wasn't about to get lured into a discussion about Fran. There had been enough rumours flying around back in the day about what happened that night, he wasn't about to talk about it to Dave Boswell. He might as well have put it on Facebook.

'Don't tell me,' Emo piped up, 'you're both gay.'

Jason reached under the table and swiped Emo's legs upwards so savagely, he fell backwards off the bench tipping his pint over his shoulder. Jason threw £20 at him. 'You can get another round in while you're getting that filled up again. Twat.' Dave chuckled into his beer.

Seven or eight pints in, Jason heard the sounds of raucous shouting and cheering in front of the pub before he saw who was making it. Nine or ten men emerged by the sea wall surrounding and supporting C.K. Blaine. They hauled him up the steps, his body moving almost like it was made of liquid and dragged him to a nearby table, partly occupied by two young ladies. The other men, locals, fishermen that Jason knew and liked, swarmed the table and the women swiftly gathered their belongings and moved on.

Dave sauntered over and said hello to several of the men, Jason nodded from his seat, wanting to join them, but not wanting to get too close to Blaine. He needed to watch.

Blaine was paralytic. His arms were slung straight out in front of him on the table and his head was face down, his hair scraped up into a top-knot not dissimilar to the way Tracy did Aleisha's hair when it needed a good wash. The men were slapping him on the back and someone placed a pint of Guinness in front of him. The group began to cheer and goad Blaine into drinking the thick, black liquid down in one. The entire beach was watching.

Blaine staggered to his feet, several strong hands ready to steady him, and he raised the pint to his face. 'Here's to the trawler men of Whitstable!' he shouted and he sloshed the

60

drink in the direction of his mouth. A great waterfall of inky liquor washed over either shoulder onto the pebbles behind him as the men cheered and hollered. Blaine's eyes bulged and his mouth was a yawning hole as he gulped back the remainder of the Guinness. Soaked to the waist, smiling dreamily, Blaine lifted the empty glass, upturned it and placed it on his head.

As his audience burst into enthusiastic applause, his entire body spasmed and a violent projectile of vomit smashed across the length of the table. His body shook in great convulsions as the jet of sticky fluid blasted the bench, sending half empty pints of lager scattering, drenching cigarette packets and immersing the fishermen in tar-like sick. When his heaving finally came to a stop, the men were strangely quiet. Joe Rigden, a mountain of a man, slowly stood. He had what looked like black baby food all over his shirt and splattered across his arms. He clenched his fists.

Jason took a deep breath.

The whole beach fell silent.

Joe swiped his great branch of an arm down hard and fast. The people around Jason gasped. Blaine swooned backwards, but rather than strike him, Joe Rigden brought his muscular limb down hard on the table with a thud and swiped the puke off in one swoop, sending a tsunami of sick onto the beach at the far end of the bench.

'Get this man another drink!' he ordered, then clapped Blaine solidly about the shoulder, pushing him back down onto the seat. Blaine sat bemused and blinking, pulling up his tee-shirt to scrub the chunks of sick from his ridiculous beard.

Dave wandered back over with fresh beers for his gang. The sun was sctting and promised to provide one of Whitstable's finest, breath-taking sunsets. Jason saw with annoyance that the D.F.L.s had their cameras at the ready.

'That idiot is some writer or something,' said Dave. 'He went out with them last night on the trawler for a story he's writing. Puked the whole time. They said he spent the whole trip curled up, whimpering like a girl in the cabin. He's been buying them drinks since midday. He actually asked them to keep it quiet. Nob. He was on an assignment or something.' Dave was vacantly looking at the bubbles in his pint. Jason could tell he was going to bail out soon.

'He's a writer for a Sunday newspaper, Dave. He's got a column.' Jason said quietly, watching Blaine swaying, staring at his new pint, puffing his cheeks out and dry heaving slightly.

'Woo! Get you. What? You gone and swallowed a dictionary or something?' Emo had taken a little livener to perk himself up whilst in the Gents and now appeared almost completely sober.

'Jason has hidden depths, don't you mate?' Dave winked at him but Jason wasn't listening. He was trying to decipher what Blaine was now saying. He was shouting, at no one in particular, in fractured half sentences.

'In production….filming starts tomorrow. You'll see the cameras….wrap in a few weeks. Out on Valentine's Day. Tragic….murder. The flood…..'

The fishermen were beginning to peel away.

Finally, Blaine stopped talking and just sat with his head dipping, almost touching his arms which were folded in front of him on the sticky table. He could easily have just surrendered and had a few hours' sleep right there. Jason knew - he'd been in that position many, many times. Instead, he lurched upwards, shouted goodnight to his last few companions who shouted, 'We ought to call you Sea-sick Blaine from now on, mate!' and laughed at him trying to mount the steps in the sea wall, holding the railing like he was on the Titanic as it went down.

Jason said goodnight a few minutes later. 'I'm off too.' Dave slurred. 'I'll see you at 6am tomorrow. Emo, don't get fucked tonight. I'm not sitting in the van for half an hour again.' Emo gave them both a cheeky grin and swaggered off to join a group of girls, juiced up, ready to party.

62

C.K. Blaine was very drunk. His progress was remarkably slow. The sun had gone down and the temperature had plummeted. Blaine was walking with both hands stuffed in his pockets, juddering with the cold in his sick soaked, clinging tee-shirt. He ricocheted between cars, walls and fell into several gardens, his hands unable to break his fall. He became fascinated with a ticking street lamp for several minutes, staring up at it with a childlike wonder. His gait would waver between a side to side dosi-doe and a surprise forwards surge, accelerating until he made contact with whatever was in front of him. Jason drifted in the shadows, silently slipping between black alleyways and hidden corners. He was *invisible*.

Blaine finally barrelled down a tight alley off the High Street like a pinball. Jason reached the mouth of the alleyway just as Blaine approached a terraced house. He fumbled about for his keys and finally began stabbing at the lock making a loud chinking. Several curtains flickered and finally the door was opened from within. Blaine, with his full weight on the lock fell over the step and into the house. Only his legs remained jutting out on the pavement. Jason sniggered. He stood in the shadows as near as he dared. He couldn't see who had let him in, but a girl began shouting.

'Dad, you are drunk! What the actual fuck? How embarrassing is this? Get up! God. When will you grow up! It's bad enough that you've got stupid girl-hair, that you've got a bloody *beard*. That you pretend you can surf! But this! Well you can stay there. I'm going out.' There followed a silence of a couple of minutes. Jason stood his ground. He didn't want her to see him but he wanted to get a look at her. He remained in the opening of the alley diagonal to the house.

She emerged through the door, stepping across her father's legs which remained motionless. She pulled on a jacket and started to walk at speed, muttering furiously and looking at her phone. Jason began to walk but she crossed the road and came towards him. She brushed past without looking up, her features illuminated by the lunar-like glow of her phone. The beauty from that morning. He thought about her smiling sweetly up at his son, making the love heart. He knew just who she was texting.

She turned into the alleyway and Jason listened as her footsteps receded. He leaned on a wall directly opposite Blaine's house and lit a cigarette. The door was wide open, yellow light streamed out onto the pavement. The television was on, echoing the same northern melodrama from several of the other houses, the acoustics enclosing them in a strange soundstage for their own drama. Blaine was unconscious lying right across the threshold, the key still gripped by his outstretched hand.

Jason padded across the road and stood over Blaine's feet. He looked about for witnesses, nosy neighbours that might come out to see what the commotion was, but the road was empty. He kicked Blaine's leg. He kicked it again, harder. The body came to life and rolled over with a long groan. Blaine shielded his eyes against the street light as he looked up.

Jason took a long drag from his cigarette and let the smoke curl out between his teeth.

'I hear you're making a new film,' Jason said in a low voice. He crouched down. Blaine struggled up onto his elbows, blinking; with each blink, becoming more sober. Blaine nodded, his eyes were bloodshot but alert. 'Steal someone else's life for this one, did ya?' Jason stood abruptly and flicked his cigarette at C.K. Blaine. Blaine batted it back out onto the road, jolted backwards, scrambling up onto his knees then slammed the door shut in Jason's face.

Jason Jenkins burst out laughing, then laughed to himself all the way home. The stalker becomes the stalked, he thought with a new, menacing spring in his step. Now, it was time to get those answers he'd waited twenty years for.

****

It was Friday and Tracy was sitting at Jason's kitchen table drinking tea and chatting with Joe when he let himself in from work. The other lads were off to the pub. He listened to the Transit roar away and wished he could go with them. He hated swap-over day.

Aleisha had been staying with Tracy in the week and with him every other weekend since her mother died. He knew there would be a time when Tracy would insist Joe took on the responsibility for more contact. He'd have preferred not to have to see or talk to Tracy at all, not because he didn't like her, but because she represented failure. He couldn't look at her without knowing he had really screwed up and that he had damaged people in the process. And he couldn't look at her without remembering what he'd never had – Sasha.

Aleisha ran into the hall and threw herself at Jason. He picked her up and she wrapped her arms and legs around him like a baby chimp. Jason buried his face into her soft golden hair and breathed in the sweet saltiness of her skin and for a fraction of a moment felt the glowing goodness of pure love. It was the only moment of joy he ever really knew and deeply felt. In each and every moment he had like that, he saw a glimpse of a different way of being. But as he grasped for it, it was gone again.

He carried her into the kitchen and set her down on Joe's lap. Tracy had her diary out and was chewing on a pen. She looked up and smiled and tried to catch Jason's eye. He avoided it. He heard her sigh.

'They've changed my shifts, I'm afraid you two are going to have to have Aleisha more. I'll write down the days I can't have her. How long you working for Jason?'

'Until the job finishes, a couple of months, or til my back gives out. Whichever comes first.' Jason dragged a chair out and sat down cautiously, exhaling with pain.

'Have you taken anything for it? Seen a doctor?' Tracy's face was close and full of concern. He felt cross that she cared. He felt the familiar resistance to her compassion, her kindness - it made him feel uncomfortable, yet full of guilt.

'Don't be daft woman. I'm fine. Here's some money.' Jason passed over a thick roll of notes. As Tracy took it she rested her hot little hand on his. He looked her in the face. She wasn't a bad looking woman. She had aged well considering the grief she'd had. She looked at him tenderly, her eyes searching his. Jason wriggled in his seat and slowly withdrew his hand. He couldn't look at her any longer, because all he really saw when he looked at Tracy, was *Her*. Or rather, the absence of *Her*. The very fact that Tracy was the best he could do, made him feel completely inadequate. And yet he knew that had he really made an effort with Tracy all those years ago, if he had really just given himself over, accepted her and her love for what it was, he could have had a different life. Not one yearning, mourning a life he could never have had, spending years taking any substance imaginable to block it out, blur it, to ignore the rampant feelings of self-loathing. He just couldn't open up to her. He couldn't let her love him. He didn't feel he deserved it.

'Joe, take Aleisha to watch a DVD in the front room, son.' Joe dutifully slouched off holding his daughter's hand, more like a much bigger playmate than a parent. 'What's up with you? You seem, I don't know, pent up. Someone wound you up?' There was the concern again, in the eyes, in the face. It made his stomach churn with self-pity.

Jason let out a long sigh and lit a cigarette. 'Nothing. Just thinking about some stuff. Listen, do you know if Joe has a girlfriend?' Her face brightened and she leaned towards him conspiratorially.

'Yes! I've met her!' she whispered loudly, 'She's lovely! She came round with him a few days ago to meet Aleisha.'

'Serious then, if she's meeting his kid. How old is she?' Jason felt slightly put out that Joe had told his mother before he'd told him. He didn't like the thought that his place was just being used as a shag pad without him even being introduced to her.

'She's fifteen. Lovely looking girl. Her name is Isobel.'

'Young. She stayed here the night before last. Do you think her parents are alright with that?'

Tracy screwed her face up and smiled knowingly at Jason. He vaguely remembered a pink bedroom, long ago. Remembered hiding in a wardrobe until parents had gone to work in the morning and bunking off school, a Spandau Ballet poster on the wall, giggling under covers and squeezing into a single bed. 'We were fifteen, remember? It's not that young,' she said.

'But we were *both* fifteen. She's underage. I just don't want Joe getting into trouble.' Tracy laughed a deep, sarcastic belly-laugh that made Jason cringe at his own hypocrisy. 'Yeah, yeah, yeah. Whatever. Have you met her parents?'

'Nope, but Joe says they don't give a monkey's about her. The mother is some *executive* in London, doesn't even live with her kids. Can you imagine? The dad is some film maker. In fact, he made that film *Burn* that you hated so much, back in the 90s.' Tracy chuckled. 'Could have been about you, Jace!' She jangled her car keys out of her handbag and Jason realised he just wanted her to leave. 'He's got half the town shut down filming some new thing. Looks like a complete tosser. Needs a proper shave. I can't imagine he'd care even if he did know about Isobel and Joe. Too wrapped up in his own life if you ask me.' Tracy stood and put her coat on. Jason felt the same relief that she was going, followed by the same shame that he had ruined her life and that she was alone.

'I've seen him around.'

Tracy stopped and looked upwards, frowning, thinking. 'Hang on, don't you think it's odd that he lives here now? I mean, that film he made. It really could have been -'

'Tracy, it's not odd. Loads of arty people come here from London, don't they? That film wasn't about Whitstable. It wasn't set here. It wasn't about - you know.'

'No Jace, I don't know. Why don't you tell me?' Her tone had changed. They were on the topic Jason had used all his mental power to swerve for twenty years. The topic that was like a malevolent black hole on a feeding frenzy, sucking him and Tracy towards it to oblivion. He stared at her.

'Don't.'

'What happened that night? I know I covered for you, but you have never told me. I covered for you because that was the night we made Joe. I thought having him would make everything better.' Tracy's voice caught with emotion and her eyes became glossy. Jason put his head in his hands. He needed a proper drink. 'Jace, did you hurt anyone that night? Tell me. There were rumours. You were covered in burns and blood. Did you?'

Jason stood abruptly and strode to the kitchen sink. He wanted to pour a big glass of vodka and knock it back, but he didn't want to in front of her. Instead he took a tumbler and turned the tap on hard, the sound quenched the feeling of rage that was building. The feeling that he wanted to light something, make something burn.

Tracy walked to the door as he turned the tap off and sipped the cool water. He stared out of the kitchen window at the depressing, messy garden. The truth was, he didn't know what happened that night either. Apart from Fran, there was only one person that did. The person that followed him. Conrad Blaine.

'I still love you,' Tracy whispered.

Jason forced himself to turn, he wanted to see her face, to know if she meant it, but he was too late.

She had gone.

Chapter 7

Sussed

October/November 2014

'Seems like most of the people in town read your column last Saturday. That must have been exciting, going out on a real fishing trawler?'

She sat opposite me with her legs crossed, her fingers primly laced around her knees. She was dressed very chicly, simply. The very fact that she wasn't in anyway sexualised made me think about just that, all the more. Her hair was scraped back into a chignon and her face was bare, her skin dewy and fresh. She seemed remarkably composed considering she was on a first date. I was a nervous shambles.

We had shared several drinks, on the afternoon I had left Giles to carry out my 'survey'. I'd used my question 'When does a D.F.L. become a local' as a way of finding out more about her. I knew she was a D.F.L. like me, but what I hadn't known was that she had first moved down very early on, in the mid-90s as part of a protest group opposed to the building of the A299, the Thanet Way. I vaguely remembered it, but I'd chosen to ignore the scores of dishevelled, smelly crusties and concentrate on the Whitstable I wanted to believe really existed: The quaint fishing village full of charming shops, warm people and a sunset to die for. The illusion held - up until the night I followed Jason Jenkins that is.

Rachel didn't seem like the other female D.F.L.s I'd met though. I would never have guessed. She was quiet, modest, popular with everyone and she knew everybody. In fact, I felt slightly irritated that *she*, in fact, was more assimilated than *me*. Maybe this was a new phenomenon – assimilation envy. I told her that and she said, with a sigh, 'Assimilation is a myth. A D.F.L. will never be a Local. Fact.'

I found out she had a first degree in Art History, that she had an MA in Arts Administration. Leaving Whitstable, she had travelled all over the world for both work and recreation and had finally ended up as a curator in some of the best galleries in London. She told me, in the most matter of fact way, that she had been in an on-off relationship for years that was currently 'off' and was childless. I asked why she'd come back to Whitstable in her thirties, why she'd finally wanted to settle here? Her answer was intriguing. She'd said that there were memories here, pulling her back. A link to someone that she wanted to keep alive, to honour.

I too had a link to someone, but one I'd long since wanted to destroy. Links with the past we were both powerless to break - we had something genuinely in common.

Now I was finally sitting opposite her again, I realised I still didn't know much about her beyond these facts and she wasn't giving much away. She had a way of keeping eye contact that was disturbing. I was finding it hard to concentrate.

We'd both been busy over the weeks since we had met and hadn't been able to hook up until now. I'd attempted to engage her in a little gentle text flirting without much response, but it had finally resulted in a dinner date. I'd forgotten how attractive she was and was enjoying the sensation of being with the prettiest woman in the room, albeit with a slightly smug sense that I was easily the sexiest man in the room. We'd moved to a corner in the main bar full of boisterous customers.

'The fishing trip was a real buzz. I loved every second. Those guys have a tough life. I mean, it was pretty lumpy when we went out, but they go out all through the winter. Respect.' I put my fist to my chest. She was looking at me, shaking her head slightly in awe. I leaned toward her and looked into her clear blue eyes. 'It's very grounding, having an experience like that, being one of them - being part of their crew. You know - being accepted. I feel I've made some true friends for life. Like, they really valued my contribution.' She was now nodding at me, clearly enraptured.

'You weren't sick then?' I felt a wave of paranoia. Had she heard something? I looked at her and her eyes widened, her pupils dilated. No, I was sure she was teasing. I just smiled and shook my head. 'Well, I'm sure your readers think you were really brave. How wonderful that they think you've been fully accepted by the local community. Now, tell me about your film, Conrad.' She changed position, leaning forward slightly, an elbow on the table, cupping her chin in her hand. This seemed to indicate that she liked me. This was going much better than I thought it would. She was interested.

'We've been shooting for a week. Done a lot of the exterior location stuff, just a few more then its interiors and scenes on set now. I haven't had much to do with it, bar the odd re-write of a line. It's looking good though. I'm thrilled.' I took a nervous gulp of my Pinot and tentatively shuffled my chair forward a few inches so I could get a little closer.

'There's a lot of anticipation about it – especially in the town. People are excited to see if you get the story right. *Their* story.' She leaned forward a little more. 'What I'm marginally intrigued about, is where you get your ideas from, Conrad?'

'Um, well. Like most writers, I *observe* people. I gather snippets of conversations, I study relationships, create backstories. In a way, I suppose, I steal lives.' I laughed lightly. She tipped her head to one side.

'It's just, your first film, it had an air of familiarity about it.'

I scratched my beard, looking around.

'Not just the seaside setting, Conrad. The story, the plot. The actual characters.' She tipped her head over to the other side. Like a Corvid, she was weighing up whether to steal something shiny, or snatch a stone in her beak to smash a small, vulnerable mammal in the skull and eat it. 'In fact, every single thing about it.' She was swirling her wine around, watching the liquid eddy and cling to the glass. Her voice had become quite clipped, professional. I leaned back into my chair.

I wondered for a moment if this was an elaborate set up. Was he here – Jenkins? I'd had a disturbing dream about him the night after the fishing trip. I had been very drunk, passed out when I'd got home and had dreamt that he'd come to my house. I'd woken up in a panic, checking the windows and doors and cursing my over-active imagination. And here I was, obsessing once more. I took a deep breath and looked into her wide, honest eyes and saw only genuine interest. Attraction even. Dare I say it, *lust*.

I decided I could lie convincingly, once again.

'Well, the character was an everyman of the 90s really. It was written purposely in a way that meant it could have been any seaside town,' I repeated, used to spouting the marketing patter, but this time it sounded like the falsehood it was, right as it came out of my mouth.

She slowly leaned right back in her chair, re-crossing her legs the other way, crossing her arms in front of her, looking rather school marm-ish, in a slightly S&M way.

'Except it wasn't was it, Conrad?' She raised a brow expectantly.

I went cold. Rachel was looking at me with a peculiar expression and her voice had become deeper. I realised that I was quite drunk then and she had only sipped her wine, barely touched it in fact. She was pursing her lips in a knowing way, her eyes squinting at me, sizing me up, full of, what I hoped was flirtation. Yet I couldn't be sure.

'What do you know?'

She slid those clear eyes side to side to check who was listening and said, 'I know how you got the story.'

I looked wildly about me. Who was this woman? Was she working with Jason Jenkins? Was this a honey trap? What did she want?

She leaned forward, her voice now completely humourless. 'You didn't meet me by accident a few weeks ago. I knew you were there, in the pub. I'd gone looking for you. We need to talk about that evening sometime.' She nodded at me. 'It's ok. Your secret is safe with me. There's a good reason why I've never said anything. I can't tell you about it yet, though.'

'But how do you know? How long have you known?' I was dumbfounded. I wanted to keep my mouth shut, I was conceding too much. I wanted to turn back time, to change the subject, to go back to the flirty date I thought we were having, but she'd got me intrigued and scared in equal measure.

'Let's just say this is a small town and people talk,' she said, smiling slightly. 'Please don't worry about it, Conrad. I've known about it for years. It would have stayed a secret too, but something's come up. The situation has changed.' She looked about her again. 'We'll talk another time. Anyway, all of this - it makes you seem more, er, how shall I say? Complex. I'm partially fascinated. I'm tempted to try and save you from yourself.' She reached forward and patted my hand and right then I didn't actually care if she knew I'd stalked a man and witnessed something horrible. I didn't care whether she knew that rather than report it, I'd turned it into a profitable film. She found me fascinating. Partially.

As she pulled away from our promising proximity, I heard a cackling laugh from the bar area that I recognised. Still buzzing slightly from the shock of her revelation, I nervously searched the throng of Saturday night revellers for a familiar face. When I found it, I knew what I had to do. The face was so well known to me, yet it was changed beyond belief. It was grotesque. My daughter, with a hideous mask on. An orange facade, with thick black eyebrows reminiscent of Laurence Olivier in the *The Entertainer* and pale, almost white lipstick. Her hair so backcombed, it would have given Amy Winehouse a run for her money.

She was wearing a super tight mini dress and emerald satin hooker shoes. She was with a group of girls who looked exactly the same. The group were getting ready to leave the bar and I knew, without any doubt, that I had to follow her.

I hadn't seen or spoken to her for a whole week since the fishing trip. I couldn't remember much beyond leaving the pub and heading homeward. Lately, she wasn't always sleeping in her bed. I knew I would have to tell Pippa what was going on soon, but I was putting it off.

She was out of control. She was out of *my* control and I needed to get her back in line.

'Rachel, I've had a wonderful evening, but I've got a tide to catch tomorrow with my kite.' Her face returned to its usual downcast form and her eyes lost their sparkle. It gave me a little pleasure to reject her after her revelation.

'Oh, wouldn't you like to come back for a coffee? I only live close by.'

I wavered, then I caught sight of Isobel again, she was giggling with a friend and was dancing, shaking her buttocks and grinding. I felt sick.

'Look, I like you and I'm not going anywhere. Let's have coffee this week instead. I want to see you again. I need to find out what you know.' She nodded and smiled demurely. For once I had said the right thing.

We kissed cheeks lightly under the street light and she walked quickly off without turning back. Even though I wanted to go back to her house, the unwelcome vista of Pippa loomed in my head and I felt immense relief that I had an excuse not to go. Rachel had been hard to read. I wondered if she was just shy, or maybe inexperienced with real men. There was something nagging at me beyond the fact that she knew what I'd done. I just couldn't catch it.

I ducked into the shadows as the posse of girls staggered out of the pub and headed off up the road, singing, shouting, accosting young men as they passed, their heels clacking, holding each other up for support and warmth. Like a many-headed killer virus, they infected all that passed on the way to the remote venue, dragging young men into their epicentre, only to chew them up and eject them, humiliated and chastened, on to the street. And my daughter, it turned out, was the ring leader. Not an innocent, press-ganged and bullied by her powerful friends. No - the instigator, the agent provocateur, the head witch.

At the venue on the beach, I zipped up my jacket against the cool sea breeze and I hung back behind the beach huts until they were in. I waited, watching the chunky bouncers with their thick necks and sausage fingers joking with the girls and getting lippy with the lads. When they weren't looking I sprinted across the beach and came up to the building where they couldn't see me, the cold autumn wind loosening my hair free and was swirling through my beard. I must have looked like a madman.

I peered in from a distance, knowing I was in the shadows and I watched. The place was only half full; it was still early in the night and the brisk wind was putting people off from making the walk. I identified Isobel's group fairly quickly. They moved like a single organism: intertwined, limbs interlaced, faces squashed together for repeated selfy iPhone shots, attempting to manufacture the generic but bizarre sexy-innocence of their reality TV idols. Their tongues lolling, displaying sparkling studs, or doe-eyed and simpering, pouting furiously.

The bass got heavier and the lights got a lot lower. I had to move much closer to the windows to keep sight of her. I was lucky she was in her heels, her natural height meaning she stood out from her friends. But when the crowd started dancing, it became difficult. I saw flashes of her illuminated like snapshots by the strobe – eyes closed - arms in the air - face blissed. A man moved near her, behind. She pushed into him, smiling in a way that I knew meant she knew him intimately. I'd seen hundreds of women dance like this before, but never Isobel. And of those hundreds of women I'd seen dance like this, only one came to mind. The woman who was the object of Jason Jenkins' desire all those years before. The dance that didn't just devastate Jason, but broke the hearts of nearly every male in the club. That female, whose wholly innocent and unconscious rejection of Jason and any other suitor that night, had set him off on such an epic bender, such a debauched, unpredictable and catastrophic rampage, it came echoing down the years to that very moment with the potency of a Taser gun.

I stood watching my daughter turn and dance with a man, a grinding sexual dance that demonstrated a familiar carnality, their legs entwined, her arms around his neck, their eyes locked as they bumped. Just like Jason, watching from the side-lines all those years ago as the beauty on the dance floor chose someone else, so I stood and became passed over for another man. My little girl demonstrating I was no longer the most important male in her life.

There was a fragment of a voice on the wind, a shout on the air, then a big fist grabbed my collar. 'Oi, sicko, what are you doing lurking out here?'

I was being dragged away, but I struggled to take one last look – to see who she was with. Just as I lost my balance, the youth turned.

The same weasely features, the same tiny cats' teeth and squinty eyes. The time Taser connected. The man dancing with my daughter was Jason Jenkins' son.

* * * *

By Monday, I still hadn't seen Isobel. She wasn't answering her phone or replying to my texts. She had managed to come home several times without me seeing, to change her clothes and eat. Her sister insisted she was 'alright', but she hadn't slept in her bed since Friday. I sent her one last text – 'call me or I will phone the police and report you as missing'. A scare tactic. I had no intention of calling the police. The very thought of them potentially bringing Jason Jenkins and me together to sort out the whereabouts of my daughter filled me with revulsion. Instead, I decided to hang around at Isobel's school and waited for her to come out.

In the intervening period since our first date, Rachel had abjectly ignored my texts. I was almost demented. I barely knew this woman, yet she had got me obsessing about what she knew and what she might do with the knowledge. My fantasies swung from her using the information to seduce me, to her entrapping me and cutting my genitals off, with very little in between. The Rachel in my head bore very little resemblance to the calm, polite woman with freckles I'd actually met, yet with each text unanswered, the myth grew.

Isobel strode out of school alone, glued to her phone, looking sullen and petulant. I followed her into town where she disappeared into MacDonald's for twenty minutes before joining the queue for a bus. She boarded it and went straight upstairs, as I knew she would. I slipped on and sat at the back on the bottom deck, my newspaper held high at each stop for cover.

The weather got worse as the bus lumbered up the hill out of Canterbury. The windows steamed up as rain slapped the glass in waves and leaves stuck like confetti. I wanted to get up and make the unsteady climb to the top deck and confront her; tell her to stop this nonsense and come home, drop the bad boyfriend who was no good for her. I knew, however, she would just walk away and get off the bus. Or worse, make a scene and get me arrested. I slunk down lower into my seat pinned down by a blanket of misery that was smothering me.

The stop light came on at the bottom of Borstal Hill. My phone buzzed just as Isobel emerged at the foot of the stairs, mobile pressed to her face, absorbed in her conversation. I had only a second to look at the text. It just said, 'Meet me and I'll tell you more'. I waited until the last possible moment, then I got off the bus, partially hidden behind school children and students. I ducked into the entrance of the fish and chip shop until she had crossed the road, then I jogged over and trailed her, holding back by a hundred metres or so. She seemed so involved in her conversation, the risk was low. I turned my attention to the text, feeling an excitement that I might actually finally be on top of the events of that night, to know everything and be able to leave it behind once and for all, to stop it from potentially wrecking the bright future I was carving out for myself. I replied 'I'll meet you soon,' and when I looked up, Isobel had vanished.

I was at a loss to know what to do. I walked up the road another quarter of a mile, feeling exposed and alone. She could have been in any house, watching me from within. I stood and scrutinised the houses that surrounded me and realised I felt unsettled, displaced, that I was somewhere I really didn't belong.

I'd ended up at the top of a hill, with an imposing set of flats dominating the foreground and woods stretching far beyond. I turned and looked back. The view of the town stretching before me. Each house in every direction looked the same. The majority were shabby Council properties. Unkempt with scrap piled up outside, rubbish on the lawn. There were a few pathetic exceptions, probably the proud elderly, with neat hanging baskets and rows of bedding plants that did little to raise the place from the dismal. I felt an urge to run. As I began striding back down the hill, a group of boys of mixed ages emerged from an open front door. I quickened my pace, realising I would have caught their attention. They followed.

I was walking as fast as I could when the first missile hit me square on the back. I didn't stop to find out what it was, I broke into a run. They immediately took chase and were at my heels, shouting insults, foul mouthed obscenities I barely understood, squealing with glee and lobbing anything they could pick up from people's front yards, aiming at my back, my head.

Suddenly a gruff voice shouted, 'Oiyt, fuck off you little shits. Leave it!' and the sound of the feet thundering after me ceased. I ran on a little further before I stopped and turned.

Standing in his front garden, naked to the waist despite the cold, late autumn weather, stood Jason Jenkins' son.

The boys ran back up the hill laughing as the skinny youth picked up the rubbish they'd left outside his house. As he forced it into the overflowing bin, he looked at me, scowled and nodded. I knew Isobel was in the house, I knew I should walk towards him, confront him and be a man. Instead, I turned on my heel and ran home.

When I next looked at my phone, there was one message, from Isobel. It just said, 'Sorry Dad'.

* * * *

I picked Rachel up in Harbour Street in the V-dub at 8pm. The sky above Whitstable was already popping with colour with dozens of back garden Guy Fawkes parties in progress. She smelled so fresh, of soap and crisp white flowers. She smiled tightly and nodded at me. I leant forward to kiss her cheek, but she awkwardly turned away and coughed. She had ignored me for another two weeks until she suggested we meet for dinner again. It was confusing. And yet by a miracle, here she was, looking naturally beautiful and seemingly unaware of any anxiety on my part.

'Let's get going then,' she said, 'I'm starving.' That's when she smiled and my hopes were lifted once more.

I drove through the town and turned off at Joy Lane towards our destination before I got the courage to ask. 'How do you know? I mean, what do you know?' My voice sounded small and needy.

'Patience, Conrad. I need to know you can be trusted with this knowledge before I tell you anything.'

'What does that mean?'

'Well, why do you think I'm talking to you about this now?' She was looking out of her window, up at the fireworks.

Was this a trick question? My gut answer was that she was going to blackmail me somehow, yet she didn't seem the type. I wondered, again, if she was working with Jason Jenkins to screw me just before my next film was due to be released, knowing if the story got out about *Burn*, I'd be in trouble. And yet, why would Jason Jenkins want to bleed me? It was me that knew the truth, it was more likely *he'd* want to keep *me* quiet. That led to only one other possibility.

'There was someone else there that night and now they want to tell all.'

'Not as stupid as you look.' She turned to me, this time there was real twinkle in her eyes. 'You're nearly there.'

I wanted to stop the van and shake her until she told me, but I knew I'd never get the truth if I did that. I was already in a foul mood and was aware that actually I may have been allowing my mind to over-think.

Isobel had come back the week before and announced that she was in a relationship: No, she did not want me to meet him. No, she did not want me to tell Mum. No, it was none of my business whether she was having sex or whether she was using contraception.

All she would tell me was that his name was Joe. I casually asked if she had met his parents and was told, 'sort of'. That was it. She shut down, avoided me, and never answered my calls, texts or tweets, refused to be my friend on Facebook then blocked me. I had no option but to let her get on with it.

We arrived at the award winning pub on the marsh and the restaurant was already two-thirds full. We had a great table in the right hand dining room on the furthest wall, a clear position to see the rest of the diners in the intimate, candle lit room, yet secluded enough to have our secret conversation. Rachel took her coat off and again was wearing a simple shift dress. She looked like she was ready for the boardroom rather than a dinner date. Her understated style seemed somehow contrived, yet she looked so fresh and pretty. She was sleek and groomed but classy and approachable, but still, it somehow seemed like a performance; not really who she was.

She ordered a soft drink and I had water. I knew I needed to be clear headed for the night. I understood I was way more into her than I'd first realised. That was confusing enough without the desire to know her secrets.

We chose our food from a chalk board and ordered at the bar then sat at our spacious wooden table. She remained tight lipped and sat for a long time looking at me with the same intensity that had first intrigued me when we met in her office. I tried not to think why, but my paranoia was building. Was she falling in love with me? Was she about to try and exploit me? I couldn't tell. It was bewitching.

'Why do you suppose you are here, Conrad?' she finally asked. Her voice was clear, gentle and straightforward.

'Er, to eat dinner? No? To, er, find out what you know about *Burn*? I don't know.' I was panicking now. She looked unamused and another few minutes passed. She just sat very still and gazed at me with the Zen-like calm of a Siamese cat. Or the icy composure of a CIA agent about to launch an interrogation.

'I meant, why do you exist?'

I hadn't expected this and I burst out laughing. 'You're not going to start chanting on me are you?'

She smiled a little sadly. 'No. Not really my thing anymore. Maybe when I was a protester back in the 90s. What's your answer?'

I remembered her first reason for moving to Whitstable. It seemed so unlikely now that she had followed that lifestyle. Again, the feeling that she was just a façade, one she even believed herself perhaps, but it wasn't real.

'Really? You really want to know. Christ. I haven't thought about that for a long time. Well, not really very deeply, er, like ever.' I felt a little sick, out of my depth.

'Oh come on. It's *the* question isn't it? I like to get to the core of someone right away, see what colour they are all the way through. I know you're capable of some questionable things, but what's C.K. Blaine really made of?'

Interesting she wanted to know that about me, yet she wasn't being herself. My head was spinning. What am I made of? If this was a test it was a sick one. She was starting to make me angry. And I was starving. I felt faint and I just couldn't unscramble my thoughts from my panic. I decided to stick to safe ground.

'On an animal level, to procreate. Um, on a personal level, to make art, create. Procreate and create. That's my answer.' I snapped. I felt cross, caged and victimised. This wasn't fun. This was way too deep for my liking. The possibility of meaningless sex with a pretty woman that wasn't my wife seemed to be drifting out of my reach with every second. I mused that the bare facts so far were that she had shown *zero* real interest in me at all, bar for agreeing to physically meet me.

'No.' she said this in a simple way that meant, you are merely a man. I felt my defences rising. I wanted to shout at her, but then she'd have never told me her side of the story. And I'd completely blow any chance of taking her to bed.

'No? Well, you don't know me. At all. How can you say that?' The whiny voice again. This was an inaccuracy. She, in fact, knew a lot more about me than I knew about her. It was unnerving.

'Conrad, there are plenty of cultures in the world that believe we have a greater purpose here than our physical form, that we are more than we buy, make or own. That the challenges of life are chances to learn, to develop beyond the material, don't you agree?'

'No. Sorry, Rachel, what has this got to do with *Burn*, with that night that you have some information about? What has this got to do with how you know I allegedly stole someone's story?'

At that moment our starters arrived. She waited until she had eaten it all before she replied. She ate in a very purposeful, economical way. I observed her closely. She was a master of self-control. I looked at her body under her clothes. It was rakishly thin, taut. The body of a gymnast, a dancer. Someone disciplined, someone who'd shut down. It was hard to believe that this woman, attractive as she was, had once been a rebellious, dreadlocked activist. I wondered what had happened to her to make her so – joyless.

'I need to know whether you are capable of redemption.' She patted each side of her mouth with her napkin, rose and left for the ladies. She left me bemused, angry, feeling got at, irritated and totally, completely non-plussed. Redemption? I had never even really known what that meant, beyond a bible bashing, American mid-west sort of way. Anyway why the hell did it matter? Again, my cranial voice, 'Who is she?', 'Who is she working for?', 'What does she want?'

She returned looking calm and composed. She stared squarely at me. Her face was now more open, a little more forgiving. This did not help me to relax. It has the opposite effect. I felt manipulated.

'Well?' she said.

'You said something about wanting to save me when we first met. Is this something to do with that?'

'Maybe. First I have to assess whether you are capable of it. I can't save you. You have to be capable of it yourself. Only then would you deserve to know the truth.'

'Rachel, what is this? Some sort of test?' I lowered my voice. 'Are you going to blackmail me?' She laughed properly for the first time and clapped her hands together.

'No! No, Conrad. But this is sort of what I'm getting at. Your state of mind. Your state of consciousness. What I know can only be entrusted to someone who is highly conscious - aware. Someone with their ego in check. And I'm not sure that you have those qualities.' She patted my hand - it seemed patronising. 'But that doesn't mean you can't develop them.'

'Wait a minute. Are you from some *cult*?'

She smiled wryly. I felt even more manipulated than before.

'Oh dear me. You've got a long way to go. Look, maybe I led you here on false pretences, but I have a task I need to carry out and a time frame to work to. Let's call it a project. I've got a few months to make some highly sensitive information be known to the right people. Those people are both trust-worthy and capable of hearing this information without feeling the need to react, respond, blame, judge or seek revenge, or they are not. If they are not capable, I have to decide if they ever will be. If they never will be, they quite possibly will not benefit from the truth, but rather, they might suffer from it until they are ready. That is all.' Again, the discipline. She delivered the speech dispassionately, like a lawyer informing you of your chances on a murder charge. Yet there was still a vulnerability about her blatant unhappiness.

I understood that this was a hugely important thing she had just said. The real reason she was actually even giving me the time of day. But I still didn't get it.

'I actually really don't understand what you just said.'

She smiled kindly. A rare glimpse of the genuine her, letting me in slightly.

'We both know you followed a certain someone that night, and we both also know you witnessed someone else drawn into the drama he caused. But what you don't know is that it wasn't just the three of you there, there were two other people besides that. Both know the whole truth, saw the whole

84

scene, so to speak. Although neither of these witnesses were in your film Conrad, because you were unaware they were there. I also know what really happened too. And no, I wasn't one of the people in Tankerton that night. I didn't see it, but I know what happened and I know you used what you saw from your perspective and made it almost verbatim into a film. And I know, what you *think* you saw, meant you gambled with a moral decision before you did it. *And* I know you chose fame and success and money over doing what should have been the right thing - going to the police, or actually, just even telling someone - anyone.' She spoke in a soft lilting whisper, her eyes cast down at the table. From another seat in the room, it may have been mistaken as the whispering of sweet nothings, or of a shy confession of love. 'So, let me recap. I know the whole truth, the other person you witnessed, who you believe came to grievous harm was fully aware of the truth, and so are the two other people who were there beside you. Only you and the person you followed – Jason Jenkins - don't.'

I was chilled to the core. Images of Jason cavorting, charging, rampaging through the burning night flashed before me. I felt the air in the room vanish.

I ran outside.

I stood on the sea wall, watching the glimmer of the half-moon reflected across the dykes on the Seasalter flats, I saw the shock of a firework exploding in Whitstable seconds before I heard the boom that echoed around the shoreline and I tried to stop my mind from detonating like the night sky.

When Rachel joined me some time later, I still couldn't think straight. She had paid the bill and when she reached me, she put a cool hand on my shoulder for some seconds.

'Let's get out of here, shall we?'

She took the keys to my van out of my pocket, unlocked it, got in and threw them on the driver's seat. It was only when I pulled over at the Horsebridge she spoke to me again.

'Well thank you. I had an interesting evening. Want to do it again?'

'I don't know. I want to know the truth, Rachel.'

'And I want to give you a chance to show me you can be responsible with the truth. What I've heard tonight doesn't bode well so far. There's a lot at stake. I have a lot invested in this myself.'

'You're messing with my head.'

'On the contrary Conrad, you simply have a very messed up head that is obscuring who you really are. Your head is your own worst enemy. Good night.' And with that she gave me that sassy, Jodie Foster lopsided smile and disappeared into the night.

****

I lay in bed, listening to the last sounds of fireworks, the muffled distant gunfire-like reports and chilling rocket screams. I had so many questions and very few answers. One new thing I now understood, a sobering fact that we had both been unaware of for decades – neither Jason Jenkins nor I really knew the whole truth. Him, because he was so cataclysmically wasted he couldn't even have seen his hand in front of his face, and me because I was unaware there were others present. Others who clearly played some role in the tragedy I thought I'd witnessed.

To my knowledge, the person, the victim, who was blighted by Jason's rage, was probably dead. But Rachel had said two others were there and they knew the truth. Who were they? Then there was Rachel herself. Why did she know? Who told her? What does she want and why does she only have a few months?

What the fuck *really* happened?

So many unasked questions, so many things I should have said to her. My feelings vacillated from extreme hatred for her, for her violation of my life, just at a time when things were going well for once, to an almost unbearable need to be with her, hear her speak and look at her, touch her.

There was one burning question I could not get out of my mind: If I'm being tested, if I'm not deemed worthy to cope with the truth, how could Jason Jenkins be? There still remained a real chance that I was at risk from him. That Jason would want to come after me, hunt me down. Not to take revenge for the version of that night that became *Burn*, but to find out what really had happened.

Whatever way I looked at the situation, one thing was a fact. Jason Jenkins was *guilty*. Not just for what happened at dawn, on the summer solstice twenty years before, but for killing his own mother. And my insurance policy was that Jason had blurted out his confession that night as he lit the killer match that made him a double murderer. 'I killed her,' he had screamed through his tears. 'It's my fault my mum was burned alive!'

As I drifted off to sleep, my questions turned into images from that night, which in turn became imaginary, vile shadow people watching me from behind burning structures, ready to strike, ready to ruin my life. Ready to send my future up in flames.

Chapter 8

Birds

Late November 2014

On November 21st, Doris Jenkins would have been sixty-five, had she lived. She'd have been a pensioner had she survived the fire that engulfed her own home some twenty-two years before.

Jason sat at his kitchen table, in the half light of dawn. His hangover had been so intense, he'd decided to get up and planned to go back to bed as soon as the vodka had deadened the savagery of it.

He sat in his frayed dressing gown listening to the faulty tap dripping and next door's baby crying. He did not pay these things any attention. His full focus was on trying to remember his mum. He thought back to her last birthday in 1992, the same year he had lost Sasha to his cousin and the same year he had found his passion for fire lighting. She had been diagnosed with Multiple Sclerosis in that May.

Jason took a long burning sip of the vodka and held it in his mouth for a moment, savouring its surgical taste and the numbing of his tongue and his senses. He scanned his memory like a researcher turning the dial through a microfiche, images flying past, especially ones that were unpleasant, until he found some from his early childhood. When Dad was less vitriolic and the drink hadn't yet turned him nasty.

He remembered his mum always having time for them no matter what. He remembered her machine gun laugh and her physical strength, he remembered the batterings he got off her if he strayed from her rules; how she would be beside herself with guilt after them. He remembered her proud poverty and her particular brand of morals, part her own interpretation of Catholicism, part survival in a small town:

You look after your own. Family come first. If someone hits you, hit them back harder. Never show your weakness to an outsider. Never trust anyone you're not related to. Work hard. Lie if you have to but make sure you don't get caught; lastly and most importantly - *Remember that you're going to die alone*.

She was a tough girl. She had to be.

Jason finished his drink and poured another. Without choosing, his mind presented an unwelcome memory. He wanted it to pass.

When he was thirteen, he saw his dad punch his mum at Sunday dinner - just because she hadn't cooked Yorkshire puddings.

John Jenkins had been for a mammoth session in the pub and had got in at 4pm, slept on the sofa for an hour, then Jason had been given the task to wake him for tea.

At first he wouldn't awaken. Jason had used the fire iron to prod him so he could stand at a distance and wouldn't get hurt if his dad had lashed out. It took six, seven, eight prods until John Jenkins stirred. When he did, he was immediately on his feet, shadow boxing and swearing, still inebriated and full of rage.

Jason had shouted, 'Dinner!' then ran from the room to the kitchen and to his mum.

She had pushed him away and growled, 'Sit down, it's bloody ready'. This hurt but he understood why it had to happen. It was an act – to protect them; to protect her.

A few minutes passed and his dad, John, appeared in the door frame, swaying. His short stocky body bunched with muscle from digging roads, his face flushed with rage and self-loathing. They all knew anything could happen and that something probably would. His mum ignored her husband's malevolent presence and carried on slamming pots down, cracking plates onto the kitchen worktops ready for serving; throwing used utensils into the sink from a distance, with a vengeance.

John Jenkins pushed himself away from the door frame and staggered to his chair and sat, head bouncing slightly, staring at the table. As was customary, like so many other rituals Jason's mother had developed out of fear, John's dinner was served first. She placed his meal in front of him, then quickly served up the children's food and then, lastly, her own. She took off her pinny and sat with them. She nodded to the children to start eating, but held back from beginning her meal until John began his. She waited.

Jason chewed his roast beef slowly, not daring to look at his dad. The silence made time drag.

'Where are the *fucking* Yorkshires?' John said quietly.

Doris Jenkins cleared her throat. 'I ran out of flour. I'm sorry.'

'You don't have roast beef *without* Yorkshires.'

Again, his voice was calm, less slurred than it should have been.

Jason's sister began to cry quietly. She knew what was going to happen. They all did. She attempted to muffle her sobbing, knowing it would just make him angrier. Jason saw his mum squeeze her daughter's leg under the table to show she understood.

In an instant, John's fist shot out and smacked Doris' face, cracking her nose, snapping it to one side. He hit her with such force that she fell off her chair and lay groaning on the floor.

John rose unsteadily. Jason knew what his dad was going to do and he knew he had to stop him. He moved around the table as quick as a flare. He shoved his father as hard as he could in the chest to prevent the kicking he was about to give his mother. John Jenkins reeled backward, a look of utter shock and fury on his face.

He crashed into the wall, smacking his head on the doorpost and passed out.

Jason and his sister went to their mother, wanting to hug her, but knowing to maintain her pride, they were not to touch her. She punched Jason hard on the arm.

'Get that bastard out of my sight.'

Jason dragged his dad upstairs put him on his own single bed, then padlocked the bedroom door. Doris had fitted a lock when the children were small. She could lock them in at night, safe in the knowledge John Jenkins would not be able to enter the room, or that they would be unable to intervene when he gave her a pasting. His dad had never taken it off. An admission, perhaps, that he knew he was out of control.

Jason had come downstairs and helped his mother back into her seat. Jean had already soaked a tea towel in water and got a bag of peas from the freezer.

His mother sat silent and proud, and let her children clean her up.

She'd looked at Jason. 'It's broken son. You're going to have to snap it back in.'

Jason put one hand round the back of her head, put a knee on her chair between her legs and took her nose in his other hand. Jean ran from the room crying and hid in the living room.

Jason tried, but he was scared of hurting her further.

'Just fucking do it, son,' she said, her voice quivering with suppressed rage. She had attempted to smile and held him momentarily by his bony shoulders. Jason never wanted to see her like this again. He vowed he would never raise a hand against a woman. He promised her, in the look they exchanged, that he would never let John Jenkins hurt her again. She understood.

He put all his force into his fingers and the cartilage cracked. He could feel it give a little, the firmness swaying beneath the skin, the gristle crunching slightly under his fingertips. That's when the blood really began to flow. But the worst of the pain, the physical pain at least, was gone.

That night, Jean and Doris slept in the marital bed and Jason slept on the threshold across her door.

The next day, Jason took his dad a cup of tea at 10am. He awoke slightly confused, but not unused to waking in a different place other than his own bed.

'Do you remember?'

John took long sips from his scalding hot tea, staring at the end of the bed, at not much at all.

'Nah. A bit,' he said.

'What happened yesterday – what you did to our mum? That won't happen again,' Jason said. He stood.

His dad had looked up, 'I'm proud of you son. You're a man now.'

And that was that. He never beat her again, in front of them at least, but the abuse didn't go, it just changed. It just became more insidious.

As the memory receded, Jason began to feel sleepy. He washed up his glass and stood at the sink looking at the dreary November garden. The day was young, but already he could tell it would be dark, flat and lightless. Without work, he had nothing to get up for or stay up for, so he went back to bed and slept dreamlessly until 3pm.

Jason awoke with no hangover. He'd achieved the holy grail of alcoholic abuse – taking enough hair of the dog to neutralise a bastard hangover, get pissed enough to sleep, then wake up fresh as a fucking daisy. He sauntered into the kitchen in his underpants, scratching his arse and yawning.

'Hi.' Isobel was sitting in her school uniform with her long legs stretched out and her feet crossed on his kitchen table. She looked up from her phone and giggled as Jason swiped a tea towel off the table and tried to cover his genitals.

'Alright?' Jason didn't know what to say. She was staring at him with a haughty confidence he had rarely encountered in the women he'd met. He wanted to tell her to get her feet the fuck off his table, but doubted she'd have obeyed him.

He could see why Joe liked her.

'I'm Isobel. You're Jason, right?'

'Yeah,' he croaked, his throat catching in a tickle then spasming into a smokers' cough so savage he had to bend over double while he was in its grip. The coughing became so violent, he let out a rip-roaring fart that lasted several seconds. Only when the hacking-up abated and he wiped the tears away, did he realise the girl had been videoing the whole thing on her smart phone.

'That'll be on YouTube later. I'll get Joe to send you a link. Right, I'm off. I'm only here to pick up the clothes I left last night. I bunked games to get home early. Hope you don't mind - Joe's given me a key.'

She swung her feet off the table and rose in one movement. She moved passed him, at least six inches taller and snapped a photo of him as she passed. 'Nice to meet you, *Jason*,' she said, giving him a brief, dazzling flash of perfect teeth and flicking her long wavy hair over her shoulder.

'Sound.' Jason stepped backwards away from her, feeling small and intimidated. Then she was gone, leaving a sweet scent in the room and a dirty tea cup covered in lip gloss on the table.

Instead of the cup of tea and sandwich Jason intended to consume, he reached into the freezer for the vodka. He could still smell her perfume and thought of Isobel's hair, height and beauty. She wasn't that different from *Her*.

The same yawning sadness filled his guts - he actually groaned with the pain of it. He could barely believe it could still paralyse him twenty years later, but it did. He sat in his pants at the table and unscrewed the golden metal cap, his fingers sticking to the icy surface of the bottle as he poured.

The thick vodka slid out in a plume of dry ice and sat heavy and cloudy in the glass. He felt the same rage building. The feeling of it gathering momentum, a need for release. His gaze settled on the gas cooker.

A solution.

He knocked the vodka straight back, throwing his head back and shaking it with his eyes shut. He had to get out. The house felt gloomy and oppressive. He needed the air, to be near other people, to stop the *thinking*.

****

Jason sat at the bar and drank four pints of lager, slowly, methodically until his mood improved so much he found himself humming tunelessly along to 'We're on a Road to Nowhere' playing on the juke box. He hadn't noticed Mack get onto the barstool next to him until he spoke.

'Thought I'd find you in here.'

Jason stared at Mack bemused, but curious. To his knowledge, Mack had never come looking for him or had ever sought him out. Mack was drinking his usual pint of bitter and whisky short and put his folded up paper on the bar. He stared ahead unsmiling.

'Did you? Why's that then?' Jason asked with caution.

'Because it's about time *yous* and *mes* had a little chat, pal.'

Mack turned and looked at Jason. There was the usual playful glint in his eye, that dangerous intelligence that could pluck out a victim and attack with a whip of venom that would amuse anyone that heard, but wound the recipient for a lifetime.

No one knew how old Mack was. He was aging better than anyone expected. Jason estimated he was at least fifteen to twenty years his senior. He had deeply lined but handsome face, bushy black brows and a thick head of steely silver hair. His eyes were a deep green and were framed by dark lashes that any girl would have been proud of. Jason had always known that women liked him. Tracy said it was because girls couldn't resist a bastard.

At that point, maybe the way Jason was looking at him, something in Mack's eyes softened and he chuckled. 'I won't bite.'

'I've not had a good day Mack. What'll you be after?' Jason tried to sound polite but the words came out curt and tight.

Mack sucked the air in through his teeth and leaned on the bar, still looking at Jason. 'Thought it was about time we put some skeletons to rest.'

Jason felt his skin shrink and prickle with sweat. 'Why would we need to do that?' he asked, becoming aware that others at the bar may be listening.

'Because, son, it's time. Things change. Scores have to be settled.' Mack winked at him and his heart beat faster. What Mack was referring to, he wasn't sure, but he felt he was being led into a deadly trap that he was defenceless to avoid.

'What do you want?' Jason was feeling paranoid now.

'Come back to mine and we can talk. Finish your drink. We can have a smoke. It's about time we faced some facts.'

Jason didn't want to go back to Mack's. That was not what he had planned. He was not friends with Mack and never would be. He wanted Mack to fuck off and leave him alone. He needed to sit by himself and get wasted, to remember his mum and get the day put to bed.

'Alright. I'll get some more fags.'

Mack smiled and nodded at him once in confirmation. They left and got in his battered old Ford Orion.

Neither man spoke on the ten-minute journey to Seasalter. Jason had reached an almost zen-like phase of drunkenness where he was physically present but was practicing no-thought. The almost constant pain he had in his stomach had dissipated. He sat smiling slightly, enjoying the motion of the car, looking at the early evening darkness and feeling remarkably at ease, despite a general underlying sense that something quite bad was going to happen.

Mack pulled onto the gravel hard-standing in front of his tiny wooden shack on Seasalter sea front. The structure was built directly onto the beach, with little or no foundation. It was scarcely more than a shed. Jason was expecting the interior to be sparse. A shambolic, filthy bachelor pad full of empty whisky bottles, over flowing ash trays and discarded clothing. He was shocked to see the sitting room they directly entered was decorated like a grand Victorian drawing room in the style of the old fashioned ones he'd seen in Sherlock Holmes adaptations for TV. The wallpaper was dark green and floral, there were tasselled standard lamps, a deep, luxurious Chesterfield sofa and a wall lined from floor to ceiling with books. Mack had no television but did have a very elaborate computer with two monitors. On the coffee table were several large, glossy books about art, architecture and sculpture. The room smelled of a delicious pot roast. Everything about it made Jason realise for the first time that Mack, actually, *really*, had his shit together.

'Sit,' Mack said, indicating the leather sofa and sat on the velvet upholstered armchair opposite. He pulled out a drawer in the desk under the computer and retrieved a leather case, then set about constructing a big joint. Jason gazed around the room at the books. He'd left school at sixteen with a hand full of CSEs. There had been no question of college. He had never read a novel or at least, never finished one. And here were all these books. Hundreds of them.

'What are they all about?'

Mack looked up, amused. 'You don't know anything about me, do you, son?'

Jason shook his head, the alcohol still keeping him feeling safe.

'I studied Classics and Philosophy some time back. It's an on-going interest, but lately, I've been majoring in the Human Sciences.'

'But how come you ran a pub then?'

Mack laughed and said sarcastically, 'I-just-like-beer.' He lit the spliff and took several leisurely drags before passing it to Jason. 'Don't be surprised if someone pays you a visit soon, Jason.'

Jason coughed out a lung full of smoke.

'Is that some sort of threat?'

Mack sat back in the armchair and smiled. 'You've always been so touchy. That's half your problem. You react. You should try and be a little less *reactionary*. Smoke, son, it'll calm you down.'

Mack stood and turned his computer on. The machine came to life in an instant and after a few moments of clicking around on the confusing screens, music, orchestral music quietly filled the room from every direction. It was sombre, strange and moving.

'Jason, I'm going to tell you a little story, then I'm going to feed you probably the best meal you've had since your mother died, then I'm going to take you home.'

Jason continued to drag on the spliff, hoping it would send his fear packing. Instead, he sat rigid, feeling increasingly uncomfortable, held hostage. He was unsure what skeletons were being put to rest, or who would be paying him a visit, or why, but he knew that Mack was very serious. Mack never ever spoke to anyone unless there was a reason.

Mack sat back on the chair and Jason handed the spliff back to him. He drew on it and exhaled slowly, closing his eyes, listening to the soulful strings.

'You're here for a reason Jason. It's about something that happened a long time ago. It's something you probably always knew would come back to bite you, you just didn't know when.' He opened his eyes and passed the spliff back to Jason who was sitting awkwardly, feeling terror chewing up his insides. 'Finish that, you'll need it,' Mack said, settling back into his chair.

'Now, then, it's story time. This is a true story and I want you to remember it, because it has a message. In 1963 in

Glasgow, my home town, a young sectarian terrorist, a Catholic, only nineteen years of age, strapped a home-made device to the underside of a car outside a Protestant church. It was faulty, hurriedly made. It detonated as he stood to walk away and blew his own legs off. He survived – just.

'Once he was better and every day until she died after that, his mum would put him on a go-cart and wheel him down to Suchihall Street where she would park him up and leave him there to beg.

'Everyone knew who he was, what he had tried to do. He was never punished by the police because he was never arrested. A rare occasion where community, family, both churches, the law and the Universe, colluded to set the most effective and long-reaching punishment. He had no option but to sit in the public eye, hour after hour, day after day, begging strangers, neighbours, family and adversaries for forgiveness and for clemency. That was natural law. It was beautiful.'

Jason sat mesmerised. The skunk had kicked in and Mack's voice, with the sinister music, had taken on a deep melodic cadence that had him both entranced and paralysed with dread. All the while, Mack's gaze never left Jason's eyes. The strange green of his irises glowed in the lamplight and his accent became deeply Glaswegian, the sounds curling and halting in their faintly aggressive lilt.

'What's the message?'

'You tell me, pal.'

'Don't fucking blow people up.'

Mack laughed deeply. 'You're priceless. Almost right, sonny. The message is that for every crime, there will always be the right punishment, and it will always, *always* come about.' Mack stopped smiling and just sat staring at Jason. It was unbearable, Jason wanted him to stop.

'What do you know?'

'Not now. Now we're going to eat.'

Mack did as he said. He served Jason a beef stew and dumplings, then took him home. He knew where he lived, despite never visiting before. Jason didn't ask how; it would have been futile. He'd started the journey holding back tears, but before long he gave up and let them flow. Somehow it felt appropriate to weep, to let it just come out. He felt oddly safe.

Just before he got out, Mack spoke.

'Want to know the good news Jason?'

'There is good news?'

Mack laughed unpleasantly. 'If you accept your culpability. If you welcome it, want it even. You may find people will forgive. You may even find a way to forgive yourself.' He leaned across Jason and opened the car door. 'Until next time.'

Jason watched the tail lights of the Orion disappear down the hill and stood for a moment, swaying, feeling the chill on his cheeks, feeling the dread in his heart. He knew what Mack was asking, but he also had his own, more pressing agenda.

****

The next morning, Jason drank half a bottle of vodka then reluctantly made a visit. He sat in the Fairview Retirement Home holding his dad's hand. They had cleared the breakfast away. A breakfast John Jenkins increasingly no longer ate. He had been given his meds and now Jason had probably twenty minutes before his dad would drift into unconsciousness. He would then sit slumped in his chair, soiling himself, before he was roused again for lunch.

John was slipping away. His eyes rarely met Jason's. His hands were ice blocks, the life leaving his extremities, lifelessness inching its way to his core. Jason needed to be there, just to be with him. His only connection to the past, to his mum. Yet looking at his father now, looking at the absence of him, he got no respite, no answers.

He left after twenty minutes and walked slowly, very slowly to the crossing. He steadied himself on a wooden post nearby. He hadn't studied the train times - but.

On the level crossing, Jason stood astride the tracks and looked again, as he had so often, at the beautiful curve of the parallel steel.

He was rarely so alive.

The air had a scent of earthy metal from the rain that morning and of seaweed and salt. There were many small birds in the hedgerows beside the line, hopping in and out. And he thought of his mum, that day she told him she was ill. May 1992.

****

He'd come in from work washing pots up at the crap chain pub at the top of the hill. She'd made him a cup of tea. Her speech had been dispassionate, forthright. She had been diagnosed with MS. It wouldn't change anything.

Yet it did. It changed everything.

The change came in the form of his dad's complete failure to accept it. But that came later. That night, she urged him to go out with his friends as he had planned. She didn't want sympathy or him being unnaturally clingy. Life would go on.

So he went out. He had been dealing for Fran. It was something he'd picked up to make a bit of extra. Fran was well connected and sound. He was at least five years older than Jason, but had a young heart and found it comfortable to be with much younger people. Because of his links to the protest movement, he had a ready market.

That night, the night Jason found out his mum had a terminal illness, they made a mint. Some shite American band called Fugazi were playing at the Assembly Rooms. Jason hated these gigs. He went in, knowing full well what he would get - hippies, ex punks and weirdoes off their tits, listening to incomprehensible music, jumping inanely up and down on that sprung floor. The music was a barrage of noise - no one could be heard when they spoke. It didn't seem to matter. Jason was selling speed, weed and acid that night for Fran. It was a good night. He stood in the corridor by the bogs, the awful racket of the band muted a little by distance and the double doors, but the stench of the toilets and the annoying fucked up hippies with their dreds and Patchouli oil, as a downside.

He couldn't stop thinking about what his mum had told him. He, and she, didn't know much about MS, but from what she said, it wasn't good. She was already suffering. He realised he'd noticed the weakness of her grip, the trembling of her fingers some time ago.

He sold his last wrap of speed to a skinny lad with a Mohawk who was already bouncing. He wanted out, wanted to leave. He'd made £300 so he left abruptly, without telling Fran or anyone and walked to the harbour.

It was a really warm night. Jason had sat with his legs dangling over the water. After a few minutes, he became aware he had company.

'You ok?'

She sat next to him. He leaned his head on her shoulder and started to sob. Soon, her arms were about him, soon after, their lips were kissing. Jason stood up and hoisted Tracy up with him. He led her to a nearby rowing boat set on the quayside by the fishermen's huts, pulled back the tarpaulin and pushed her inside.

'I'll give you a blow job,' she said. 'Just don't cum in my hair.'

After, they pulled a tarpaulin over themselves. They slept in the little boat until dawn when Tracy's uncle, a cockle man, discovered them there and smacked Jason about the head with a yellow Wellington boot.

****

In front of Jason was a train. It was coming very fast. He didn't like it, so he moved.

He was remarkably calm. Astonished, how two simple steps were all that it took to change the course of his life.

Once it had gone, he sat for a while beside the track. The birds were back, chirping and chattering, hopping in and out of the bushes. They were oblivious to what had happened seconds before, instantly free of the threat of the train.

Jason Jenkins watched them.

He intensely watched them, like he'd watched nothing else. And in that watching, not only did he find peace for a moment, he had a realisation: he wanted to live. For the first time since he could remember, he wanted to be alive. Not just exist, but be fully, really, properly alive.

He strode away with purpose, his mind, for once, full of hope and adventure. At the end of the alley way, he heard a woman's heels tapping towards him.

Jason looked up.

A smart woman, a familiar woman, was walking his way. He stopped in shock. He thought of Mack and his warning about a 'visit'. She had completely blocked his path and was looking at him straight in the eye.

Jason glanced back at the railway, thinking about the little birds. He looked at her and saw that she was like them – beautiful, free. He wasn't surprised to see her. It made sense.

'Hello Jason,' she said. 'It's been a quite a while.'

Chapter 9

Pseud

December 2014

I got Pippa's blunt text while I was replying to Rachel. It was soon to be Christmas and the girls were breaking up from school.

'I'm having both the girls Christmas Day,' it said. I had no idea whether she had spoken to them about it or not. I wasn't particularly bothered about having them with me on Christmas Day, but I certainly didn't like the idea that I didn't have choice, or that it was a forgone conclusion. I ignored the text, put Pippa out of my mind and reverted back to my fantasy where my film was a resounding success, where Rachel made the whole Jason situation dissipate and I could get to know her better.

My communication with Rachel had been erratic and frustrating over the period since the confusing evening we'd spent in Seasalter. She said she was busy with 'another project' which I took in a typically paranoid way to mean she was seeing another man. She was answering my increasingly long and embarrassing messages with 'sure' and 'cool' which I interpreted into wildly elaborate meanings ranging from 'get out of my life you freak' to 'I cannot live without you'. My involvement with the film was now minimal as post production was in full swing. I knew I probably wouldn't be called upon again until the pre-release publicity at the beginning of February. I should have been spending the time on holiday, writing something else, visiting friends or pursuing hobbies. Instead, I was increasingly agitated. Her talk that night had unsettled me beyond words. I spent most of the time imagining Jason Jenkins was around every corner, ready to pounce. Or worse, Isobel held hostage, in order for him to exact revenge for stealing his story from that grim night all those years ago.

What I couldn't do though, was look back. I found it impossible to clearly remember the facts about what actually happened. I had my version – *Burn*, but the truth eluded me. I just obsessed about how, if it came out now, it could ruin me for good. Then there were the other mystery people that I had been completely unaware of for twenty years. Every time I went out, every time someone looked in my direction, I began to wonder if it was them who *knew*.

I felt my paranoia intensify as soon as I left my house, which increasingly, I didn't. I trawled through hundreds of Facebook profiles to see if I could ascertain who else, besides me, Jason Jenkins and his victim, might have been there.

Like peeling back the layers of an onion, I realised how interweaved the people in the town were. The inter-familial, cross-generational ties that went back decades, to place, occupation and name. I found Joe Jenkins' profile and unhappily scanned through several photographs of my own daughter, tongue lolling with a piercing I didn't even know she had, or in a faux-innocent pout. There were fewer people of my age, Jason's age on there, but enough to get a broad picture of who knew who. Never before I had I felt so separate, isolated; so *other*. If the community in the town was an onion, I wasn't even part of the same vegetable. The only thing I had in common with any of them was that I'd gone on a rampage with Jason Jenkins and I was human.

Rachel had finally texted to ask if I wanted to get together over Christmas. The mental movie I created had us sipping bubbly in her little house, real fire, some mellow tunes - romance. I answered simply, 'When?' and got a reply immediately, 'Tomorrow morning'.

I had already planned to kite surf with Wade, so I arranged for her to come with us for a dawn patrol in Swalecliffe. I couldn't see any harm in her seeing me in action.   She'd probably be drawn to my raw physicality. I imagined her running towards me on the windswept beach with a towel, then massaging me later with warmed oil, telling me how awesome I was.

The front door slammed and snapped me out of my thoughts. Both the girls were home early, the school kicking out just after lunch for the Christmas holidays. I tentatively wandered downstairs and could hear them arguing in the kitchen, cupboards slamming.

'Hey you two, what's all this about?'

They both huffed loudly, then Miranda spoke. 'Mum wants us to both go up there for Christmas Day, but Isobel says she won't. She wants to stay with her *boyfriend.*'

I cleared my throat and stood with my hands on my hips, trying to appear authoritative yet liberal.   'Well, I'm aware of your mother's wishes. I think you're both old enough to make the decision this year and from now on, about where you want to spend Christmas, don't you?'

Isobel stuck her upwards facing palm towards me and looked at her sister with righteous justification. 'See? Told you! I ain't going. Now - I've got somewhere to be.'

'Not,' I said.

'What?!' Isobel shouted.

'"I'm NOT going," not "I ain't going."'

'Fucksake!'

I held my arm as a barrier across the narrow stairs.

'I think you meant to say, "For Fuck's sake"'.

She chopped at my arm, passed and thundered up the stairs.

'Dad!' said Miranda with her lip quivering. 'Mum had it all planned! Winter Wonderland in Hyde Park. Skating at the Natural History Museum. A proper Christmas dinner. Now she's ruined it!' Miranda stormed past me up the stairs and slammed the door of her room, loud music erupting immediately afterwards.

I bounded up the stairs to Isobel's room and tapped on the door.

'What?!'

I put my head in. Her clothes were strewn across the floor and she was already changed from her uniform and straightening her hair.

'Just wanted to say, good decision. I mean, whatever your decision, it is fine by me.' I smiled sheepishly, feeling a glowing sense of victory that she wanted to stay with me. That I had won.

Isobel's eyes narrowed. She stopped straightening her hair. 'You support any decision I make about who I spend Christmas with?'

'Yes, absolutely. That's what I said.'

'Thanks.' She gave me a genuine smile and came across the room. She put her arms around my neck and kissed me on the cheek. 'Thanks, *Daddy*.'

I squirmed a little with smug pride. I'd got my girl back.

'Erm, can I have some money?'

'Yes, go on then. It is Christmas. My wallet's on the side downstairs.'

Isobel grabbed her bag and walked passed me at the door. 'Thanks again Pops. Love ya!' Then she was gone.

Half an hour later I was sitting at my desk, writing about how there will always be a special bond between father and daughter, when I got a text from Miranda. 'Don't see the point in staying here one second more so I haven't. I'm on the train. Your present is under my bed. Happy Christmas, *Dad.*'

****

I picked Rachel up at 6.30am in the V-dub and we drove to Swalecliffe where there were already several kites swooping across the slate-grey surf. Wade was on the grass

106

above the beach huts putting his kit together. It was absolutely Baltic.

'Have you had a chance to think about what I said?' Rachel looked fresh and youthful. She didn't have a scrap of make-up on. I felt my heart flip and realised I liked her more than I wanted. I realised she represented a new start.

'I have. But I'm confused. It's all so muddled. And I didn't really get what you were on about. I mean, you know, I'm just trying to live my life, you know. Be free. I'm, like "live and let live", yeah?' I looked into her eyes with my best lost-boy expression, hoping the floppy hair and beard might soften her attitude.

'Well, we can talk more another time, Conrad. You're compardre is waiting. Break a leg.'

'My spine more like!' I felt like she'd let me off the hook and indicated that she wanted to take the relationship to another level. I made sure I held my stomach in flat as I dragged the kite across the grass and down towards the surf.

We were out there for an hour. I was conscious the whole time that she would be watching. I did myself proud. It was such a masculine performance, no woman on earth would have been less than impressed. We pulled our kites back up the beach and I jogged over to the van.

It was empty.

I thought, maybe, she might have sheltered on the veranda of a beach hut and was just making her way back, so I took the kite apart and packed up the kit. It was only when she still hadn't come back and I was in the van that I realised she'd gone. I looked at my phone. She'd sent one message, 'Sorry. Bored.'

Then, two days before Christmas she called me. 'Want to meet up, then?'

I must admit I was feeling a bit wounded. I simply couldn't understand what was not to love. The rough sea, the raw air, real men - *in rubber*. She was playing games with me and I didn't like it.

'Well, only if you're not going to disappear.'

'Yeah sorry about that. Turns out I don't like kite surfing after all. And for future reference, I wouldn't bother taking any other women to watch it. You, I mean.' She laughed lightly. It was confusing. 'So, Conrad,' she said, 'perhaps I could come and see where you live?'

I relented. I was desperate to impress her. I instantly imagined a scene where she slinked into my house and Isobel and I were playing a yuletide board game, some Sinatra on the stereo, wine mulling in the kitchen, filling the space with the scent of spices and citrus fruit.

'I'd be honoured. Tonight? You could meet my eldest daughter. She's staying with me for the whole of Christmas.'

'That would be lovely. I'll come at 8pm. Why don't we get a take away? Make an evening of it? Give us a chance to talk.'

'Perfect.'

I couldn't believe how well it turned out. I immediately booked an appointment to have my hair and beard trimmed and spend a couple of hours cleaning the house. Isobel came home and I told her there was someone coming round who I wanted her to meet. She looked suspicious and frowned, 'A woman? But you're – old. Er, and married. To my *mother*.' I laughed - she didn't.

'No really sweetheart, I'm getting a take away in, want some?'

'Dad. Do I look like I eat that shit? I'll be about for a bit. But only because I want to check up on you. Mum won't be happy.'

This was something I hadn't thought about.

'Does she need to know?'

Isobel put her fist on her hip and tipped her head to one side.

'How much?'

'Hundred. I've got one day to buy *all* my presents.'

'Ok. I'll get it out later. She's coming at eight. Please be here.'

She shrugged and disappeared into her room.

Rachel arrived at exactly 8pm, dressed exquisitely under her long coat in gold patterned statement cropped trousers, kitten heels and a cashmere jumper. Her hair was loose and she smelled as warm and as spicy as the mulled wine I had prepared in the kitchen. I'd had just enough time to string up the fairy lights along the mantel piece before she came. I only realised then that there was no Christmas tree.

She kissed me softly on both cheeks, in what I thought was a particularly tender way. I was glad I'd put the serum in my beard. It was now soft and long and came down to my collar. I'd been careful to dress smartly. If tonight went well, it could prove an important turning point.

'Lovely house. Very, um, sea-sidey.' She looked around at the stripped floors and white walls decorated with an eclectic mix of Whitstable paraphernalia and London art.

'Well, we tried to keep it authentic.' She pulled a face, which I interpreted as "Ooh, brave, modern authentic, not Victorian railway-worker authentic". She was impressed. I handed her a glass of mulled wine. 'Here's to us.'

She cleared her throat and said, 'To me, and, very separately, to you,' then took a sip. 'So Conrad, where do you write? This isn't a big place. Surely you need some space of your own?'

'Oh, I'll show you! My little den. Not many people are allowed in my inner sanctum you know. You're very honoured.' I led her up the two flights of narrow stairs and into my loft. I sat in my leather writing chair and she sat on the swivel office chair by the desk. 'Want to see the first cut of the trailer for my new film?'

'Yes please. As I said, there's quite a buzz about it. Townspeople remember the flood well. The *real* stories of that night. They're anxious you get it right. *Very* anxious.'

'Oh, but of course!' I said, nervously. 'Well I've definitely got it right. I've done my background reading. The story is told through the letters of a local woman – her correspondence with her husband from when she's sixteen. It ends up with a terrible tragedy on the night of the '53 flood. I used a real name, someone who really lived here. Got the idea for the ending from local history books and talking to pensioners. You know - research. But with my own unique twist!'

It took me a few minutes to get the machine fired up and set up the file.

'Mind if I look around?' Rachel said. She had already stood up and was wandering the few paces around my small loft. I didn't mind. My degree certificates and other awards were framed on the walls, as well as photographs of me with the actors from *Burn* at the Venice, Cannes and Berlin festivals. The highlight of the room was my 'Bafta Wall'. Images of the awards ceremony that night and my Bafta on a shelf in the middle. 'Wow!' she said quietly.

'I know,' I said, putting the trailer on pause until she was ready to see it. 'I can still hardly believe it myself.' And now she was about to see what else I was capable of. I smiled to myself. Good old Bafta. That's clinched it.

'No, not the gong. This – these!'

I swivelled around on my comfy leather seat and Rachel was standing with a clutch of Minnie's yellowing letters in her hand. She placed her glass down and was opened one out.

'It says "from Minnie". It's addressed to someone called Robert.' She opened another. 'So is this – and this one too. Conrad, is Minnie the real person you based this on? Are these hers?'

I took a long, what I hoped would appear languid sip from my wine which was now cloying and cold. 'Um, sort of.'

Rachel took another letter out. She hadn't yet discovered the latest letter – the one I had promised Joanne I

110

would take to the local paper. My pause button had been pushed. The guilt and shame freeze framing me into inactivity, I was on mute.

'Wow, this is incredible. But you just said you "got the idea from local history", are you protecting your sources? How did you come by these?' She fired the questions at me so fast I couldn't think.

'I, um, acquired them earlier this year. It's all confidential. I, er, can't talk about it.' Rachel was carefully leafing through one letter after the other.

'I take it you have her permission?'

My face reddened. 'Oh, very much. All the legals are covered.'

For the first time ever, Isobel made an appearance at a useful time. She popped her head up into the loft and said an uncharacteristically cheery hello.

'Come up, let me introduce you. Rachel, this is my daughter, Isobel.' They stood facing each other. The height difference was massive, yet Rachel seemed unfazed. Isobel had a sinister smile on her face and slowly and candidly eyed the older woman up and down.

'Well. Who'd have thought my dad could do so well? What are you? Thirty-five, forty?'

Rachel laughed. 'Ish. I try not to think about it. You're very tall, Isobel. Don't get that from your Dad, then?' Isobel burst out laughing. I reddened yet more. At least I wasn't as short as Jason Jenkins.

'I like her.' She sat down on the chair next to the desk. 'I tell you what, Dad. You go and get the Chinese and I'll get to know your girlfriend.'

'I'm not his *girlfriend*!'

Isobel laughed. 'Dad, I'll show her your trailer. It's ok. I use your computer *all the time*.' She looked at Rachel. 'You would not believe his search history!'

Isobel turned to stare at me and fluttered her eyelashes. I absolutely did not want either of them in the room without me. Especially not now Rachel had discovered the letters. How stupid had I been? But I could hardly order them out or tell her not to read any more. That would have aroused suspicion. I had to play along.

'Ok, but now you two – no swapping nasty stories, got it!' I nervously got up and Rachel slid into my seat. She looked like a cool CEO of an international fashion house. She smiled enigmatically. Isobel patted me on the back as I descended the stairs.

'Don't get too much for me, Pops. I don't eat take away, remember,' she giggled.

****

I ran to the nearest Chinese, cursing myself for not ordering it before. It was all going terribly, terribly wrong. Completely different from the narrative I had set out in my head that afternoon. I felt my control slipping away and panic setting in.

While I was striding back to the cottage feeling slightly tipsy and ravenously hungry, I thought about what Rachel had said that night in Seasalter. Did I think I could find redemption? Some other words she used seemed familiar now too. 'Presence', 'awareness'. I realised I'd heard Pippa spouting some of that stuff after reading a lot of hippy books her and her friends had swapped. She'd even attended something called a 'mindfulness' course. It had been one of her fads, all long forgotten. Rachel had been a new age protester. Of course she was going to be into all that. Pippa never really believed it, or lived truly by those principles, but all her friends talked about 'being truly present' and listening to the 'higher me' all the time. Usually while they drank themselves into oblivion. Well if Pippa could adopt being 'spiritual' as a lifestyle choice, so could I. Especially if it meant calling Rachel and the two mystery witnesses off over that night twenty years ago. And, if I got to shag her, then that was an extra bonus.

I could hear chatter and laughter from the loft as I let myself in. I set the meal out on the little table in the middle room and called the girls down. They took their time and I felt impatient.

'Did you miss me?' I said as they came into the room.

They looked at each other without smiling. I had that sinking sense I have always had that I've been talked about, that I've missed something. I tried to read their faces but they were neutral.

'Let's eat.' They sat next to each other, opposite me. They shared a calm silence I hadn't bargained on. I felt excluded by their gender collusion.

'Rachel, would you like to come and spend part, or all if you like, of Christmas Day with us?' I said this while we all helped ourselves to the meal. I poured white wine.

'When you say "us", I hope you don't mean me?' I looked up at Isobel who had reverted to the stony faced hostility of a few days before.

'Yes, that's exactly what I meant, Isobel. Remember, you aren't going to your mother's, are you?'

'Nope! But I'm not spending Christmas Day here either.'

I thought back to the conversation we'd had. I had indeed said that she was free to spend it with whomever she liked. I had naïvely assumed that the only options were me or her mother. Rachel raised her eyebrows, grimaced slightly and looked away.

'Can I ask where you will be that day then?'

Isobel rolled her eyes and nervously drummed her nails on the table. 'I'm spending the night of Christmas Eve with my boyfriend and then all of Christmas Day with him and his mum. Sorry. I just want to be around a proper, normal family.'

I looked at Rachel. How would she think I should react? I was being tested alright. By every woman in my life. I decided to try out the pseudo spiritual tactic. No resistance.

'Ok sweetheart. That *is* what I said. You are old enough to choose. I hope you have a lovely day. Perhaps we could do something together on Boxing Day?'

Both the women looked at me and sat blinking. I smiled and started to nibble at a pork ball.

'Come on you two, it's going to get cold.' I started humming along to Bing Crosbie playing quietly in the background. 'Mmm, mm, this is *good*!'

'I think I'll eat this in my room and give you two some space.' Isobel got up with her plate. 'Thanks Dad. Hope you're not coming down with something.'

'No Isobel. It's just at this time of year, I feel it's best to be generous and grateful for everything we have. I love you sweetheart.' And I did, but I was also bloody furious that she was going to be with Jason Jenkins' family and not me.

I wanted to put my theory to the test. I needed to speak first. I put down my cutlery and cupped Rachel's free hand and in mine, she did not resist and let her hand go limp. It was cool and slender. I felt a wave of desire which I ignored. I needed all my faculties to get through this.

'You asked me why I think I'm here. You asked me if I think I'm capable of redemption. Well, what I haven't told you is that I've begun my spiritual journey, Rachel. Since I came by those letters you saw, I've had to address what it means to be alive. To really be present in one's own life, and take responsibility for it. To forgive. That's what my film is about. Human consciousness. The woman that wrote those letters was highly conscious. I can only dream of the moment that I could attain her level of, um, being.'

Rachel was looking at my hands. Her face was unreadable. I tried to see if there was a flicker of excitement, some recognition of the jargon I had spouted. She just sat. 'The thing is, my wife is highly unconscious. She's an abusive

114

alcoholic. She's a control freak. I've lived with it for years and only had the courage to ask her to move out once I knew my screenplay had been accepted.' I took my hands away and closed my eyes, squeezed them hard. I had no idea if she was looking at me or not. 'I've started on my path to enlightenment, Rachel. Truth, forgiveness, being present. That's what I'm trying to practice, but I need…' I looked up and she was staring at me. 'I need a guide. Will you help me? Will you teach me how to find redemption?'

Wallop. Got her!

She put her hands round my face and said, 'Dear Conrad. I've never met *anyone* quite like you. I'm not sure I'm qualified to be your "guide" but I can be your friend. You have gone some way, with everything I've discovered since I've been here, to giving me the answer I needed. You remember? Are you conscious enough to receive the information I have? Well, I'm beginning to form a cohesive opinion.' She smiled, slightly.

I was in.

****

After our meal. Isobel went out and we returned to the loft where I showed her the trailer for *Flood*. She sat enthralled, captivated. I watched her as she watched my film. She looked so beautiful as the light from each shot - scenes I wrote, flickered across her face. It was like a work of art creating another work of art. I laughed to myself. I felt 'present'. Maybe this was what all Pippa's books were banging on about. Enjoying each moment at a time. And, of course, skirting around all the horrible bits.

At the front door, as she prepared to go, she moved to kiss my cheek, but I caught her on the lips and got to slip a fraction of my tongue into her mouth. She left very soon after, saying she would call. She said 'Conrad, tonight was important, you know that don't you?' I felt something move in my pant area and I knew she was right.

****

On Christmas Day I was restless. I couldn't stand being by myself. All I could think about was Isobel. My little girl with that family. By half ten, I'd made a decision. I didn't know where her boyfriend's mother lived, but I did know where Jason Jenkins lived. I decided to stake him out. I dressed for the event in camouflage, with a high scarf and a low hat. I thought I could pass for a hardy dog walker, off to Duncan Downs, if questioned. Albeit, of course, without a dog.

I approached his house just as Isobel and Jason's son left. There was no sign of the toddler or Jason. I followed them. Luckily, they went on foot and ended up in a house near the station in a cul-de-sac. There was little cover, bar a few shrubs, but I managed to get in under one before neighbouring families left their houses on the inevitable Christmas run-around of obligatory visits. I inched my way closer and finally got a view of the living room and the distant dining room from behind a spikey plant. I quickly saw that the grandma, Jason's ex-wife, seemed to have custody of the child. There was no mother around. Isobel's boyfriend, to his credit, sat and played with the child. Isobel had my camera – *my camera!* And was taking shots as they unwrapped the presents, Jason's ex was fussing around, stuffing wrapping paper into recycling bags and making frequent trips to the kitchen, which was out of view, presumably to prepare dinner. She regularly fetched cups of tea and coffee and juice for the baby. Isobel chatted with her easily. They stood close, touched hands, embraced. There was no front, no arrogant testiness. I had never felt so jealous in my life.

I had sat watching for about an hour when footfall crunched on the drive behind me. I ducked down. Jason

116

Jenkins sauntered up the path carrying a huge Argos bag full of wrapped presents and another carrier bag full of tins of lager.

I was in agony. Not just the cramp from crouching in one shape in the freezing cold, but in my heart. I wondered, had Isobel known what kind of man Jason was, would she still choose to spend Christmas with him? I felt I had to do something. I resolved to storm the house and free her before he burnt her alive. I was just preparing my ambush when he came into the living room. Isobel, the boyfriend and the toddler were nowhere to be seen. Jason was alone with the woman.

There was something about the way his ex-wife approached him that made me reappraise the state of their relations. She held out her arms tenderly and Jason fell into them, his face buried in her hair. His shoulders began to shake and heave and I realised – could it be? Jason Jenkins was crying! I laughed out loud, then ducked back down. I carried on watching. She had put her hands either side of his face and was wiping the tears away. I stopped laughing. I stopped wanting to laugh. The couple stood looking at each other for a long while, then they held each other and leaned foreheads together. It wasn't sexual. I realised what I was witnessing was love.

I reversed backwards through the shrubs, getting scratched and stabbed until I was able to make a bolt for the road. I headed for the High Street right from the bridge at the boring end of town and walked all the way along until I got to Harbour Street. Every car that passed was full of smiling, happy people. The pubs were full of men, having a pre-dinner pint. Laughter and good cheer emanating into the cold air. I did not want to join in. Again, the eerie sense of separateness, of being totally alien, crept into the very guts of me.

I headed home. I opened a bottle of Jack Daniels and I drank it, the whole lot. I sat swaying on the sofa. My film

Burn playing on repeat on the giant flat screen TV just a few feet in front of me.

There I sat in Miranda's leopard skin patterned onesie, cradling my Bafta until finally, mercifully, I passed out.

Chapter 10

Road

New Year's Eve 2014

Jason tapped lightly on the open window and heard the sound of someone rising from a creaky chair within the dark room. The interior door, beyond the shared entrance hall, swung open and the figure receded back into the half-light. Jason put his shoulder to the warped outside door and was immediately engulfed by the stench of incense, dogs and skunk.

After a few seconds, his eyes had adjusted and he wandered cautiously through the unkempt, pokey flat to the narrow galley kitchen at the rear.

Fran's slight body was framed by the back doorway and engulfed by plumes of thick smoke. He looked like an 80s rocker from a bad music video shrouded in dry ice. Jason made his way warily through the kitchen.

'Light the stove, Jace.' Fran flicked his spliff out into the messy garden. Half yard, half scrub, it had one small rusty metal table and two wrought iron chairs surrounded by empty beer bottles full of fag butts.

Jason found matches and lit the stove. Fran shuffled towards the cooker and loomed over Jason. He was so thin, had Jason put his hands around his waist, his fingers would have touched. Fran reached for a milk bottle that had the flat end smashed off it and took the cling film off a healthy bar of cannabis. He got his pen knife and cut two tiny lumps off at the corner, then took two blackened butter knives from the drawer and balanced the dope between them, placing it into the flame. As soon as the gear started to catch and glow, Fran held the milk bottle over it. The bottle was soon full of swirling white smoke. He put his thin lips around the neck and inhaled long and hard then handed the half empty bottle to

Jason. They repeated the procedure until they were both bent double coughing, laughing like chimpanzees.

'Happy new year, dude.' Fran pushed Jason into the dingy living room. A moody old dog watched cautiously and rose crankily. Fran ordered it to stay put and it awkwardly resettled its arthritic body onto the chewed up cushion.

Weak winter light filtered in through the tattered curtains. Jason sat beside Fran on the worn sofa and waited for his head stop spinning. They both sat in silence for some time. Then Jason sniggered and Fran sniggered. 'Fucking hot knives, man. It's been a while.'

'Yeah innit.' Jason was staring at the psychedelic picture on the wall opposite them. It was a painting of a triangle with multi-coloured stripes coming out from its centre, getting larger to appear as though they were light rays rushing towards him. He'd never got it before, but now he did. He realised the old dog was staring at him with a suggestion of fang about the unnaturally dry lip. Jason felt an urge to leave. 'Can't stay long Fran. Got stuff to do.'

'Just leave the paperwork on that table.' Jason placed a score under the ashtray and Fran reached in an inside pocket, got out a pouch and handed Jason a little package.

'You know I've been central to the new anti-fracking protests right? Know why?'

'Haven't got a Scooby mate.' Jason dearly hoped this wasn't going to be one of his rants.

'I had a visitation.'

Jason too had had a visitation of sorts, but not the kind Fran was talking about. He thought back to the day he nearly ended it all and saw, *really* saw, those little birds. She had appeared like an apparition. He'd seen her around over the years of course, their eyes met from time to time. An acknowledgment of a slight nod always exchanged between them, but they weren't friends, not even acquaintances. She had disappeared for many years and was a different person when she came back. Grown up, professional and unhappy looking.

She had been brief.

'Jason,' she had almost whispered, 'everything has changed.' He could see she was serious. 'It's time you knew the truth. I just need to know what you might do with it.'

'I don't understand. Is it about that night?'

'It all goes back to then. Things move on. Very soon, it'll be time for it to all come out. It could unburden you.' She smiled at him with pity, but he didn't feel judged. He was still singing inside from his experience on the tracks.

'You know what really happened, don't you? How come you never told me before?' Jason was aware that he should, by rights, be full of rage. This woman had known all these years and had kept it secret. Yet he was still feeling the resonance of his experience on the railway. The two things seemed linked.

'I would have if I could, but someone needed to be protected. I made a promise. I'm sorry. I know you have suffered.' She had put a hand on his shoulder. 'I need to be sure that you are not going to do anything stupid if and when I can finally tell you.'

'I understand, I think. What might you class as stupid?'

She had smiled and walked past him towards the railway, then turned and said, 'I'll be back in touch. It's good to see you again. Be kind to yourself, Jason.' Then she had walked briskly away.

And now, here was Jason with someone who held onto a dark secret that was perpetually linked to his. He looked at Fran's profile. He looked at the hair resting over his missing ear. A battle wound from that night. He looked down at the scars on his own hands, the burns on them that destroyed his fingertips.

'What kind of visitation, Fran?'

'Aliens man.' He smiled toothlessly at Jason. 'They told me we are raping the earth. I had to act.'

Jason felt emboldened by Fran's state of mind. It was time for him to ask the question and risk Fran's wrath.

'Have you ever told anyone what we did? What you did, then what I did, Fran?'

He took a really long time to answer. His hands were resting on his bony knees and he breathed slowly with his eyelids drifting up and down in lazy blinks.

'I never told anyone man. That doesn't mean I'm the only one that knows.'

'I know that.'

Fran's voice was raspy, unstable. The old dog began a low, almost inaudible growl. Jason wanted to ask, what did I do? What actually happened? Instead he rose.

'Thanks for the hot knives. I'm going home for a kip.'

Fran suddenly bounced to his feet. His eyes wide and unfocused. He grabbed Jason's arm.

'They told me to do what I did that night too. They visited me, three of them, from the mothership and told me she was the devil. Here to ruin the planet not save it! I was working under *their orders*!'

'Okay. Nice one.' Jason snatched his arm back. 'I'll let myself out.'

Fran laughed. 'Don't forget, Jenkins. I know what you did. I *saw* you. I saw that D.F.L. run away. And after I saw what you did, after I sent you to safety, I had to *deal* with it. With *her*.' He started laughing and Jason hurried out as the old dog staggered to its feet and limped towards him.

Outside, his mind was foggy. He wandered to the pub on the beach and ordered a lager, then sat in a bay window by himself and stared at the tall houses of Wavecrest. Twenty-one years had passed since the last New Year's Eve he'd spent in there. Fran was living in a tiny bedsit, the whole house was riddled with people crammed into large rooms divided into smaller, cramped dwellings. The party had been put on by

Fran to welcome the protestors come to town to resist the building of the new Thanet Way that had begun that year. More and more crusties had flooded into the town with a wildly mixed reception. For Fran and Jason, it was good for business. Jason had got a job cheffing and flipping burgers at the local round the corner from his new flat. Life was getting better, despite losing his mum and losing *Her* to his cousin. He had money in his pocket, an inexhaustible supply of drugs, a regular shag and he had work in *a pub.* Sweet.

Jason smiled, remembering, as the lager sent a cold chill down his gullet. He wanted to take it easy. He was so stoned; he didn't want to get the swirly-whirlies. He looked again at the tall house and he remembered that that was the night he'd met Rachel and Noelle. He'd seen Rachel around, with Fran. She was cute, pretty. Very petite, hippified, but very cool. She barely knew Jason existed, she was so out of his league. She was an art student from London but not in a D.F.L. way. She was here to protest.

Fran had a way, despite being extremely ugly and unpleasant, of getting much younger, beautiful women to sleep with him. It was probably all the spiritual hippy clap-trap he was always spouting. And he was *political*. These posh university girls loved all that. Still, Jason knew Fran wasn't right for her. Fran wasn't right for anyone.

At that point, though, Fran was shagging Rachel, the English Rose. Then another wave of them came to town. This lot were altogether different. They meant serious business. Fran had been top dog up to that point. It was *his* protest. He found them places to live, sold them drugs and shagged whatever he could that came on to his radar. The new contingent knocked him off his throne and he didn't like that one bit.

As Jason thought back over those times, he began to feel distinctly drowsy, so he finished his pint and went outside. He decided to walk past Wavecrest and round the caravan park before heading home.

Once in front of the house, he recalled arriving at the party twenty-one years before. He'd just finished his shift and got out quite early – nine, half-nine, perhaps. No one had wanted to eat. It was New Year's Eve, no one came out until ten, and then they just wanted to get smashed. He'd arrived as the new protesters turned up. There were maybe twenty of them. They were a little older than Rachel, a little older than himself. All except the head protester. She was incredibly young for someone in such an esteemed position of power. They were well spoken, educated and so very earnest. They weren't caned and they didn't want to buy any. Jason offered their leader, a small woman sitting in the middle of the floor, a swig from his bottle of Scrumpy. He had been shocked and impressed by her reply.

'Thanks friend, that's really kind, but we don't drink.' The people around them fell silent to listen to her. Jason realised there was something special, important about this woman. She was tiny, yet she had a power and presence about her that commanded attention. She had shaved hair save for a pink dreadlock coming from the top of her head. Her nose and lip were pierced and she wore eighteen-hole Doc Martins painted with green gloss paint.

'It's a party though,' Jason had said, waving the cider at her again. She laughed and shook his shoulder fondly.

'Yeah, thanks for inviting us. None of us in the Dragons drink. It's a rule we all decided on while we're here. We need to be focused.'

'Fuck. You do take this whole road thing seriously.' Everyone laughed except Fran who was far across the room with Rachel tucked under his long bony arm. He was scowling, straining to hear what was being said over the deep trance music.

'We've got big plans. We're going to occupy a property destined for demolition. It's right in the path of the new road. We have to be sober or it could go badly wrong and someone could get hurt. It's my job to make sure that doesn't

124

happen.' All around her, her people were nodding and smiling and saying 'Yeah!' a lot. Jason remembered, it did his head in. He thought they were barking. He actually thought the new road made a lot of sense. Really, who cared if a few old trees got chopped down? If it meant teenagers stopped getting killed on the old road with its crazy suicide lane down the middle, much the better.

'Jason!' Fran had bellowed throwing a £50 note at him. 'Fuck off up the offy and get some vodka and fags, there's a good boy. Leave the politics to the grown-ups.' It got him a cheap laugh from the Whitstable contingent, but Noelle didn't laugh, she smiled apologetically.

'Nice to meet you -?'

'Jason, Jason Jenkins.'

She shook his hand. 'I'm Noelle. Just Noelle.'

Jason never did go back to the party and he never did any work for Fran again. He kept the £50 and spent it on his mates doing shots and speed until 4am in the pub on the edge of town. But that wasn't the last time he would see Noelle. What a shame she hadn't decided to protest somewhere else, he thought, as he stared at the tall house.

He thought of Fran, sitting emaciated and yellow-skinned in his smelly flat and how he'd got the value of that fifty back off him ten times over in the last twenty years. Then he thought of his apparition. Of Rachel, after seeing those little birds, so different in her smart clothes from the little crusty girl she was back then. Back with her strange message that now seemed much more like a warning, or even a threat. Despite that, the possibility of finally unburdening himself seemed like a chance at freedom.

Jason trudged home. It was 2pm and already getting darker. The day had never really got light. He stopped, swaying a little outside the home his father was in and thought back to his visit on Christmas Day. His dad had gone downhill. He was in bed. His breathing was laboured. He had woken only to curse and swear at him. He'd called him a murderer. Jason had been too upset to conceal it from Tracy when he had arrived at her house. It was a relief to share it, but left him feeling vulnerable and irritated by her kindness.

He looked up at the ornately decorated cornices on the roof of the care home, the weirdly mosaicked designs on the walls. He decided to swerve the visit. Besides, he had a serious case of the munchies. He walked across the line without looking up the track and said, 'Hello birds', as he crossed, then giggled to himself.

Despite the usual sadness, for his mum, his frail old dad, his lost life, for *Her*. Despite all that, for the first time he could remember, there were gaps forming between the sadnesses. And shining through those gaps was hope.

****

Tracy arrived at 9pm. She had suggested on Christmas Day that they babysit for Joe and Isobel and spend the evening together. Jason had been too emotional after seeing his dad to object and had agreed this was a good idea at the time, now he wasn't so sure. He didn't want another deep and meaningful and he wasn't sure he'd be able to maintain a convincing silence if Tracy started to question him.

She came in, poured herself a large glass of white wine, kicked her shoes off and curled up on what used to be her sofa. It was almost as though they'd never split up.

'Want to watch a film?'

This appealed to him. He could sit on the other sofa and drink and wouldn't have to talk to her.

'What have you got in mind? I'm not watching anything with Julia Roberts or Hugh Grant in it.' Tracy laughed, her face rosy and her eyes bright.

'An old favourite? What about *Trainspotting*?'

Jason nodded and got the DVD off the shelf. It had been long enough since he had last seen it to tolerate it again, but wasn't sure hearing what had been the soundtrack of that time would do his thinking much good. It was better than being made to talk about his feelings though.

'Come and sit here with me Jace, you're at a funny angle.' Tracy patted the cushion next to her and he dutifully moved seats. She wiggled her feet up next to him, and smiled sweetly, squeezing her eyes like a Persian cat.

He felt trapped. The film began and the familiar high octane music started. His chest was pounding along to it.

'What do you suppose they meant by "choose life"?'

'Are you going to talk all the way through it?' Tracy shook her head and laughed.

'It's just a weird thing to say, innit? You don't *choose* life. You're alive!' Jason kind of got what she meant, but he knew what the film meant too. You'd only really get it if you had actively avoided living for twenty years. He drained his Stella.

Tracy managed to stay silent for another twenty-five minutes. Then she paused it to go to the bathroom. She came back in and didn't press play. Instead, she swivelled round on the sofa and sat crossed legged to face him.

'Do you remember Jace, this came out the year Joe was born?'

'I know it was about that time, yeah.'

'But don't you remember? We went to see it and I was really pregnant. I cried and cried at the scene when the baby dies. We were in the cinema above the fish restaurant. Don't you remember?'

Jason thought hard. He remembered the film, but that might have been because he'd watched it and heard the soundtrack so many times since. He couldn't remember taking her to the cinema, he couldn't remember her crying. He couldn't remember anything about that year at all.

'Jace, you alright?' The unwarranted sympathy again. Like she was scrubbing a cheese grater at his insides. He wanted to run screaming from the room.

127

'No. I don't remember the fucking film, or going there, or you crying, alright?' His voice had risen a notch or two in volume more than he'd meant. He thought of Aleisha. Tracy looked hurt. He couldn't stop himself. 'I don't actually fucking remember much about you being pregnant if I'm honest, Tracy.' Her eyes pricked with tears.

'But that was one of the happiest times in our relationship!'

'I don't remember it that way. I don't remember him being born and I don't remember what it was like just after either. The whole thing, that whole year is a blank.'

'Why?'

'I was very, very, very drunk. Now let's finish watching the film and stop going over this stuff.'

She sat staring at him, her lip quivering. He knew why she was upset. They'd been different together lately, he'd thawed, let her in. Now he'd slammed her out again.

'Do you remember getting married?'

'No. A bit. Sort of. I don't like to think about then.'

'That's not true. You do think about then, don't you?' Her voice shook. 'It's all you do bloody think about. Then. *Her.* That night. The reason you're so angry is because it's all you think about every day. Your head is always in the past, you're never really here.' She tried to take hold of his hands, a beseeching look in her eyes. 'Jason, look at me. I'm here - right now! Wake up!'

He threw her hands off. 'Oh fuck off, Tracy. Don't start all this crap again. You'll be banging on about bloody therapy and treatment and all that. Leave me be.'

'So you admit you don't remember much from back then?'

'Fuck all'.

'What about that night then?'

She'd got him. If he admitted he couldn't remember, it would leave her open to interpret what might have happened

that night - her way. If he said he could remember, she'd want
to know about it.

'I don't want to talk about it.'

'Well I do!' Tracy's chest was heaving; her eyes were
wet. 'I've wasted two decades of my life on you. The very
least you can give me is the truth for once.'

Jason looked at her and his guilt bit him hard. She was
right. What harm would it do after all? She wasn't going to
turn him in.

'Ok. I remember some of that night up to a point, then
it's a blank. What I do know though is that some cunt followed
me and he saw it all.'

'Do you know who?'

'That fucking writer, Blaine.' Jason swigged his beer
and crunched the empty can in his fist. 'That film was based
on what he saw. You were right.'

'But, in the film -'

'Right that's enough. I don't want to talk anymore.'

'Did you do it? Did you hurt that girl?'

'Tracy, I want you to leave.' Jason kept his voice low.
He knew if he lost his temper now, he would shout, swear,
worse and he didn't want to go there. He could already feel
the fire burning in his chest.

'Did you kill someone or did he make that up?' she
shouted, crying hard.

'Tracy, *leave.*' Jason stood and Tracy snatched her
shoes, rushed past him out of the room and out of the house
barefoot. He heard her slam the front door and all he felt was
intense relief.

Jason headed to the kitchen, intending to put it all right
with a stiff drink. Instead, curiously, his body stopped dead at
the foot of the stairs. He climbed them quietly and pushed the
door open into his granddaughter's room. She was tiny for
two, still barely speaking. Health visitors regarded her as
underweight, below the lowest centile, whatever that meant.
But her nature was so sweet. Aslumber, she still had the plump

129

cheeks of a baby. Her golden curls were splayed about her on the pillow and she whistled softly into her favourite bear as she slept. He stood and looked at her and failed to retrieve any such memory of Joe the same age. He felt a new sadness burden him and he retreated from the room and drifted down to the kitchen.

He got the vodka out of the freezer and a glass from the drainer and he poured himself a large one and lit a cigarette. He tore a strip of paper from a utility envelope left on the table and lit it with his zippo. The paper curled and twisted exquisitely. He tipped it up, keeping his fingers clear until the flame accelerated and he dropped it into the ash tray. He lit another, and another. The vodka remained untouched. Jason felt a growing compulsion to do something he hadn't done, had managed to deter with alcohol and drugs, for a long time. He wanted to light something – something *big*.

He rose and pulled on a hoodie then stumbled into the small back garden just as the sky lit up nearby with fireworks. Music blared out from noisy neighbourhood New Year parties. He dragged an old armchair into the middle of the long grass. It was damp, sodden inside. He'd intended to take it to the dump before his car bit the dust, so it had sat there for six months at least. He went to the shed, knowing exactly what he was going to use - his own carefully honed recipe for napalm. He'd discovered, after his latest flat screen TV was delivered, that Dixon's polystyrene packaging was far superior to the product packed by Argos. He dissolved a fair amount in some of the petrol for the old lawn mower that no longer worked and decided he might as well use the rest of the jerry can. He took two propane bottles he'd nicked from a local roofer, knowing they'd come in right handy, and rammed them into the arms of the chair, shoved the jerry can under the seat and doused the whole thing in his special concoction.

'I'll give you fucking fireworks,' he said and threw the match towards the chair then stood to one side of the shed.

The chair left the ground with great force and a boom so loud the shed windows blew in. A chair sized fire ball rocketed through the rickety fence, into the public footpath behind and came to rest on its side by a discarded Tesco shopping trolley. As it burned ferociously, the old jungle track, 'Terrorist' by Renegade thumped in his head and saw *Her*, Sasha, dancing, totally lost in the bass. The arms blew off the chair in time with the drums, the fabric and foam curled back to reveal the glowing wooden frame, like Fran's old dog curling his lip back, snarling.

Jason laughed out loud. He felt so alive, yet so at peace. Almost the same feeling he'd had when he'd heard the little birds, except there was one big difference: the delicious chaos. He headed inside as neighbours ran out of their houses from their celebrations to investigate the explosion.

He poured the vodka back into the bottle, switched off the kitchen light and went to bed.

Jason had finally made a decision. He wanted to live. He didn't want to miss Aleisha's life like he'd missed Joe's or his own for that matter. He wouldn't hassle Rachel, but it was time to get some answers. He couldn't wait for her to decide when the time was right. That meant there was only one way to fill in the missing pieces.

It meant it was time to finally do something about C.K. Blaine.

Chapter 11

Break

January 2015

I sat, stroking my beard, deep in thought, but enjoying being in a warm and busy café as the weather raged wild outside. I studied each local male that passed with a forensic interest. There were virtually no Londoners in the bitter January rain. The ones that did come, stood about, looking miserably up and down the street, wondering why on earth they'd bothered. I scanned each eerily similar male for a familiarity, attempting to see if I might recognise them - if I shaved twenty years and a lot of beer belly off. I'd had no luck so far.

I'd taken to doing this in the last week. Setting myself up in the best vantage places in all the cafés up the High Street, apart from the Kebab ones of course, under the ruse of writing with my laptop, but really, it was reconnaissance. Or rather, my own witness identification operation. It was proving frustratingly futile. I'd come to believe it could have been any of the world-weary, potato faced, middle aged men I saw.

This was one of my two favourite cafés because it was run by locals, had a good view up and down the High Street and did a damn fine breakfast. I could legitimately perpetuate the fallacy that I was a much loved, fully accepted member of the core community while in reality, I was like a highly trained spy, senses taught as a tripwire, eating a smoked salmon and cream cheese bagel with a cappuccino - all as a clever cover.

I was planted in the window seat right opposite the High Street supermarket and an old fashioned ladies' underwear shop, when I spotted Jason. I ducked down behind a programme for the local theatre effort and keenly observed him. He'd stopped outside the shop and was talking to a short woman with the hood of her dark green coat pulled up against the horizontal rain. She seemed familiar. The coat, the boots, looked too expensive and well-tailored for the type of woman I assumed Jason would know. Her composure, the way she carried herself jarred too – at odds with someone who would talk to him in the street at least. Just then, my mobile rang. It was my editor. I felt a rush of panic whenever he rang that maybe I'd been found out; that he'd discovered I was really a fraud, then I smiled and confidently answered, knowing several pretty waitresses were earwigging.

'Peter – I,' before I could speak, Peter Gordon, the Rottweiler editor of the Culture section of the weekend paper I wrote for, exploded with a barrage of expletives. I had to hold the phone away from my face, it was so loud and offensive. Once the volume dipped down, I put the phone back to my ear and caught the tail end of it.

'- you fucking twat. So they're running it tomorrow. Thank fucking god my Sub is shagging the Editor's PA over there or I'd be none the wiser. They've got *examples* for fuck's sake!' He was breathing hard. I could imagine him, puce faced and sweaty in his office.

'Peter, what was the middle bit? My connection isn't good.'

'What? The bit where I tell you some arsewipe has sent an anonymous letter to our arch rival weekend paper with an exposé of where you sourced, illegally, immorally sourced they claim, the material you turned into your latest film attempt. That? Or the bit shortly afters where I tell you you're going to be my *ex* weekend columnist unless you pull your finger out of your gay arse and come up with something I can print head to head with it that transforms their story from headline grabbing revelation to utter dog shite?! You've got until 4pm. I want hourly updates. Get started - NOW!' he bellowed down the phone then hung up.

I looked about. The ladies in the café were all silent, smirking into their teacups. The owner of the café, a tall, dark, intimidating local I knew enjoyed taking my money but little else about me, was smiling at me for the first time ever, his pretty wife nearby, unnecessarily wiping a table over and over, lips pursed, supressing a giggle. I swung my head around and looked across the road. Jenkins was there, the mystery woman had gone. He leaned on the metal bars in front of the supermarket, hood up, staring, not taking his eyes off me.

I quickly paid and left, not looking at Jenkins. I just scuttled along the High Street and up to Cushing's View where I began hyperventilating, hoovering in blasts of North Sea air. I sat on the sea wall and sent the same text to Isobel and Rachel. 'Was it you?'

I didn't expect to get a reply. I then did something I was at pains to do. It was a measure of my desperation and really the last resort: I rang my wife.

After another barrage of abuse, she agreed to take some emergency leave and get on the next train. That gave me approximately three hours to try and fix it myself without having to seek her help to PR me out of this hole. I took three very deep breaths and began walking slowly towards the harbour as I called Rachel. She spoke first.

'Was it me? It depends what it is. Are you alright?'

'No.'

'I'm on leave, come round. I'm the first house next to the celebrity chef's restaurant. See you in a minute.'

Having brushed up on my new age clap trap since I'd realised her game, I knew what I was going to say as soon as I told her. And in a way it was true. Out of every bad situation there is an opportunity for good to come out. I was well on my way to finally getting romantic with her.

It only took me two minutes to get to her door which opened as I arrived. Her house was small, draughty but beautifully decorated. Very minimal, simple and chic. She led me through to the sparkling white kitchen where there was a pot of coffee already brewing.

'Tell me, what's happened?' She perched on a stool at the breakfast bar. She was dressed in yoga pants and a warm fleece, her hair was scraped up into a bun. She looked about twenty.

I took a deep breath.

'My editor just rang to tell me our rival paper has been given a tip off that I stole a load of letters from a dead local and turned them into my new film without permission.' I slugged at my coffee, knowing it was only going to make me more wired, less able to deal with the unravelling nightmare.

'Is that true?'

I thought about lying, but I needed her help. 'Sort of. The woman involved probably wouldn't have minded. But I never asked her.'

'I see. The letters I found in your office. So your producer, director, where do they think you got the story?'

'From my own head?' I knew it sounded bad. 'Listen, I have realised, since I met you that, er, life will give you whatever experience is good for the evolution of your consciousness.' I stood shaking slightly from the caffeine, nodding sagely at her.

She smiled kindly. 'In that case, dear Conrad, can I suggest you just go with this. Let them print it. Let the truth come out. It certainly can't change the past.'

'Rachel! I need to find out who did this to me! As far as I know, only you, possibly my wife and daughters and the woman who gave me the letters know that I have them. I can't see how you would benefit from exposing me, I can't imagine it was my wife or daughters, so it has to be her, the woman I got them from - Joanne Kemp! She'd copied the first few hundred words of a letter out for my class. Maybe she showed her husband, or a friend – who knows!'

'Ah, the source of your "research" – looks like you've got a bit of soul searching to do.' Rachel hopped off the stool and calmly walked across the room. She took my cup and set it down then took both my hands and held them in hers against her heart. I was sure she was about to kiss me.   'Conrad, Conrad. Stop it. It doesn't matter who "did it to you". It's happened. You can't do anything about the past and trying to influence the future is futile. Why don't you just go with the flow and allow it to play out? Trust your gut feeling. You *do* know what to do.' I didn't understand a word of what she just said, but I was enjoying feeling her warm skin, her heartbeat through her fleece so much, I was prepared to agree to anything.

'Are we ever going to be more than just friends?' She smiled. 'Ever?' I performed my up-and-under glance through my golden locks. 'It would cheer me up.' She let go of my hands, and, for a fraction of a moment, I thought she was going to lead me upstairs. Instead she sat back on the stool.

'Temporarily maybe, but the situation would be the same, just with an extra layer of complication to it.' She looked at me with concern then. 'You can't control the future, Conrad. No matter how many scenarios you rehearse in your head. It will unravel as it's meant to. With or without your thinking.'

I nodded but I thought about Pippa. She controlled everything she did, she could control the future. It's what she did. I became aware of the time and knew I had to go. Rachel saw me to the door.

'This is a chance for you to do the right thing. Forget your career, the success of your new film, money, your wife. Deep down, if you listen to your instincts, you will know.' She gently pushed me out of her house. 'I'll be interested to see what you do.'

I walked backwards and was just contemplating whether to blow her a kiss when she said, 'Oh, and Conrad – you've got a bit of, something – what is that? Fish? In your beard. Bye.' Then she shut the door.

I trudged the short way back to my fisherman's cottage with a heavy heart. Something was niggling at me. I couldn't shake it off. When I got to the alleyway I stopped dead and a blinding clarity came to me.

I could just tell the truth! I could actually just let the whole sordid tale come out. I could just let it happen.

I laughed out loud. Not a shallow, amused laugh, or a sarcastic clever-clever laugh, but a real, machine-gun belly laugh that took me by surprise. It was so simple. What had I been so afraid of? In one action, I could free myself not only from the past, stealing the letters, but from fear of the future. I felt instantly unburdened in a way I hadn't in years. I laughed again. Then it seemed so obvious – why not tell the truth about *Burn* too? What harm would it do? There need by no mention of names, just the facts. Well, not *all* of the facts, not the really bad facts, like the ones that implicated me as an accessory for example. But to confess! To be able to shake Jenkins off my back forever – it was so beautifully simple.

I broke into a run to my cottage and flew up the stairs to my desk. I spent the next hour writing a detailed confession of my actions on and after the night I followed Jason Jenkins and the way I had appropriated and used Minnie's letters. I was just about to email it to my editor when I heard Pippa's shrill voice from bellow. I saved it.

I slowly tiptoed down to the living room, where she was stomping about, rearranging cushions and tutting at discarded clothing. Before my body had even emerged into the room, she stopped, hands on hips and said in a low growl one might use to discipline a dog, 'Thank God I'm here. I got a taxi from London. I'll manage this from now on, Conrad. I'm back.'

I was sent immediately back upstairs. She gave me fifteen minutes to explain, in bullet form, exactly what I did and in what order. I left one crucial bit out. The letter to the local press. I liked that I still knew something no one else did, not even that bitch Joanne Kemp. And I liked that she thought I cleverly came up with the huge plot twist at the end. I wanted to own that, to have something that was my creation, even if I'd never have thought of it in a thousand years. Then she dictated a five-hundred word piece to go to the Editor entitled,

'Rest in Piece' with the sub-title, 'Why Writers Should Be Brave with their Historical Sources'. It was an assertive, aggressive article about how I had single handedly uncovered and exposed the truth about a local murder that might have otherwise gone unknown and forgotten. I had, apparently, boldly taken those letters and bravely crafted them into a beautiful story that paid homage to the woman that wrote them.

Pippa glossed over the legals, but insisted we had our story straight. She demanded to know exactly what Joanne had said and decided we would say that we'd come across the letters in the top of an old wardrobe we bought at a house clearance, if asked. If anyone mentioned Joanne Kemp, I should deny she had anything to do with it. Beyond that - let the public decide, she said. She then spent an hour on the phone to the film's funders, the producer and director and the marketing people. All saw the potential of this new development. They decided to get all the crew to sign a secrecy contract and leak a statement that they had done it. She was texting my editor every forty-five minutes. At 3.30pm she rang him, satisfied that the copy was ready to go.

He loved it.

He got hold of some photographs of the flood in 1953 to run with the story and persuaded me to write another piece in the lead up to the film's release in February about what life was like for women in the town back then, to interview people who'd survived the flood. I agreed but looked at Pippa in horror. She wrote, 'Don't worry, I'll bloody write it,' on a piece of paper in front of me.

All the while this was happening and I was being 'managed', Rachel's words echoed. I clung on to the idea of telling the truth, telling myself as the clock ticked that I would stand up to Pippa, tell her what I needed to do. But it never seemed the right moment. As we waited to see if Peter Gordon and the legal team gave it the final go-ahead, I realised my chance was diminishing. My golden opportunity was melting away like butter in a pan, transforming into liquid, then evaporating. I felt sick in my stomach. For a while this felt bad, then I realised, it was how I always felt, it was just that I'd had a strange respite from it while I thought I'd could seek redemption. I could feel the anxiety, the buzz of being scared of what was to come next return, and it felt like a warm blanket. I looked at my wife, talking in a clipped efficient voice down the phone, jotting in a note pad, stabbing at her iPad and, with a sinking heart, I realised we needed each other.

Once the story was dispatched, Pippa opened a bottle of Prosecco and we went to bed. I resisted the fantasy at first, but couldn't help imagining it was Rachel. Afterwards, Pippa said, 'Conrad, you better have told me everything. I might not be so willing to bail you out if you're not telling me the whole truth.' She played with the hair on my chest. 'Remember, Conrad, it was *me* that made you.'

I kissed her on the mouth to shut her up.

When the girls came in from school, arguing, harassed, shocked to see their mother, Pippa forced them to sit down on the sofa to have a family conference.

'Tomorrow, there's going to be a bit of a fuss about your dad in the papers. I want you to know that the story *we* wrote is the truth.'

They stared blankly at her.

'And what I mean by that, is that this is the version of the truth that we, as a family, are going to stick to.'

The girls looked at one another.

'Because if either of you do not stick to our version of the truth, you will have your phones taken away and your allowances frozen. Instantly.'

Isobel stood up, 'Whatever. By the way, this was on the doormat. Not sure who it's for.' She threw a jiffy bag onto the coffee table, sighed and thumped up the stairs to her room. Miranda looked from me to her mother.

'Is Dad in trouble?'

'No, no darling. Not at all. This – the film, the papers, it's all a game you see. And Dad, who's been a *very* silly man, lucky for him, he has me.' Pippa went over and hugged our youngest daughter and smiled at me triumphantly. I felt my life contract, wither. I was back in my box, all the more prison-like for having had some freedom, yet she had saved me. My reputation, my film, my past and my future. I thought about her warning. Maybe now was the time to finally tell her it all. Tell her about Jason Jenkins.

Pippa picked up the jiffy bag. 'Conrad, do you know anything about this?'

In big marker pen someone had addressed the package to Mr K. Hunt. 'I'll take it back to the post office.'

'It's been *hand delivered*.' Pippa began to unseal it and shoved her hand inside, 'Oh fuck! What the hell?' Miranda recoiled in disgust and covered her mouth as Pippa pulled her hand out, her fist around a large turd, the faeces right up between her fingers and under her nails. She screamed and ran to the kitchen where I could hear her shouting 'Fuck! Who would do that? Fuck!', while she blasted the dog poo off and washed her hand in bleach.

Sometime later, when she had had several showers and a nap, she came up to my attic. I knew I should feel sorry for her, but I actually just felt grateful it hadn't been me that opened it.

'Conrad, that package was meant for you. Do you think the two things are connected, you know, the letter to the paper about Minnie's story, now this? Could it have been the Kemp woman who you took the letters from?'

I knew the answer, but to tell her, I'd have to reveal everything. I waited. Maybe I could still tell the truth, about *Burn* at least. Maybe if Rachel heard I'd done that, I might pass her 'test'.

'Oh, I don't want to talk about it now,' she said, eyes shut, rubbing her brow. 'What a day. Tomorrow, when we know both stories are published, we are going out for a family breakfast in the middle of town. I want people to see us and I want us to hold our heads up, front it out.' She wrapped her dressing gown up tighter. 'And Conrad, you can shave that beard off before we go. You look like a joke.' She turned and thudded down the stairs. 'Don't forget to put the dishwasher on before you come to bed.'

I looked down at the dark hole at the bottom of the stairs where she had just been. I bared my teeth. I knew then, I would never, ever be free of her.

****

The three of us sat, squashed in the window seat, at my other favourite café opposite a new, much needed supermarket; albeit, sadly not a Waitrose.

Pippa stage managed the whole thing. We had full English breakfasts. She and Miranda were wearing something that apparently said, 'effortlessly casual, yet assured' and I was newly shorn, feeling vulnerable and alien with my bald chin. I kept reaching to stroke my beard, and it was gone. I felt Pippa had violated my human rights. At least, my right to be a man. I wasn't hungry and I pushed the food about. The cold yolk congealed into the beans, making me retch slightly. Pippa was loudly reading interesting things out of the paper – neither my paper nor the rival publication, and I was to respond in a way that said, 'Nothing to see here, business as usual'.

Pippa took a sly look at her smart phone and she squealed. Several people eating breakfast at the bar looked over. I sank into my seat. She grabbed my arm and whispered hoarsely, 'It's bloody worked! My Twitter account has gone berserk. You are actually trending my darling! People are calling you brave, bold, honest. We've bloody done it!' I gave her a thin smile. If my bacon was saved, how come I didn't feel good about it?

141

I looked across at the supermarket and leaning on the plate glass window opposite, was Jenkins. His hood was up, casting shadow over his face, but I knew it he was looking at me. He moved slowly to the entrance of the shop and his son joined him from within. He lit two cigarettes, passed one to the youth that was sexually violating my daughter, then he leaned back on the plate glass window and continued to stare.

'Daddy, who's that man?' Miranda asked as Pippa continued to check her email and other social media. 'Why is he staring at you?' Pippa's head snapped up. She scowled at Jenkins over her reading glasses.

'Do you know him, Conrad?'

Again, a chance to tell the truth. To abolish any power Jenkins had by bringing the real story behind *Burn* into the open. And why not, now I was nationally known as a beacon of the truth, of the right for a writer to ferret out long lost untold stories? I stared at him and he smiled, his signature exhalation of fag smoke, creeping from the cats-cradle of missing teeth.

'No, course you don't,' said Pippa, returning her attention to her phone. 'Look at the state of him. He's clearly deranged. Don't worry Miranda, he's probably on smack.' Miranda frowned.

I had to sign several autographs of my article in the café before I left. Pippa almost had the punters form an orderly queue. I was like a dysfunctional, sham book signing. I'd hoped Jenkins would be gone by the time I left, but there he was leaning, smoking, grinning. We walked towards the harbour and I realised he was following. I wanted to shake him off. It was clear that it had been him who'd sent the dog shit. He was upping the ante. I remembered back all those years to the point at which I had realised he wasn't just a sad, crazy pikey on a bender, when I actually knew he was dangerous, when my own life was at risk. Now, I started to fear for the safety of my wife, my daughters. How had this got so complicated?

'Um, let's go to the Gorrell Tank, my van is there. We could go for a drive? That would be nice wouldn't it?' Pippa and Miranda looked at me, aghast.

'Who "goes for a drive"? I'm not in my seventies! Besides, I need to get home and monitor how this story is breaking and developing. This is our future, Conrad!'

'Why is your van always parked there, Dad?'

I really didn't have time for this. Jenkins was closing in. We had a double murderer on our heels and these two were asking stupid questions.

'He can't parallel park it in our road. It's too big.' They both laughed.

Jenkins was alone and he was nearing, twenty, then fifteen feet behind us. Striding in that strange familiar lumber, fists deep in his pockets, hood up.

'Let me just move the van then? Find a free parking space.' I pleaded.

Pippa and Miranda rolled their eyes and groaned. I shepherded them across the road, not waiting for the lights to change, waving apologetically as a taxi driver blasted his horn and shouted out of the window, 'Fucking D.F.L.s! Don't you have traffic lights in that London, you *wanker*!'

Jenkins stood by the railings on Cromwell Road, lighting another cigarette, surveying the car park beneath as I herded my family, my vulnerable women, down the steps, across the concrete, to the comparative safety of the VW. I unlocked the van and practically pushed the girls in. I started the engine without putting on my seat belt and pulled away fast, only to find the vehicle lurching, rocking about from side to side. I stopped and jumped out, leaving the engine running, Dire Straits blasting from the stereo. Jason was standing with his arms spread out on the rail, looking like a totalitarian dictator surveying his domain.

Every tyre had been slashed. Not just a little, but shredded to ribbons.

I jumped back in and drove off regardless.

'What's wrong? Why is it *undulating*?'

'The tracking's out, that's all.' Pippa stared at me with total displeasure for several seconds then her phone buzzed. I drove to Belmont Road and abandoned the van at the garage. It was far enough away from Jenkins to alight and they could fix the tyres. The girls were furious and demanded I order a taxi to take us home. I was happy to do so, safe in the knowledge we would be unlikely to cross Jason's path that way. We stood in silence until the same angry taxi driver pulled up. I was still too anxious to care or even mind that he charged £12 to take us to our cottage. Only when I got in and slammed the door shut behind us did I stop feeling sick. I sat on the sofa with my head in my hands, panting gently, trying to take stock of the events, the connections, who was on my back, who I was dealing with. It was a mess.

Pippa squeezed my shoulder and said 'You've had a hard twenty-four hours. It'll be fine,' and disappeared to find her laptop.

My phone hummed in my pocket with a text message. It was Rachel. 'I'm disappointed. I've made my decision. You're on your own and staying in the dark. Sorry.'

I texted back 'She made me do it! Meet me. I can explain!'

I could hear Pippa laughing on the phone with my producer, setting up meetings, interviews, turning my revelations into an event.

My phone hummed again. 'Last chance. Meet me next week when the dust has settled, when she's gone.'

Yes! I still had a chance. I stretched my arms out, feeling some of the tension leaving my shoulders, I reached for my beard to be met by unwelcome rasping stubble, just as the letterbox creaked open and another parcel landed on the mat with a dull thud. I sprang up and ran to the window, too scared to open the door, but I could see no-one. I picked the package up.

'What was that?' hollered Pippa from the kitchen. 'Not another one of those disgusting parcels, darling?'

I cleared my throat as I turned the jiffy bag over. 'No, no. Just the crappy free paper. I'll put it in the bin.'

'You know, in case we get any more, we might want to think about talking to a lawyer about that Kemp woman. I don't suppose she'd want people finding out she failed to carry out the will of a dear little old lady? What a stupid idiot!'

I stood and stared at the package. It wasn't from Joanne Kemp and neither had the other one been. Joanne Kemp hadn't slashed my tyres. I looked at the marks on the envelope that vaguely resembled the letters that only a semi-literate imbecile would form. 'To Ben Dover' it said in scratchy biro, hastily written after the package had been sealed, the pen puncturing the surface in several places. I shoved it up my jumper and bounded up the stairs then opened the skylight in case it was a repeat of the package from earlier. I lay newspaper on the floor then cautiously unsealed the edge and shook it gently.

A small metal object thumped onto the paper. It was a shiny zippo lighter. I got a pen and flipped it over with the nib, not taking any chances. And what I saw made me feel faint with terror.

Jason Jenkins had carefully printed and cut out a photograph of Isobel and taped it to the lighter. It could only mean one thing - if I told anyone, anyone at all what happened, he would hurt my daughter. I stared at the lighter and thought back to the woman I saw Jason manhandle that night. She could have only just been out of her teens herself. He'd killed his mother, he'd undoubtedly killed the young woman, now he was coming for Isobel. I knew any normal person would have gone to the police immediately, yet I knew if I did, I'd lose everything.

I sent another text to Rachel. 'I think I'm ready to come clean about *Burn* if I have to. Please just tell me the truth about who else was there.' I lied.

'I'm glad. I can't promise I'll be able to tell you anything new just yet though. Come to my house, Thursday at 7pm.'

I stared at the photo of Isobel, taken, by the look of it, on Christmas day. The suggestion of decorations in the background, the familiar fabric of his ex-wife's sofa. Although I knew what I should do, I wasn't ready to tell anyone about *Burn*. Not now. Not after the near fuck up with the letters. What I *was* ready for, however, was to sort Jason Jenkins out once and for all. Rachel had told me she knew him. She knew the truth. And that lady was damn well going to help me get rid of him.

Chapter 12

Twist

January 2015

With Tracy not speaking to him, a total absence of employment and a continued abstinence from drinking, Jason had more time on his hands than he could manage. An unhealthy amount of time. He knew, deep down, he was going too far, but his compulsion to have contact with Blaine, to mess with his head, was too much to resist.

In a week, he had carried some of the most classic wind-ups he could think of. After starting off gently with the dog shit, the tyre slashing and the lighter with a photo of Isobel taped to it, Jason had bombarded Blaine with at least one prank a day until eventually there was a knock on his door one evening. Jason never got visitors and the knock sounded suspiciously like the serious, assertive knock of a Pig. He shuffled through the darkness from the kitchen to the porch, peeped through the letterbox and let her in.

'Jason. We need to talk.' Rachel bristled down the hall, her long green coat flaring out behind her as she lowered her hood and shook out her pale hair.

'Would you like to come in?' Jason said sarcastically to the empty space where she'd just stood.

He slammed the door and followed her down into the kitchen where she had already pulled out a chair and sat down. She looked less angelic than she had after his encounter with the birds on the train line. Maybe it was his sobriety, the on-going feeling of loss, the shortness of his temper and the constant cravings, but Rachel looked old, drained and like she had an axe to grind.

'What can I do you for? Want a cuppa?' He tried to keep it even, not give away any sense that his life had taken yet another, less than positive turn as he flicked the worn plastic kettle on. Revenge was all consuming and not nearly as satisfying as he had expected. And none of it, not one bit of it had choked off the near constant memories, getting sharper, more lacerating, by the day.

'You've been having some fun, haven't you, Jason?'

He smiled to himself as he filled the mugs from the kettle and stabbed at the teabags until the water turned a rich brown.

'Can't imagine what you mean.'

'Right. Some old classics in there. Glue in the door lock. Pizza delivery for Mr. Wayne King. I liked the rent boy for Mr A Koch. Nice. But my personal favourites, the ones that actually tipped him over the edge were the Facebook frapeing and the cling film on the toilet.' Jason stifled a snigger. 'Not because it's original, or especially funny, but because it just took the abuse way too far — it meant you'd been *in his house*.' Jason set the steaming teas down in front of them. 'On top of the zippo lighter with a photo of his daughter, of course. The man's in pieces. And now it's got to stop.' Jason thought with pride about the fake Facebook post he'd put up. He'd put the cling film on the toilet and decided to find Blaine's computer. The numpty had left the machine logged into his Facebook account. Jason had written 'I love cock!' as his update and posted it.

He stopped sniggering when he saw her expression. Jason sat down opposite Rachel and rubbed his face.

'You broke into his house. He's a nervous wreck as it is. Now he's having a complete meltdown'

'Good.'

Rachel looked at him for some time. 'You don't trust me do you?'

'I don't trust anyone.'

'That's a shame. I thought we had an understanding, Jason.'

'What exactly is it you want? I was fucked last time you spoke to me. I can barely remember what you said. Something about the truth? What the bollocks?' Jason was feeling really irritable. He thought of the ice cold vodka he still kept in the freezer, just in case.

'I'm glad you're more lucid. You will need a clear head to handle what will happen. You've heard of Karma right? Things come around. Nothing goes away.'

'My mum always used to say, "It'll always come out in the wash".'

'Well maybe your old mum knew what she was talking about.'

'She never got to be old, remember? Look, get to the point.' Jason sipped the scalding hot tea and felt calmer.

'Sometime in the next few months, the truth about what happened that night in 1995 will come out, it has to. The summer solstice isn't just the anniversary of that night. It's a special day for another reason, a better reason too. It won't be me doing the telling, it's beyond my control, but I've been asked to talk to you – and Blaine – about how you're going to handle it. I want to know what you might do if that happens.'

Jason took a deep breath and exhaled long and slow, unable to think of the implications, the reach of the problems and who they would effect. He couldn't get Tracy out of his head. What she had said on New Year's Eve before she left. He suddenly felt heavy with loss.

'I will give myself up.' Jason said this quietly into his tea. He watched a small cluster of bubbles spiral and touched them gently with the tip of his finger.

'Go on.'

'I thought, after that prat admitted to stealing another life, actually using old Minnie's letters and then claiming to have uncovered a 'hidden story', that I could frighten him into admitting he'd stolen mine too. I want to ruin him. I actually don't care what anyone finds out now. I've been in prison for twenty years anyway.' Jason tapped his head. 'In prison up here.' Rachel nodded slowly. 'What the fuck have I got? Fuck all. Why should that bell-end get a good life when he stole mine and held that over me for all those years?'

'Jason, he's an outsider. He didn't know the whole town knew about Minnie. But neither does he realise that most of the town knew about what you were like too. That *everyone* saw that film and thought it seemed familiar, similar to the rumours at least. Listen, I've been asked to talk to him too.'

'Who did the asking?'

'Someone else who was there that night.'

'Fran? What the fuck? He's the reason this shit happened in the first place.' Jason stopped. Rachel had a curious expression on her face. He remembered again that she's been with Fran for a while back then, although well before the summer solstice. He said cautiously, 'It's always been him you ought to be worrying about if this comes out. The police came close – they knew he'd done something because of the state of his ear, he was the last person she was seen with. The fire destroyed any evidence he'd been near the huts.'

Rachel nodded, her gaze dropping to her hands around the cup. 'Let's keep Fran out of this for the moment.'

'Then who? How come you know what happened? How come you haven't told anyone or turned me in? Are you protecting Fran? You had a thing with him back then, didn't you? Is this what this is all about?' Jason could feel his anger rising. The old pattern digging deep, the old urges pushing up the need to fire-light, twisting it up inside.

'Calm down. I grew up and realised Fran was a user. I realised lots of things that summer.' Rachel sighed and looked up at the ceiling. She was trying to compose herself, to stay in control. 'The reason I'm involved is precisely because I know what he is capable of. Look, I *am* protecting someone, but not who you think. It's complicated.'

'Fucking right it is.' Jason banged the heel of his hand on his temple. He knew only one person that could see their way through this mess and he was suddenly desperate to talk to her. Tracy.

'Tell me, what do you think happened that night?'

Jason closed his eyes. He'd never actually said what happened out loud to another living soul. He wanted her to fuck off. He wanted it all to go away. But it hadn't for twenty years and he knew, suspected at least, that this was the beginning of the end. The outcome of those events had been hanging there for nearly two decades waiting to come good – to come out in the wash. He felt powerless to stop it.

'I killed her. I burned her up.'

'And that's what Conrad saw and turned into his film?'

'Yes'

'Jason listen. I can't tell you what's going on just yet. I need to find out what Blaine would do if this got out. He's on the edge and your childish pranks have not helped. He thinks you're going to kill his daughter.'

'Oh, for fuck's sakes. I wouldn't. I mean, I've made a couple of terrible mistakes, but I like the girl and besides, Joe's smitten. I couldn't do that to him.'

'Well you need to back off, alright?'

'I'll back off if you tell me who else was there, that night.'

It was Rachel's turn to sigh deeply. She looked tired, thought Jason. Burdened. He realised he wasn't the only one who'd had to live with the aftermath of the tragedy. He saw beneath the surface clearly. She may have seemed together – beautiful, a successful woman, her own home, doing what she loved, admired by the community, but Jason saw then that she was lonely and somehow that was his fault too.

'It was Mack.'

Jason took a few seconds to process this information. It didn't add up. Save for Mack's recent, rather disturbing offer of an olive branch. He'd always been aloof at best, if not openly hostile. Mack had always made him feel like a stupid, pointless oik. A scumbag, a pikey waster. Jason thought of the story Mack told him about the man with his legs blown off. It *was* a message, but now, it also seemed like a threat.

'Looks like I'm headed for some time inside then.'

'That might not happen. Look, I just know, without doubt, that the truth is going to have to come out. You're not the only one who's lived with this. The person I'm protecting needs closure, an end to the guilt and the bad memories. And while I can't stop this happening and despite my reputation as a bit of a hippy, I don't have a crystal ball. I can't predict the future.'

'But why should I trust you? We went to the same parties twenty years ago, so what? You and me – we're different. We're not the same. For a start, you're not from round here. That makes a difference. It doesn't matter how long you've lived here, you'll never belong. And it doesn't matter what secrets you know either.'

Rachel looked sadly at him. 'I don't belong anywhere, Jason. And trust me, I'll have my reputation to lose too when it all comes out. You say you've got fuck all. Well from where I'm sitting you've got more than me. You've got a family for starters.'

Jason hadn't thought about this. He looked at her again. The lonely woman pretending she had a wonderful life. Filling the emptiness by keeping busy, working tirelessly to support local community arts, believing she could feel satisfied from the opportunities she gave to others, then going home alone. He saw then that she was like him. Too scared to share her life. Too fearful to really give herself up to anyone. Taking the easy option and staying closed off. He thought again about the absence of children. He'd never seen her with a man except for Fran. He wondered. Maybe the truth was what they both needed, for good or for ill. Maybe Rachel wasn't even being honest with herself.

'What did Mack see?'

She sighed again. She stood and pulled her hood over her head. 'He knows everything. Everything you know and more. Text me if you have a wobble, but I take it we have an agreement? You never know Jason, you might find that accepting Conrad, that he witnessed what you did, then what he did with the information, you might actually be free of it all.'

It was impossible to be free, he knew it. But he would stop stalking the man. He would do that. He indicated his acceptance with a curt nod, then she swept out of the house and quietly closed the door behind her.

He felt utterly drained. He turned all the lights off and ascended the stairs slowly, pulling hard on the banister for support. He picked up his phone and wrote a text message - 'Can we talk?' pressed send, then went immediately to bed.

****

There were three people Jason needed to see and fast. The first to know he wasn't losing his mind, the second to know he wasn't about to be screwed over and the third to know he had the story straight. *Their* story. The one that had kept them from snitching on each other, remaining business acquaintances and to all intents and purposes from a public perspective, 'friends' since that terrible night.

Tracy met Jason in their favourite sit-down chippie in town. Jason had loved this chippie so much that back in the day, after a particularly enthusiastic session at the pub, he'd had FISH'N' tattooed across the knuckles of his right hand and CHIPS tattooed across his left. The letters were now a blurry bottle green, but he didn't care. They covered up some of the scars.

They got teas and sat at their table in the familiar room with its dark-stained pine furniture and tea-towel collection decorating the walls. He thought she might fancy a nice bit of saveloy, but she didn't even pick up the menu. She couldn't even look at him.

He was fifteen days sober. The longest he'd been sober since he was a child.

It was horrific: the whispers in his head, the visuals, the sensual triggers everywhere, the sheer barrage of thoughts and feelings – *stuff* he thought either had never happened or he'd forgotten. It was hard. But he was exultant; the clarity was a revelation, the moments of peace – although punctuated by the intensity of his emotions, were pure and becoming more frequent. He felt so clear headed, so normal and so very fucking sorry.

He studied his ex-wife. She had lost weight since New Year. Not in a good way. Her skin looked flat. She had made an effort – her hair was shiny and newly cut, she had make up on, her nails were done. But there was something sallow about her skin. It hung in a way it hadn't before and her eyes were anywhere except on him.

He went back over their argument. It was one they had gone through so many times, but this time something was different. Normally, Tracy would just be there, ready to pick up where they had left off, but now she seemed distant.

'Are you hungry?' Normal Tracy would eat anything that was offered to her. He'd always loved that about her. Not like the other girls. Her unashamed appetite for life – for him.

She looked up and shook her head. Again, she wouldn't meet his eyes. She gave a cursory half smile on one side, her mouth drooping somewhat. He started to panic a little. It had been weeks. Had she met someone finally after all these years? Right now, when he was trying to be better, when he needed her?

'What do you want, Jason?' She slurred the words out like she didn't really want to have to speak to him. He realised then that she looked exhausted and he knew it was his fault.

'I wanted - want to say sorry for being a total cunt on New Year's, Trace.' He reached for her hand on the table and it shrivelled away across her lap and deep into her coat pocket.

She looked small and cold. She really had lost *a lot* of weight. 'I'm worried. About you.'

'No.' she said, now sounding drugged. 'The only person you are worried about is yourself. I shouldn't have come. I'm stupid.' She started gathering her things up with one hand. She was slack mouthed and confused. Her skin appeared to have an opaque sheen of dirt, of built up worry.

Jason was at a loss. She wasn't right. This was not his wife – this was a stranger. Had she met someone else? He wouldn't blame her. He did a mental inventory of all the men in her life that he knew of and he couldn't think who it might be.

As she stood, she started breathing more heavily, her eyes drifting up into her head.

She twisted backwards as the left side of her body appeared to disintegrate. Jason caught her just before she fell onto a neighbouring table. He could see instantly from her collapsing face - one half melting like wax - that she was having a stroke.

****

Jason finally, reluctantly, left Tracy in the hospital the following morning. He'd made the painful phone call to his son and estranged sister the previous evening. He needed family to look after Aleisha. Joe was in pieces; he couldn't do it alone.

Apparently, it wasn't *that* severe. She was unconscious for a long time and upon regaining albeit a drugged awareness, her face drooped like a shabby festoon blind on the left side. Jason had sat and openly sobbed. He felt so sorry for himself. He could feel the discomfort of the Consultants as they tried to talk to him. He sensed the irritation of the nurses as they worked around him, tending to her bloods, liquids and meds. He thought of his mum. How he lost her so young and he thought of his own son, his granddaughter. And yet all he could feel was his own despair.

Jason got two buses home, let himself into Tracy's house and packed an overnight bag with several nighties, a dressing gown and her toilet bag, then got two buses back to the hospital.

It had been the first time in many years he'd been in her bedroom. They had occasionally, in the past, had drunken sex since their divorce, but this had stopped when Joe had got sick. Their mutual blame of each other nullifying any need to reach out. He noticed with tenderness that she still had photographs of him on her dressing table, her walls; their wedding, the christening and various Christmases, anniversaries. He was surprised it didn't annoy him. It just made him feel sadder.

All the way on the bus, he kept thinking there was something he ought to be doing but he couldn't get past Tracy, the thought that she might go and leave him. He wept on the bus, several people moved away from him. He realised he looked a mess, unshaven, hood up. He looked mental, but he didn't care. He felt angry too. How could she leave him? He needed her. He was nothing without her. He'd always, *always* assumed he would go first. He didn't want the sole responsibility of looking after a son and a grandchild. It just wasn't fair.

By the time Jason returned to the hospital, her relatives were there. He handed the bag over and was, at first, politely marginalised, then openly rejected. Tracy's aunt finally swooped the curtain across in his face saying 'Just go to the pub, Jace'.

****

Jason sat watching his dad sleeping in bed. The only sound in the room was the rasping heave-ho of his lungs. The knackered, encrusted old bellows struggling to draw fragments of air in and barely expelling the dirty air out. John's lips were slightly blue and dry. His face had sunk and was pale yellow. Jason stroked his dry head, scattering parmesan-like particles of skin across the pillow. He'd visited to feel like he had back up, but never felt more like he was alone. He looked at his dad, doubting the thing he always thought would be true – that he would be glad when he was dead. Instead, he just missed his mum more and was doubly scared of his passing.

Jason realised what would help. And what would help was cold, thick, cloudy vodka, straight from the freezer. On the way out, the nurse asked after Tracy and he broke down. She took him to the kitchen and offered him a sherry. He looked at the half empty green bottle and imagined the rich burn of the amber liquid on his lips. He declined. She put her hand on his arm, looked in his eyes and told him to expect the worst in the next few weeks. That his dad would be gone.

Jason floated out of the home. He became aware of his surroundings only when he was stood in the middle of the railway lines, staring at the glinting curve, unable to see what was coming. He heard the little birds, but did not want to look at them. He did not want to be reminded that nature carried on, was oblivious to his agony. He waited until he could feel a slight rumble underfoot. Then the train was ahead of him, bearing down. He locked eyes with the driver, saw the shock and fear and heard him slam on the brakes just as he walked towards the railings and disappeared through the gate.

Jason couldn't do it yet. He had to be around for Tracy and to see his dad out, even if the old bastard had made his family's life a living hell.

He remembered there were still two people he needed to see. He set off to the café in the high street just as the train came to a lurching stop.

****

157

Jason stood across the road outside the new supermarket and watched Mack through the café window opposite. He was quite sure Mack had seen him, but was ignoring him until he'd finished his coffee and his big, billowy paper. Eventually, Mack folded the paper up, put on his cap and coat and wandered out of the café. Jason stared at him and Mack slowly made his way through the traffic jam in the High Street, banging the bonnet of a bright yellow Hummer that attempted to squash him up against the backside of the Porsche in front. He stood before Jason, pulling suede gloves on.

'What do you want, son?' Mack drawled, eventually looking up.

'I want to know what you know.'

'Tsk, tsk, pal. That's no way to talk to an elder. Very disrespectful.' Although he sounded playful, his eyes warned that he was less than happy that he'd been confronted. 'In fifteen minutes, meet me at the back of the pub no-one goes in and we'll talk.' Then he slowly walked away.

Jason didn't want to go into the pub that no-one goes in, for lots of reasons. When they say, 'no-one goes in' what they meant was, no-one in their right mind would go in. It was, in fact, a pub that lots and lots of people go in and liberally frequented by members of his and Tracy's extended family. Even at the back of the room, Jason would be spotted, approached and questioned at length about his health, his dad, his son, granddaughter and anything else that might have happened in their living memory that one of his ancestors might have been vaguely connected with. Jason ruminated that this just proved that even Mack didn't really get it. Even though he'd lived here so long, even ran his own boozer, he just wasn't from the town and never would be.

There were two other reasons why he didn't want to go into the pub no-one goes in. First, it was full of proper piss heads, like him, who would force him to drink. Second, it reminded him of the night C.K. Blaine had followed him. As Jason shuffled through the permanently open door and entered the low ceilinged, thickly carpeted room, he could remember it clearly.

It had been his first stop on his big night out and he'd ducked in to see his Nan Gann on her birthday. Jason loved his Nan, but there were others in the Gann clan that he was less friendly with. People who had made certain comments when his mum had died. People, who, even though years had passed since her terrible death, still tutted and whispered when he'd entered the room that night. It made Jason twitchy. A bit antsy. He had done his best to ignore the bastards.

His Nan had always done her best to keep the peace, but there were just too many of them in a small town. There was always going to be friction. Jason, at heart, was a Jenkins and a Jenkins was always viewed by a Gann with, at best, contempt, at worst, murderous antipathy. As Jason had approached, he had avoided eye contact with several tasty distant Ganns and put his hands over his Nan's eyes, then surprised her with a loud 'Boo!'

Nan Gann was already hammered and it had only been 10pm. With another port and lemon placed in front of her, Jason had caned three pints straight down in quick succession. He had discovered, that night, that his cousin had finally split up with *Her* – Sasha. He'd heard that she was looking for a good time and he finally knew he was ready to make his approach. It was that night *or never*. Jason was hoping to see his cousin in the pub no-one goes in, but Robbie had not shown up. Rumour had it, he'd taken the break up really bad.

He remembered feeling increasingly agitated, chatting politely about his job and had put up with Nan asking if he was seeing a special young lady yet. Finally, she had shoved a tenner into his hand, signalling that he had been forgiven for puking up on Aunty Susan's carpet the Christmas of 1978. It also meant he had to give her a kiss and she performed the face-grab as usual, ruffling his super slick hair. 'Mind the bloody hair!' Jason had shouted. How they had all laughed.

He'd then had a crafty line of billy in the toilet and the rest of the night went ballistic from there.

Jason now stood frozen at the bar, the ghosts still seated around him, in that very room. He thought of *Her* - his last memory of her that night, dancing. He shook his head to unrattle it, but it persisted. He leaned on the bar for support, hood up, remembering and feeling increasingly troubled. He couldn't meet the barmaid's eyes, or answer her questions about his wife, his dad or anything. He ignored her. He ignored the drunk old gobshite cracking jokes about zippo lighters and he ignored the old dears rambling on at him about how good looking his granddad had been. He just took his revolting, generic flat cola and sat at the table nearest to the back of the pub. A disturbing row of giant stuffed animals which Jason dearly hoped were raffle prizes, sat cheerily behind him along the back shelf. Even Jason was aware that their garish cartoon appearance was in stark contrast with his own miserable countenance.

He waited. Exactly fifteen minutes after they spoke, Mack walked in.

He ordered a pint of ale and a scotch and joined Jason, nodding respectfully at the old boys who watched on with curiosity. Jason was vaguely aware they were second cousins of his dad. Or something.

Now Jason had Mack in front of him and had no idea what to say.

'Seems to me like you need some help, kid.' Mack took a long sip from his pint and set it down, studying the thick foam on top with the moon shaped indent of his lips at the edge.

'What the fuck does that mean?'

'I know Rachel told you I was there. So what? Why should that bother you? You know I won't talk. I haven't said a word for nearly twenty years.' He took another sip from his pint. 'It seems to me, however, that you might want to. Talk I mean. You can talk to me.'

Jason thought of Tracy, how she was always on at him to 'open up' and 'talk about his feelings'. Little did she know that he did everything in his ability to drown out any feelings, until they no longer existed.

'Rachel said you know everything "and more". What does she mean? Do you know why all this has to come out?' Jason suddenly felt so tired. 'Fuck it Mack, I want it over with. If it's going to come out, let's just get done.'

Mack looked at him and narrowed his eyes. 'Now listen. You're not the only one involved in this. Don't you go shouting your mouth off after all these years until the time is right, you understand?' Jason didn't.

'What I did - I should pay for it. I should have come forward then. I wish I had.' To his shame, he felt like he wanted to cry. It felt liberating to tell someone his darkest thoughts in the full knowledge they knew everything already and didn't seem to want to judge.

'You hold tight, son. You'll get your chance to pay your dues and explain yourself soon. And I might have a way to help you forget it all too.'

Jason stared at his long-time adversary. He wasn't sure, but again, it sounded like Mack was trying to help him.

'How exactly do I forget something as fucking bad as that?'

Mack knocked the whisky back and set the small glass down gently on the beer mat. He sucked air through his teeth and looked at Jason intensely through his thick eyelashes. 'What if I told you that there is a way to put this behind you, change your behaviour, who you think you are, the past, everything. Make it all completely different and it would just take one day. What would you say?'

Jason thought about *Her*, about Blaine, about the stupid, devastating events of that night and how they'd shaped, warped and ruined his life ever since.

'I'd say, whatever you've got, give it to me.'

Mack laughed.

Jason didn't bother asking him what this miracle cure was. He didn't care. He had one more visit to make. He had something he needed someone to do. They sat in silence until Mack's beer was finished, then they parted with a contractual nod, without saying another word.

****

Jason peered through the dirty windows, through a gap in the ripped curtains into the darkness and then tapped three times. He could see shapes shifting and stirring. He saw the room lighten as a door was opened at the rear of the flat. Jason made his way through the brambles and nettles at the side of the building to the backyard with the rotting shed and rusty furniture. Fran was sitting on a wrought iron chair, naked and about to light up a pipe. Jason took a step backward. Fran had lost even more weight. His dreads were thigh length and, thankfully, covered most of his body. It was still a shock. His skin hung from him and Jason was reminded of his dying father just two streets away.

'Smoke?'

'No thanks.'

Fran took a huge toke from the pipe and puffed the smoke out into the January chill.

'You're naked, mate.'

'They told me clothes are poisonous.'

'They? The aliens?'

'No. The people in the radiator.'

Jason was pleased. This was exactly how he hoped Fran would be.

'I know them.' Fran looked at Jason. 'They told me something. About a man called Conrad who wants to shop you. The D.F.L. you saw that night. You didn't think he saw you, but he did - and now he wants to tell.'

Fran looked up and shrugged. 'Let him fucking try. I just want to get my fucking ear back.'

162

Jason stopped himself laughing and thought in a way he never could had he been wasted. There were some advantages to the clarity sobriety brought.

'Are you missing your ear then, mate?'

'I want it back. It's out there somewhere. The radiator people have told me how to put it back on.'

Jason thought some more.

'I know where it is.'

Fran leapt up and shrieked, throwing his arms in wild arcs. Jason was scared he might try and hug him. He saw curtains twitching in the flat above. He tried not to look at Fran's shrivelled, dangling member. 'Fucking tell me, *man*!'

'I'll tell you, but the man that knows about me, about you – *he* has it and he won't give it back. Listen Fran – *listen*!' Fran was shaking violently, Jason wasn't sure whether it was the cold or his state of mind but he needed to make his point and leave. 'His name is *Conrad Blaine*. He lives opposite puke alley along from the pub that used to show home porn films. Number 37. He's got *your ear*.'

Fran pulled his crusty grey dreadlocks back and revealed the remains of his ear – the bottom half, just a jagged hook.

He said, in a robotic voice, 'I'm going to take my ear back. I'm going to make that man give me my ear. I'm going to silence that man forever. Then the radiator people are going to help me reattach it.' He stiffly turned and walked towards his house. The loose skin hanging from his saggy arse rippled as he stepped up and into his filthy kitchen. The ancient, malevolent dog shuffled after him, then he slammed the swollen door shut.

Jason walked slowly towards his home and smiled to himself. He knew he had set something in motion that he had no control over. It almost had the same thrill as fire lighting.

Almost. But not quite.

Chapter 13

Empty

February/March 2015

I flicked on the coffee machine and shuffled to the bathroom feeling a little hung-over. I'd been out with the producer and director the night before, going over the final points of the premiere. The girls had got themselves up and off to school without waking me and I allowed myself the luxury of a lie-in until late morning.

I still couldn't get Rachel out of my mind. She'd swallowed my line about being willing to let the events in 1995 come out into the open and helped me get Jason off my back. There had been no more pranks or threats. The paranoia still lingered but the anticipation about *Flood*'s release was building. The whole 'Minnie's letters drama' had only served to fan the flame of interest especially as people believed it was my own tireless detective work that had revealed the final truth – the crucial twist at the end of her story. The essential contents of Minnie's letter to the press, still hidden behind a panel in my loft. I had been booked solid for appearances and interviews in the last week, all to be timed with the first public screening. I should have been ecstatic. Yet, well - it was Pippa.

I was grateful she'd helped, but I couldn't honestly remember agreeing that we were back together – without even so much as a romantic prelude. She was still in London, in the week, but now expected me to speak to her on the phone every night and do 'family stuff' at the weekend. I hadn't been kite surfing for weeks. Wade had ignored my calls. I missed my freedom, I missed the possibility of meeting unknown women, of a romance with Rachel and most of all, I missed my beard. I'd secretly started growing it again. Whether she approved or not and I was determined to have at least a beardette by the premiere.

It was only after a few minutes sitting on the loo reading *More!* magazine that I noticed the bathroom mirror. From the angle I was at, I couldn't read the words but could see that someone had scribed something in what looked like shit. Thick clumps of shit. Someone else's shit that I could now smell. *Man's* shit. I abandoned my own attempt and slowly walked to a place in the tiny bathroom that allowed me to see the words. My hangover got worse and I felt a stinging clump of bile rise to my throat. I pinched my nose.

Written on my family's bathroom mirror, in a strange man's shit, was the sentence 'I want my ear.'

****

After I cleaned it thoroughly and destroyed the foul and bizarre statement, I dressed warmly and left the house. I felt agitated. I couldn't eat. I had stupidly trusted Rachel and relaxed. I'd thought the threat from Jenkins had receded. I'd allowed myself to indulge in elaborate fantasies about how successful the film would be in order to stop thinking about how unhappy I was. Everything was beyond my control it seemed. And now, this maniac was back in my house, writing mad messages in shit.

To my best knowledge, Jason had both his ears. Yet we'd found that ear on the beach. How that could possibly be connected with him, with that night? I desperately needed to speak to Rachel. She knew Jason, knew what he was capable of. When we'd met the Thursday before, I'd convinced her that I'd come to my senses, that I wanted the truth to be known, even if it meant my reputation – my liberty even, would take a knock. She sat all big blue eyed listening to my bullshit and then begged me to hold back until the time was right. She'd confirmed that she knew Jason and would talk to him, give me a chance. Then the contact had stopped again.

165

I had tried to get her attention by hand-delivering a ticket to the premiere, scheduled for February 14th at the BFI Southbank. I knew she was at home when I posted it. I heard voices from within. I heard her voice and a man's voice, a voice with a strong Scottish accent. It made me furious. But I'd heard nothing back. She wasn't answering texts or emails. I was lucky I was so busy with publicity stuff or I'd have gone mad. Now, with the ear-in-shit message, I needed some answers.

I stomped along the High Street, looking at the drab shops and locals through a February vignette. I was pretty sure the town wasn't really this dull. The people not really that parochial. I was just viewing it all through an anxiety veil. Everything had been applied with a bleak winter filter.

Today I especially hated *the people*. The way they clustered in the winter months, oblivious to the cold, chatting – about what? Their weird accents. They couldn't even say the name of the town right – 'Whisssaple', I heard, especially from an elderly mouth, again and again. It made me mad. Their chumminess to each other and absolute refusal to be civil to anyone from elsewhere, particularly London. It was discrimination.

I didn't really know where I was going, or have any purpose. I passed all the cafés that were good places to be seen and was just negotiating the queue of pensioners at the bus stop when I spotted Jenkins. He came barrelling out of a tall pub ahead. He managed to right himself just before the road, then curved back and set off towards me in a stuttering gait. It was 1pm and he was absolutely steamed.

I dived into the nearest open doorway, through a metal fly curtain and into a peculiar smelling shop. I heard voices at the back - two women. I moved out of sight of the till and pretended to look at the shelves. It was a health food shop, selling thousands of vitamins, minerals and organic, wheat free, gluten free products. I waited. I picked a tub off the shelf and pretended to study it in case Jenkins should look in as he lurched past.

'Good afternoon, Sir. Would you like me to tell you a little about Horny Goat Weed?'

I looked properly at the plastic bottle. A supplement for erectile dysfunction and aiding sexual desire. I put it back and looked at the small pretty woman who had spoken. When our eyes met, she jumped back and put her hand to her chest.

I couldn't help but smile. I knew this was going to happen more and more, now I was back in the public eye. She recognised me. Desired me. I moved towards her and started to explain that I'd be happy to sign an autograph, when an excruciating noise sounded so close to my head I fell to my knees on the floor. I looked up and the small, woman was now standing next to Rachel. She was holding the rape alarm at arms-length.

'What did he do?'

'Nothing. I just know he's not right.'

Rachel hugged the silver haired lady as I got to my feet. 'In what way "not right"?'

'You know him?'

'Yes.'

'Want me to do a reading?'

'Yes.'

I staggered up, rubbing my head, squinting at the pair. Rachel nodded at me. I had no choice but to let the silver witch-lady reach out, force my coat sleeve up and put her incredibly hot hand on my arm. She closed her eyes and mumbled, swooned a little. I laughed and I felt her nails dig into my skin.

'He's – empty, Rachel. There's nothing there to work with,' she said, yanking my sleeve back down.

'Thanks. I think I knew that already.'

The lady moved closer. She was tiny but fixed me with her pale, brown eyes in a way that made me do a bit of sick into my own mouth. 'You know nothing about us – the people

167

in this town. You're not welcome in here again. Be gone!' Then she vanished into the dark interior of the shop.

Just then, Jenkins lumbered past. He was walking sideways, diagonally and marginally forwards enough to make a slow progress. Once he'd passed, Rachel pulled me back through the heavy chains out onto the street. We stood and watched him cross the road, narrowly missing being hit by a bus, an aggregate lorry and several 4x4s. He finally almost fell down Skinner's Alley and out of our view.

'What the hell were you doing in there?' I said, a little too emphatically.

'It's a shop. I was buying stuff. And she's a friend. What were *you* doing in there?'

I hung my head.

'She says you're empty, Conrad. I'd say you're *full of it*. Let's go for coffee.'

I followed her along the High Street and we ducked into the same café I'd been in only a few weeks earlier when my editor had called. It was busy and bustling enough for our conversation to go unheard.

'I thought you'd called him off!'

Rachel was still struggling to get out of her coat. A green coat. I realised I'd seen her with Jenkins that very day. I felt suspicious.

'What's happened now?'

'He's been in my house again and scrawled "I want my ear" in his own shit on my bathroom mirror, that's what!' Rachel stopped pulling at her sleeve and looked at me, visibly shocked.

'Say that again.' There was something about the look on her face that made me scared.

'It said, "I want my ear".' She yanked her arm out, then abruptly sat down opposite, her eyes darting from side to side, gathering her thoughts.

'Conrad, this is serious. I don't want to alarm you but whoever wrote that probably won't stop there.'

'But what does it mean? I can tell by the look on your face you know something. *What's wrong with the people round here*?' I had raised my voice loud enough for the burly owner to shoot me a warning look. I held my hand up as an apology. He snarled in response.

'You're not going to like this, but I'm afraid this does all, yet again come back to the night you followed Jason. As I have said to you many times before, you two weren't alone.'

'And I take it one of the other people that were there is fairly easy to spot because they only have *one ear*? And now, apparently, I have it!' That's when I remembered what Pippa had shrieked at me on her birthday – the day we found another ear on the beach. There had been a new age traveller in the 90s too. It had to be him.

'You don't know what you're dealing with. Look, I know your film is out next week. Its half term right? Why not take the kids up to London and stay with your wife? I'm sure you'll be hobnobbing with celebrity types anyway. It might be good for you two, and the girls. Get away from here, have a break from it all, yeah?' She sounded ever so slightly desperate. There was something in her voice, her eyes that I didn't like. She'd lost her calm and peaceful demeanour. She was scared too.

'I had been hoping you might want to come with me?' I felt the wrongness of it the moment it came out of my mouth. I realised she'd never had and never would be interested in me. I looked at her face and what I saw was not the chic, together woman that I desired, but a lonely, desperate spinster that had been playing with my feelings. I felt crushed and resentful. In that moment, I realised the stupidity of my intentions and she'd made me feel like a fool. 'Actually, you know what Rachel, I will *fuck off back to London*. You've caused me nothing but hassle. You can keep your mindfulness shit and your small town politics. Having a break was the best idea you've had since I've met you.' I stood up and pulled on my Crombie, pleased to see she looked upset. 'And by the way, you're not *all that* either!' I marched out of the café as the manager paced menacingly from behind the counter and I slammed the door behind me.

Bitch. Who was she to tell me when I could or could not tell the truth about something! I went home and packed the girls bags. The school could bugger off with their stupid 'no holiday in term time' rules. My girls were coming to see their daddy turn into a huge success, back in civilization and as far away from Jason Jenkins as possible.

****

It had been a while since I'd been to the Southbank and as I wandered into the Benugo Bar to meet with the BFI events co-ordinator and the film's producer, Douglas, I sensed a long lost swell of pride and excitement in me. I could feel eyes following me as I walked tall, passing young wannabe film makers and cultured middle-aged women who eyed me with a mixture of suspicion and admiration. The BFI person – her name was instantly forgettable – got me a cocktail and carried on checking arrangements off on her list with the producer. Neither of them sought my input at all, so I decided to observe the clientele while I waited for any consultation or discussion about the premiere.

Despite the slightly Italian sounding name, the bar area was decorated in what I thought they must have decided was very British 'eclectic' design. Hideous lime green and fuchsia rugs clashed with purple wall paper featuring huge white swirls, blocky standard lamps and chunky white lighting. The furniture was an unpleasant mix of chesterfield sofas and battered, brightly striped velour easy chairs with modernist square settees that offered the absolute minimum in comfort. The eating area was even worse. A mass of polypropylene bucket seats in that bumpy church-hall finish that made skin crawl and teeth hurt when touched. Here were dozens of media people looking louche and at home.

I sipped my horribly sour drink and let the alcohol diffuse my irritation that the after screening party would be held in such an offensive environment. In truth, I had engineered myself a place at the informal meeting just to get out of the flat. I had no need to be there at all, but that's not what I told Pippa. She of course, was delighted that we had come up to London early, but what I hadn't bargained on was the sheer lack of space in the flat and the fact that every square millimetre of it was policed.

Whereas my space at the cottage had slowly eroded to just the attic, here I had no claim to any area at all. Over the two days prior to the eve of the premiere, I had been tutted, hissed and groaned at for sitting, leaning or standing anywhere, or moving, nudging or touching any object. She monitored me around the clock and her vision had a Big Brother-like omnipresence. I had developed a keen revulsion to her, unlike anything I'd encountered before. I couldn't bring myself to look at her in case she misinterpreted it as a come-on. I needed to get out. I had a bad feeling I couldn't shake. A sense of foreboding that was entirely separate from the anxiety about how the film would be received.

I was jolted out of my thoughts by a hearty slap on the back. I turned from the bar to see a young man who could have been anywhere between twenty-one and thirty-seven, grinning, nodding and pointing at me.

'Hey,' he said, joke-punching my shoulder. 'Alright chief? It's been too long.' I studied the man's face. He was smiling warmly at me, still nodding. He took a step back and appraised my body, overtly, up and down. 'Looking good! You been in the gym?' I took another sip from my drink as two grey haired be-speckled culture-cougars walked past, in deep discussion. They stopped when they recognised him and kissed him melodramatically on each cheek. He was a Somebody. He had a good-looking face and wore very expensive clothes. And he had a beard. I knew I had to have met him at some point, but I couldn't place him. He certainly looked like someone I ought to know.

'Yup, just compound stuff for core strength. Helps with the kite surfing, you know.'

'Yeah, wow! I only get the chance to get on my board when we go to Cornwall. You're looking good on it there, buddy.' He took in a sharp breath of air and did a slappy drum roll on his thighs. 'Sooo - '. His voice trailed off and he shuffled around me ninety degrees fixing his gaze at my producer.

'Sooo - ,' I mimicked. 'Projects?' He refocused on me.

'Ugh, yeah. Yeah! That's why I'm here. The project.' Now I was confused. He was smiling at me with expectation. Was this a new project that was mysteriously being lined up for me? I felt a tingle of anticipation. Things finally seemed to be gathering momentum.

'Yeah, me too. I think it could be good.'

'For sure, for sure. Well, it wouldn't be going ahead without your input, bro.'

I smiled at him. He nodded back grinning and wagging his finger.

'See - that's what I love about you – you're so modest.' He looked at his phone. 'Ugh, got to go. I see Caspian over there. See you soon, fella.' He slapped my upper arm and walked backwards making a phone gesture to his ear for me to call him. He turned on his heel and made a bee-line for a group of four men sitting on the chesterfields each hunched over a MacBook. They all had beards too, three of them ginger. I looked around the room for evidence to explain what just happened, as the over-organised nobody from the BFI wrapped up her meeting with my producer and click-clacked her away across the distasteful room.

'Fabulous space,' Douglas said to no one in particular, finishing his Michelob.

'Who was that man talking to me just then?'

He turned around and squinted that the group of men. 'Oh, you don't know him. He thinks you're someone important. Ignore him. Right, I'm off. I'll see you tomorrow. Get ready for the circus, Conrad!'

And there was the feeling again. Even the booze couldn't dull it - dread. I couldn't fight it, so I ordered another glass of the vile lime substance, found a stained velour easy chair, opened my MacBook and logged into brazilianandbouncy.com then waited for the heaviness to slip away. It didn't. But as I scanned the room, watching the like-minded and the like-bearded go about their networking I was reassured by one thing – I was nowhere near Jason Jenkins. I was back amongst my own.

****

'Of course, culturally, I own the town, Jonathan.'

Jonathan Ross giggled - I didn't know why. He grinned with all the menace of a randy chipmunk and continued to ask a series of questions about my life in Whitstable. I didn't like his snide inferences, the goading about how assimilated I really was or the cheap audience laughs at my expense. The studio audience weren't even laughing that much, but canned laughter would probably be added on in post-production afterwards. I wasn't sure how to react to him, so I just smiled and thought, 'What would Danny Boyle do?' After all, I was likely to become as successful as Boyle, albeit, a far sexier version, and the public loved him.

I'd agreed to go on his show because they'd paid me a large sum and I felt enough time had passed since I'd met him and his wife after the Baftas back in the 90s. It hadn't been my fault that I'd tripped and fallen face first into her generous bosom.

I had been celebrating my Bafta win for *Burn* and had necked the free wine. The place was crammed and as I'd made my way across the room, climbing over the emaciated bare limbs of aspiring actresses as they courted the elderly Bafta board members on the deep sofas, I'd caught my toe on the trim of a gown and had grabbed for anything to prevent myself landing on a glass table. It wasn't, I was sure, the first time his wife had had her mammeries exposed in public, but it did a good job of silencing the cacophony of sycophancy in the room for a few seconds. Ross had been vitriolic to start, but since I had been out of the public eye and his circle of acquaintance for so long, I didn't think it would do any harm to use his show to publicise the film.

His teasing, however, was increasingly vituperative and bitter. He played a clip from *Flood* soon after I sat on his rock hard sofa, and the audience were rapturous. He had stared at me with little concealed hatred until the cameras turned back on to him again. I knew it then: he was jealous. Here was a younger guy, with a fresh start at a long career, being tipped for yet more awards. I was fitter, more talented and hotter. And there was one thing in particular I really noticed him fixating on - my facial hair. While he still sported a quasi-Jeremy Beadle-esque effort, mine was now luxuriant and plentiful. I smiled benignly from behind it, I smiled at the camera. I didn't care if he took the piss – the public had voted. *Flood* was a runaway success and the British audiences loved it. They loved it so much, it had attracted a U.S. distributer. We were due to go state-side.

Luck would have it that shortly after the premiere and shortly before the general release, a series of freak storms had hit the South of England off the Atlantic. Flood defences that hadn't been breached in decades were totally ineffectual and vast swathes of pasture and arable land lay waterlogged and marsh-like for weeks after. Whitstable was spared, but only just.

When the film opened, the tabloids praised it as a timely reminder. They interpreted it as a message to fight Nature tooth and nail. To block out the sea and tame it. To protect our towns with yet more concrete. In this bizarre turn of events, I was required to have a breakfast with the Energy Secretary and invited to sit on a special think-tank about flooding. The press were always there. Every one of my utterances became a quote, a sound-bite.

GQ magazine nick-named me the 'Eco-Time Lord' due to the historical nature of Minnie's story. They had paid me generously for a feature article with images of me kite surfing with Wade, who had mysteriously reappeared as the film became successful. I also did shots dressed as a fisherman on a trawler in the harbour and pulling a pint in the pub on the beach. It must have been the '*Flood* effect' but all those people who had been intolerant of me before, seemed to come back to me, embrace me. In the GQ spread, the images that were published didn't look much like me. It was a better, younger, more HDR version of myself – grittier, manlier. The hits on my blog – which I had neglected, went sky high. The Sunday paper doubled my fee for the column to the point where I knew I could be financially independent from Pippa, should I choose to. It was tempting.

There was only one proviso to the pay rise and one I wasn't completely comfortable with. The paper now wanted one of their own writers, a bone fide historian, to write an historical account about the real Minnie and of the lives of women in general during and around the time of the flood. She would need all the primary evidence – the letters – in order to begin her research. I was reluctant to hand them over, but the pay was so good and the potential to make a bolt from Pippa unimpeded if things got intolerable, was too good to refuse. I still had the letter to the local paper hidden and there was no way I was going to part with that. I still had some secrets.

Celia Walden interviewed me over lunch for *Glamour* magazine, which my daughters both loathed and loved. I did *This Morning* with Pip and Holly. I got an invite to meet Elton John. What more could anyone ask for?

It was only while I was interviewed on Radio 6 Music in a retrospective about the soundtrack to *Burn*, a soundtrack that I'd had very little to do with, that the pernicious little thug who'd both made and ruined my life, made a startling reappearance in my consciousness.

The music, particularly the jangling 90s jungle, the monotonous techno and the booming miserable dub, summoned up a vista I was unprepared for. Memories I had long forgotten arose. There, like the flickering hologram of Princess Leia, the spectacle of Jenkins' shambolic cavorting quivered in my mind. It was like I'd had a month long holiday from my own brain – a brain-beach-break. For a month, I'd been transported somewhere alien, different and distracting, only to find that upon returning home, the situation – the reality of it, was far worse than I'd ever realised.

A month after *Flood* had its premiere at the Southbank, I finally came back down to earth. I'd moved back almost immediately, but had spent my days locked away updating my blog and writing my well paid column, commuting to London for interviews or attending special screenings along with the director, giving audience Q&A sessions. I could barely register the relief at getting away from the claustrophobia of Pippa's flat.

I was so busy, I hadn't thought about Jenkins, Rachel or the message scrawled in human shit for weeks. That is, until, the day after my Jonathan Ross appearance, when another parcel arrived.

I had just returned from a relaxing and highly alcoholic afternoon with Giles at the big pub in the middle of town. We'd listened to some live jazz, drank copiously. All the while I was aware of a buzz around me. People in the immediate vicinity were whispering, women shyly glanced under their lashes in my direction, men raised their drinks at me when we made eye contact. At the bar, other Londoners confidently shook my hand and told me their tedious relocation stories. I nodded, smiling pleasantly, stroking my beard, not really giving anything away – remaining an enigma. Giles thought the whole thing was hilarious and insisted on insulting me for the best part of the day, in order, he said, to keep my ego in check.

We'd almost fallen through the door with some bottles of red from an off licence when Giles stumbled on the packet. The exact same type Jenkins had used to deliver his pranks.

'You've got mail.' He passed me the packet. Typed and printed out from a computer, it was addressed, simply, to 'Thief'. I laughed at the perpetrator's pathetic effort to conceal his identity. There couldn't have been that many people in the town with only one ear. 'What have you been up to?' Giles gave me a quizzical look as we took the packet into the kitchen and he unscrewed a bottle of wine.

'How long have you got?'

'Oh shush. You're not nearly as intriguing as you make out. Are you going to open it then, Thief?' He giggled as he took two huge glasses from the cabinet and began to pour half the bottle between them.

I took some of Pippa's rubber gloves out from beneath the sink. I hadn't told anyone but Rachel about Jason's parcels. There was no way I was going to tell Pippa about this latest turn of events and I had cut contact with Rachel. I realised I was going to have to end this bullying myself if I was going to enjoy my new success. Moreover, I knew, in my gut, that this was all connected with Jenkins somehow. I could feel Giles staring at me with increasing concern as I snapped on the tiny, pink gloves and gingerly picked at the sealed edge.

I looked up at Giles. He was frowning. 'I'll give you fifty quid if you can guess what's in this parcel, Giles.' He smiled. I handed it to him and picked up my wine and drained half of it right down. Giles squeezed and prodded the package.

'Hmmm. It's soft, with a harder edge at the top and a lump in the middle. Quite long, can't tell how long, it sort of peters out. I'd wager it's a tangle of soiled ladies underwear from an obsessed fan who believes you have stolen her heart.' He looked smug, passed the package back and took an equally big slug of the wine. 'Conrad, this is a joke isn't it? You're beginning to frighten me.'

'No joke, Giles. Shall we see if you're fifty quid better off?'

I ripped the packet open and shook it. An object wrapped in a filthy bit of fleece blanket dropped noiselessly onto the kitchen counter. Giles drew closer. We both leaned over the mystery gift to get a closer look, taking hasty slugs from our wine.

'What is that horrendous smell?'

'And you, the wine tasting expert? Come on, what top notes are you getting here Giles?' I leaned closer. The tatty fleece had a geometric Aztec design on it. 'Ugh, are they dog hairs?'

'Yes. Please just get this over with. I feel sick.'

I put my glass down and pincered the hairy material between my gloved finger and thumb. Slowly, I peeled the fleece back, but it stuck, as though it was glued to whatever was inside. I realised I was sweating and wiped my brow on my shirt sleeve. I reluctantly placed an index finger on the object and ripped the fleece away. The object lay in the bright halogen lights of the kitchen for us to examine. It took a while to work out what it was. Giles laughed, then dry heaved. He shook a hanky out of his breast pocket and covered his mouth, taking a step backwards.

On the kitchen top, was a dog's ear. It was the ear of a hound. Long and smooth haired. An expressive ear, no doubt, that would have become erect when its name was called, or go floppy and inside-out on a good run. The ear was half chestnut and half flea-bitten grey and it stank of wet dog, weed and urine. The 'glue' had come from the central area of the ear, where a shiny scab of blood had clotted onto the fleece. The ear had been cut close to the head. There was visible gristle and bone at the edge. I poked it and revealed a typed, blood-stained note underneath.

'Can this get any worse?' Giles whined from behind the hankie. 'What does it say?'

I looked at the typing. All lower case, not that it mattered. It said, 'swap you this for mine - meet me tonight at the pile of whelks at the harbour at 8 - bring my ear.'

Giles and I looked at the clock in unison.

Half past seven.

'Do you have his ear, Conrad?' Giles said tentatively, sipping his wine and holding his nose at the same time.

'Of course I don't have his fucking ear, Giles! But I do have a camera with a bloody long lens. Come on, we're going spying.'

'Do I have to come?'

'Yes you bloody do, now get your coat on.'

'Let's just finish the bottle first, eh? Dutch courage and all that.' I weighed it up. It would take us barely any time to get there and it probably made sense if we were a little late. I'd watched enough cop dramas to know that the perp needed to sweat it a bit.

'It's almost finished, why not.'

Giles poured the rest of the wine and I re-covered the ear and put it in a shoe box.

'Giles, listen. This, and anything else that happens tonight, no one, especially not Pippa, must know about, right?' Giles took a gulp of wine. He wasn't really focusing on my face. It was difficult to read his eyes, they'd become droopy and opaque. '*Giles*!' He jolted.

'Of course. No one,' he slurred.

We drank the wine, wrapped scarves over our heads and faces and left the house in search of some answers.

****

Although I was absolutely blind drunk, I was unprepared for just how bitterly cold it was. We took a convoluted route to the rendezvous that took us past the Life

179

Boat Station and onto the far side of the harbour, facing the whelk shed and the restaurant at a safe distance. Right on the edge of the quayside, we ducked down behind some stacked plastic containers and began our reconnaissance. I positioned my Nikon, fitted with my Nikkor AF-S 600mm f/4G ED VR, at the opposite side of the quay. It was so dark and the lens was so long, I saw only giant grey details of fishing nets, plastic buckets, concrete and the sheds, all of it so marvellously close-up, I could barely identify what they were. The wind was howling and I wrapped my scarf tighter about my head. I began swinging the lens back and forth along the quay, remembering scenes from *The Wire*. Nothing. Giles tapped me on the shoulder.

'What?!' I hissed, not looking round.

'It's cold. He's not here. Can we go now?'

'No Giles. This is a waiting game. It's a test. He's toying with me.' I put my eye to the view finder again and continued my sweep of the empty harbour. Something at the entrance moved. I focused on it and took a couple of shots. It was dog on a long lead urinating on a lamp post near the pedestrian crossing.

Giles tapped me on the shoulder again.

'What *now*?'

'I need the toilet.'

'Hold it in.' He groaned and I looked again at the whelk store. I saw something flicker. I adjusted the ISO and focused. There was definitely something there, creeping around the pile of smelly whelks. I took some shots. He was near. I could feel it.

Giles tapped me on the shoulder again. This time I didn't take my mind off the view-finder. There was definitely something, a white shape, moving by the shells, maybe a figure crouching.

'Giles, just go and do a piss over there, bud. Keep low, don't get seen.' The wind was picking up and my hands were frozen. I could barely operate my camera.

Giles did not reply.

Suddenly, the white shape loomed up in my vision. I burst the shutter and got the menacing white object as it emerged from the whelk pile, presumably, Mr One Ear himself. I chuckled to myself. What kind of amateur would wear white on a stake out?

Giles tapped me on the shoulder again, this time, harder. It hurt.

There was something bony about the prod that I hadn't registered before. I lowered my camera and was aware that the space next to me, where Giles had been crouching, was now empty. I sensed there was someone tall standing immediately behind me. I pulled my scarf down and uncovered my ears. I felt disorientated, my vision changing from macro to normal focal length. Everything suddenly seemed so distant, even though it was all close by.

'Giles, don't fuck about buddy. What's wrong?'

There was a hoarse laugh from behind. I couldn't bring myself to turn and look up.

'Where is my ear?' The voice was husky, deep. The accent wasn't local.

'Where's my friend?' I asked nervously.

The laugh again.

'He's having a mud bath.'

I peered over the edge of the harbour and there was Giles lying face up on the mud. The tide was out and he'd narrowly missed two fishing trawlers. I couldn't take in the facts. The wine was making me more accepting of the situation than I knew I should be. Giles hadn't just fallen down there. He'd been pushed.

'What do you want?'

'I know you have it. They told me. Give it back.'

'I really don't!' I protested. Who had told him?

He laughed again and this time pulled me up by the shoulders and started to push me along the quayside in the direction of the Life Boat Station.

'You're coming with me.'

There weren't many times in my life when I'd done the right thing, or acted the way I ought to have, but this was one. I still hadn't got a look at this person, and I didn't want to either. My fear sobered me up in an instant. Giles was lying on a mud bank, about to be drowned as soon as the tide turned. As the one-eared man dug his fingers into my shoulders to push me on, I knew this was the only chance I'd get to escape.

I swung myself around, a bit like a ninja. The camera and lens flew in an arc and smashed him on the left side of his jaw. I heard something crack. He stumbled backwards, holding a hand to his face. I tried to see who it was, but the man before me was wearing a massive Rasta hat and huge iridescent snowboarding goggles. I unhooked the camera from around my neck and I did the only sensible thing I could have done.

I ran home.

As I legged it passed the fishermen's huts, I glanced over at the pile of whelks where a white plastic supermarket bag had caught, inflated and was twisting wildly in the icy wind.

I opened the door and Miranda was eating a microwave meal in front of YouTube. I nodded hello and went to the kitchen. The lens was smashed on one side where it had made contact with his chin. There was blood on it. I took the lens off and put it in the same box as the dog ear, then I took that upstairs and hid it in the cubby hole I'd made in the plasterboard in my office.

I poured myself several fingers of single malt and sat at my desk. There was something that I knew I ought to do. Something important and moral. All the way home, I knew I had to do it, now it eluded me.

I scanned the feedback on my blog while I waited for the 'something' to come to me and ten minutes later, it still hadn't. I saw with disinterest that Pippa had called six times since 3pm, so I turned my phone off. I heard Isobel come in.

I was aware, as I poured another large tumbler that she was upset and in Miranda's room crying. I sipped my drink. I wondered if I ought to go down, but I knew I couldn't move from my chair. I was in the clutch of a physical paradox – my body hyped and veins coursing with adrenalin but also so cataclysmically paralytic I was rendered immobile. I still couldn't think what it was – the *thing*, the important *thing*.

I checked the audience statistics for the film, I looked at the weather report for the next day with the drunken optimism that I might go kite surfing. Then, almost unable to see the screen I typed a long email to Rachel.

Then I passed out.

Chapter 14

Lost

March/April 2015

Jason had been given no option by his son. A month after she had been admitted, Tracy was due to come home and he was to be her carer. Joe was adamant that he would have Aleisha full-time, now he felt recovered. He said that the best way for Jason to pay his debt to his mum for being such a fuck up, was to step up and help. Jason was bewildered about where Joe had got his moral code from. With Jason's new blistering sobriety, he'd become aware of a radical change in Joe and the way he related to him. They'd always joked he was the strong but silent type. Jason had even taken the piss on occasion, that Joe was just how a mass murderer is sometimes described in the press when quoting neighbours and colleagues: 'kept himself to himself', 'was always was a bit quiet', 'bit withdrawn'. But that couldn't be said of him now. It was like he'd literally found his voice. And, it seemed, he had a lot to say. Not only that, he'd joined a boxing club, given up the fags and started running. Jason barely recognised him.

Joe had set a cup of tea before him, but Jason was bored of tea. Joe had argued that now he was sober, it had to be him. He'd looked at his son and felt unabashed jealousy. He was young, healthy, looking fitter and more relaxed than he had ever known him. Aleisha sat at the table colouring in a book with felt tips and Joe stood behind her, stroking her hair and gently twisting a ringlet around his finger, staring hard at Jason until he had agreed to be his ex-wife's nursemaid.

And that had been that.

On the morning she was due back, Jason let himself into his ex-wife's semi and put the kettle on. Tracy would need round-the-clock care whilst a community team of support was put into place. Jason already felt overwhelmed.

The house was pristine and orderly. Quite a contrast to his house. Tracy had a thing about interiors and loved those programmes about decorating. She usually did her front room and bedroom up alternate years with the latest colours and soft furnishings.

He deposited vodka in the freezer, the shed, the back of the wardrobe in the spare room, just inside the entrance to the loft and, the last ditch desperate option, above the boiler. He needed it close by.

Jason sat down heavily on the leather sofa. He was trying to fight an overwhelming desire to leave and run as fast as he could to the nearest pub. Yet there was something right in the core of him that wanted to stay more than anything else.

He hadn't been completely honest with Joe. It was true, he had gone for the longest time in years without a drink, but seeing the rapid decline of his father and the meteoric success of Conrad Blaine's latest stolen story had set him back. Witnessing it all in sober high definition was too hard.

****

It had started by accident. He visited his dad and then bumped into Bungle by the pub on the edge of town. Jason wasn't on his guard, too upset by the sight of his dad's frail form to be aware. When Bungle offered to buy him a pint to cheer him up, it seemed like the most normal, harmless and sensible thing to do. After all, in a time of need, what could be more innocent than old friends sharing a pint and talking over their worries? That pint turned into seventeen. He'd ended up going in every pub he had ever drunk in that was still open in town, on the premise that he wanted to talk to people who knew his dad. Finally, the landlady of the pub that no one goes in let him have a kip on the bench at the back. There, unconscious, he lay protected by the row of bizarre candyfloss

185

coloured, fluffy animals with their inanely happy faces, like stuffed guardian angels. She had called him a taxi home. Luckily Joe had not seen him.

Jason managed to sober up again for another week, then Blaine's film came out. It was odd seeing him in on TV and in print, when he hadn't had an eyeball in person for so long. Blaine became hyper-real again, just as he had before, yet this time, more pervasive, more 360 degrees. Jason rued the fact he'd got a 3G smart phone. He was now watching Blaine on Facebook, Twitter, Instagram, following his blog and Googling his name just to catch any other coverage, at least seven or eight times a day. Images of Blaine's stupid, fake smile and that massive Mormon-like beard, posing in clothes that a much younger man ought to be wearing, were everywhere. Whenever Jason saw a photo of him in a paper, it was as though Blaine was looking right at him, and saying 'I've done it again, you cocksucker. You'll never know what happened now. You'll never touch me'.

The morning Tracy had been due back, Blaine had been on *Good Morning* with Pip Schofield and Holly Willoughby. He had sat there, louche and smirking at her lovely boobs, while Pip tried to ask him important questions about the environment and global warming. How on earth the slimy git had become an 'expert' on the environment was a mystery.

Jason had glowered at the TV in his pants. He had wanted, more than anything to drink some vodka, but knowing Tracy was due home, he settled for taking a tyre up the woods behind the estate, covering it in petrol, igniting it and rolling it down the steep hill into the beyond. He was seventy per cent sure it wouldn't end up setting fire to someone's house. It was the thirty per cent not knowing that had calmed him down.

So now, he sat quaking on Tracy's immaculate sofa, waiting for the ambulance to arrive, dreading the responsibility of looking after her. The sheer intimacy he would have to share, caring for her body. The kindness, the patience, the understanding, that he knew he didn't possess. This in turn, made him realise what a weak and pathetic prick he was, which again made him loathe himself yet further.

He stood up and paced around the room, studying the many framed photos of Joe in school uniform, Aleisha at birthdays and Christmases in pretty dresses. Images of him at events he had no recollection of whatsoever. Pictures of Tracy. He looked at photos from their school days, in the hallway. What a pretty girl she had been. He had barely noticed. He'd been too busy looking the other way, at *Her*.

Jason heard the ambulance pull up and the chipper banter of the staff as they hopped out and opened up the back door. He resented it; their professional helpfulness.

He looked at himself in the hall mirror. He looked shady, older than his years, grey. He opened the door and strode out into the bright, cold day as they were lowering Tracy down a ramp on a wheel chair.

When he had imagined seeing her, he envisaged her appreciative face, eyes brimming with tears, gratitude emanating from her. Maybe a limp, pale hand extending toward him for help, support. What he saw, instead was pure fury. He kept checking that it wasn't her disability, her sudden otherness. But all he was getting back was hate. Tracy's mouth was set in a warped grimace, one side of it slack, dribble coursing onto her chin. Her eyes were hard and bitter, showing her opposition to his presence. Only then did Jason realise that this hadn't been her idea at all, that Joe had engineered the whole thing without her consent. And yet the sight of her moved him. Her opposition to him still so revolutionary and wounding.

'Tracy, you're home,' he managed.

'Take me in,' she ordered, in a barely audible slur.

They settled her by the dining table, where she said a goodbye to the staff then tried to get a notepad and pen out of her handbag. She only had the use of one arm and was struggling. Jason edged forwards and attempted to help. She

187

slapped his arm back, hard, and stared up at him. She violently yanked the items from her bag, scattering the other contents across the room.

Jason sat on the arm of the sofa in dismay. She was breathing hard, her temper building as she started to write furiously with her good hand. She wrote a page in giant script and tore it from the pad, then held it out in her outstretched hand for Jason to read.

It said, 'I do not want you here, but I have no option. I will get better and when I do I want you out of my life forever.'

****

The following morning after they'd had virtually no sleep until 5am, Tracy had the first assessment visit from her Occupational Therapist. Jason let her in and immediately he knew this woman disliked him because she knew he was not good for Tracy. She knew he would hold up her recovery. That he was bad.

As Tracy couldn't speak well, they had decided, via written notes and her frustrated and angry utterances that she should call him, when she needed him, using a child's maraca that had been Aleisha's toy as a baby. Oh, how he had grown to regret that in the early hours. She just couldn't settle. She was uncomfortable, the wrong temperature, distressed, thirsty and worse. As her bathroom was not adapted, he'd had to carry her to the toilet and wait by her side as she'd gone. He prided himself that he'd never changed a nappy in his life, like no real man ought to and yet here he was with a packet of wet wipes, cleaning up an adult.

After that he'd gone downstairs and drank half a bottle of vodka while flicking through a photo album. It seemed that Tracy had constructed an entirely different version of their early courtship than he could remember, or even knew existed. As he turned each page, from about 1983 onwards, he vacillated between pangs of acute guilt that he had let her down so comprehensively, to vitriolic rages of self-pity, knowing it wasn't, couldn't be his own fault. It was his dad, his dad's dad before, his mum's illness, her death, *Her*. Blaine. Finally, it was the distant shake of a maraca that forced him to put her memories away and return upstairs. By the time he got to her, she had gone back to sleep and didn't wake up again until the morning.

In the weeks since his re-acquaintance with the booze, Jason's habits had returned to normal. He drank every day, but now he did it secretly, away from Tracy and by himself. Rather than do what Rachel had urged and think about his life now and making it better, he deliberately re-lived every second of the events of his early life and 20s. If he had seen Blaine in a magazine or on the TV, or better still, in person, looking far less glamorous on the street, Jason took particular pleasure thinking about that night, feeling the anger rise. It made him feel alive.

Every morning he would wake up regretting it, visit his dad while Tracy had a nap, feeling remorseful and shaky, then, think about Blaine, yet again, enjoying success at someone else's expense. Jason hated him more than ever before.

****

One evening, three weeks into nursing Tracy, Blaine had been on Jonathan Ross. The next morning was Sunday. Jason drunk a bottle of vodka in his kitchen, then, when Tracy settled for her late morning sleep, visited Fran. He knew Blaine had been back and forth to Whitstable, so he guessed Fran hadn't had much opportunity to demand his ear back. He needed to keep the pressure on.

He'd let himself in the back without really thinking and found Fran in a full head-stand in front of the radiator, chanting in an unfamiliar language.

Jason hadn't wanted to startle him, so he'd crept back out, went around to the front and knocked on the door. When

Fran opened it, he was still muttering rhythmically. He let him in without looking at him or saying hello, just whispering his repetitive incantation.

Jason gripped him by his bony shoulders and asked, 'Fran, have you got your ear back yet?'

Fran had stopped murmuring. He was wearing just a filthy white sheet tied around his waist. He took a moment to examine, then bite a fingernail off, before finally looking at his visitor.

'Not yet. I left him a special message on his mirror a while back. I used recycled materials. He knows I want it. The man hasn't been there since.'

Jason looked about for the dog, but it was nowhere to be seen.

'That man, Conrad Blaine, he's back now. Back in the house where *your ear* is. Demand he gives it back to you. Do it *today*.'

Jason left him rocking gently on his threadbare couch, muttering to the radiator people about how to retrieve his ear. He was in no doubt Fran would do something drastic, he just didn't know, or even want to know, what.

A couple of mornings later, Jason noticed the local rag that had plopped onto the mat the previous evening. He settled down with a breakfast vodka and when he flicked the paper over on his lap and looked at the front page, he went cold. The lead photograph was of a man he recognised. The headline sent a bitter chill of shame through him.

He'd seen the puce-faced fat man with Blaine a number of times – usually as they stumbled out of the pub in the middle of town on a late Sunday afternoon. Jason liked to watch them, the pair of them, as they unsteadily made their way back to Blaine's tiny, damp terraced house. It amused him to see Blaine so vulnerable, so unaware.

The fat, gay man had been rescued from the harbour moments before he might have drowned. The man had fallen onto the mud the very same day he had visited Fran. There was no mention of Blaine in the paper, but Jenkins knew he was involved.

The paper said it was an accident. Jason knew, in his heart, it was not.

He felt sick. Yet again, something he had done had caused harm to someone completely innocent. He sunk inwards, withdrew into the torture of the past and hid there.

****

The following weeks that saw winter turn to spring were a blur of physiotherapy, speech therapy and constant visits from the objectionable Occupational Therapist. Tracy finally had a doctor's appointment where she got diagnosed with depression. Jason just sat and stared at the fake fire-place and fantasised about being in the pub. Any pub. The nights were getting easier. She was taking herself to the toilet and doing the personal stuff, but she kept having night terrors, like a toddler. He had to rock her back to sleep in the middle of the night, stroking her hand, thinking about the vodka he could be drinking.

One night, Tracy was ready for bed early. She'd had physio for her aphasia and she was wiped out. Jason helped her up to bed at 7.30pm. It was the first time he'd had the opportunity to get out of an evening for weeks. Jason methodically worked his way through two-thirds of a bottle of vodka standing at the kitchen window, dispassionately acknowledging the abundant evidence of spring.

He decided it was high time he paid someone a visit.

****

Jason was very drunk. He noticed with ambivalence that the evenings were getting lighter, and there was still a pale blue hue in the clear sky that night. It had rained earlier, releasing a scent from the soil reminiscent of warm blood.

Jason approached the maisonettes silently. No one was around, so he inched his way through the hedge to peer in through the soiled curtains.

To begin with, Jason thought Fran was decorating. In the front room was a fold-out table. But there didn't seem to be any wallpaper, paste or brushes. Jason watched. Fran walked backwards into the room cradling something wrapped in a blanket. He set the heavy object down on the decorating table and hung his head over the bulk, his shoulders shaking. Jason felt uncomfortable, but he couldn't leave. It was gripping, in the way a horror film was. Fran unwrapped the object from its fleecy covering and there on the table was the long dead, rotting corpse of a dog.

For one beat, Jason didn't know what to do, then he made an impulsive decision that seemed entirely rational in his drunken state, and let himself in round the back.

He stood in the shadows of the corridor and watched Fran chop off a paw and the tail of his old dog. He watched him cut two squares of fleece and wrap the smelly body parts up. All the while, he was chanting in an unknown tongue but to the melody of the song 'Lily the Pink'. Jason was feeling very creeped out, but he remained in the half light.

'Alright Fran?'

Jason was pleased to see the older man, the man who'd always controlled him, jump in surprise.

'How long have you been there?'

'Long enough to know you're not going to bury your dog.'

Fran looked at the pathetic carcass and stroked its one remaining ear.

'That queer D.F.L. in the harbour a few weeks ago. Was that you?'

Fran's lip was wobbling. He was bent over the carcass, caressing the dead dog's sunken face. There was a large, green bruise around a deep half-healed cut on his left jawline.

'They wouldn't give me my ear,' he said, then began coughing until he hacked up a big chewy clump of phlegm which he swallowed, noisily. 'That man you told me about. It *is* him. He has it. And I'm taking steps to get it back.'

Fran turned and looked at Jason. Jason could see that his ability, fragile as it was, to function normally, had ceased. Fran was out of control and Jason had pushed him to it.

Jason slipped backwards into the shadows and let himself out of the back door. He went and sat on the swings in the local park, feeling sick and dehydrated. He wanted to see his dad, but it was now too late for visits. He wanted to see Joe, cuddle Aleisha, to turn the clock back to – before.

He needed another drink.

It took him twenty minutes to get to Tracy's house. He let himself in silently and went to the downstairs toilet for a nip. The vodka was gone. He went into the kitchen and climbed onto the worktop. The bottle he'd hidden behind the unused blender on the upper cabinet was gone. He rushed out to the back garden, to the shed. The bottle he'd put behind the electric lawnmower - gone.

He came back in and slumped on a dining room chair in despair. His heart was racing and he felt panic. He put his head in his hands and began to keen, softly. Such was his loss, he barely noticed the movement in the darkened living room. He cried like a child. He gave himself up to it totally. As his sobs started to subside he became aware that he wasn't alone. Tracy was standing, in her nightie and dressing-gown, in the twilight.

'Jason,' she said with almost clear speech. 'I had some help tonight, after you went out, clearing up your bottles. They've all gone. I counted twenty-two.'

He gulped and looked at her. There was the kind face and loving countenance, but there was also a new stern seriousness that would not yield to sentimental nostalgia or emotional blackmail.

'I want you out of my house and the hell out of my life.' She crossed her arms.

'You need me - to get better.'

'I have never needed you, Jason Jenkins. It's you that has always needed me. But that's going to stop. Joe came by after you got drunk and went out and we cleared out your stuff. You are back there as of tonight.' Her speech was still slow, a drawl, but she was annunciating every single syllable. She meant it. 'My sister is going to come down and stay while I recover. I don't want you here anymore. Go now.'

Jason stumbled towards the hallway. He was desperate for a drink but he was skint. He knew he'd have to be creative about acquiring more. He stopped and leaned against the door. Tracy hobbled behind and watched him warily from the kitchen. This was the moment when it could have gone one way or the other. He knew what she really wanted: Jason, on his knees, crying, telling her everything he never had, swearing he'd always love her. He thought about it. All he could see was that bin on fire.

'I don't want to ever see you again, either,' Jason shouted. 'I came here to help you, and this is the thanks I fucking get. You're a *bitch*.'

She averted her eyes from him and covered her mouth with the back of her hand.

Jason left and slammed the door behind him. He was not prepared to go back to Joe with his new morals and horribly positive perspective. Instead, he walked to the all-day store and bought some bread. He waited until the shop assistant had some more customers, binned the loaf, then re-entered the shop with his hood up and went out the back to the storage area, stole a 1.5 litre bottle of vodka straight from the box and scrambled over the fence into the unlit car park.

Jason sat on the railway line for thirty-five minutes, enjoying the slight electrical buzz in his butt, hoping a train would corner and take him out. He then sat cross-legged on the pavement in front of his dad's death-home, willing him, at once, both immortality and an instant end to his suffering.

It was a mild night and a low mist clung to the ground, illuminated by the orange street lights. Jason stopped half way across the raised path over the golf course and smelt the earth - the peatiness, a fecundity that was reminiscent of blood and sex. He looked across towards the row of houses on the edge of the golf course, squinting to focus. Jason couldn't be sure but he thought he could see a small woman, pushing a large object at hip height, almost in mid-air, through the swirling mist. He took another large swig of his vodka. The moon appeared from behind the clouds and the scene took on an other-worldly quality. The small woman was walking, wading, as though through fog-covered water. Her long strides tempered by her need to navigate the bulky cargo she was pushing.

Jason sat in the moonlight and watched. She was so tiny, her face so determined. The closer she got, the clearer it was that the object she was teasing across the low golf course, was a body.

Jason sat swaying and closed his eyes. He remembered the story his dad had told him about the man that had drowned in 1953. The real story the locals all knew. And he remembered the story Blaine had stolen. He wondered whether he was just remembering the story or seeing something. He opened his eyes and she was standing in front of him, hands on hips, her eyes penetrating his with an unnerving intensity. She was as small as a child, shorter than Tracy. Her eyes were drilling into him. Jason hugged himself. He wasn't sure what was going on.

He squeezed his eyes shut and when he opened them again. She, and the body, suspended in the foggy air, were gone.

****

Jason woke up in the shed in the gardens of the home his father was in. The smell of buttered toast and coffee had roused him. He gingerly approached the back door where the care workers were preparing breakfast. One recognised him and pulled him in. He wasn't expecting this. They brought him tea and a bacon sandwich. It almost made him cry. He hadn't even had to speak to them.

When he finished, the care manager, Debbie appeared. He'd only met her once or twice. Jason had no idea what the time was, or really, why he was there. He just knew he smelled quite bad.

'We're so glad we could give you a breakfast and a hot drink on this sad day, Jason.' She was still holding his hand and nodding.

'Why is it a sad day?' Jason couldn't be arsed with cryptic shit. His hangover was savage.

'Your father, passing. The body is ready for you to see. We left a message with your son. We've been expecting you.'

It seemed unreal. No - nightmarish. He looked out of the patio doors as an intercity train rushed past over the death-crossing. How could he be alive? How could his old dad be dead? His dad who he thought would live forever. How could that be?

The Priest arrived and guided Jason upstairs then pushed him into the room where the air was dead and so was his dad.

John Jenkins, as a deceased man, seemed much younger. Jason studied him, shaking a little from his hangover, not really engaging. He felt nothing. He was not left alone so he performed what he thought he should do, based mainly on TV hospital dramas. He ran a finger over John Jenkins' face and kissed his forehead. He'd heard that it felt like marble, cold and perfect. Not with a critical Priest watching. His father's head felt clammy, a bit like play dough, with the same salty taste.

He felt sick.

He went downstairs and signed forms, signed his dead dad's body away. The girls made him more tea and put brandy in it. They had a laugh, they hugged him, wished Tracy well. He left.

He got over the crossing. There was no urge to hurt himself. Just anger. It was so early still. The roads were jammed with commuters and yummy mummies on the school run.

Jason wanted - no, needed, to destroy.

He went along the back alleys until he got to the bigger houses along Joy Lane. He took one of his Cat's off and used the thick heel to systematically smash every greenhouse and shed window he could until he heard a siren, then he pulled it back on and ran until he couldn't any more, settled down on the beach, hunkered up next to a groin and passed out.

****

He woke up in a white, stripped-bare room with one hand bandaged up and throbbing. He had no idea where he was. He heard a woman and man speaking downstairs. He was naked. The room was fresh and bright. It felt reassuringly hospital-like – he let go of any need to question it, feeling calm and drowsy, then fell heavily back to sleep and dreamt that Tracy was drowning.

When he awoke, the light was fading, it was dusk. It took him a moment for his eyes to adjust, and when they did, Jason jolted upright.

At the end of his bed, two people stood motionless, silhouetted against the fading sunset glowing through the single window behind them. They were looking over him.

'It's time, Jason,' one of them said.

And Jason knew they were right.

Chapter 15

Caught

April 2015

I knew it was on the cards, but still, the reality of Pippa moving back full-time was way more distasteful than I'd anticipated. Early, on the morning of her return, I felt a restlessness stirring in me. I paced my office, couldn't prioritise the dozens of jobs that needed doing and snapped at the girls as they got ready for school.

Eventually, I left the house and bought a take-away coffee from Harbour Street and sat on the beach, looking out at the sea at high tide. It was eerily still, more like a lake; the spring tide bringing the water much further up the beach than normal, waves gently lapping the pebbles. It should have been enough to ease my stress, but even the sun on my back didn't lift my spirits. In my immediate and distant future, all I could see and feel, was entrapment. I wasn't sure how it had come to this. I'd had ample opportunity to end the relationship, especially now I was financially solvent.

I mused while I sipped my cappuccino. It was more than just being scared of being alone. I was scared of having to be an adult. Being with Pippa was like still living at home – or at least, in some sort of correctional facility where my time was strictly controlled and I was afforded the occasional 'jolly'. I actually didn't know what I would do, or who I would be, without her.

And yet I'd had a tantalising taste of freedom. Admittedly, a few things had gone a little wrong. But I had learnt stuff about myself. And I had my beard. I set my take-away cup down on the sea wall and took a moment to stroke my face-mane. It felt good.

Behind me, a figure caught my eye. Rachel, turning from the alley next to the pub run by the celebrity chef, round to the Community Arts Centre, checking her smart phone. I felt a twinge of something in my loins, accompanied by a stab of dread as the vista of Pippa bustling into the house in a few short hours, arose in my mind. Maybe I *had* been too harsh on Rachel when I rejected her in the café? Now all the stress of *Flood*'s launch was over and I was preparing to take the film on the festival circuit, starting with Cannes in May, I wondered if I ought to reconsider. Maybe I ought to give the little lady another chance to be my special friend?

I got my phone out and texted 'Hey, just saw you. You're looking lovely today on this spring morning. Fancy a coffee?' I sat for fifteen minutes, gradually getting more wound up and infuriated as no reply materialised. I had made a fool of myself, again. How did she manage to do this?

I finished my coffee and shoved the empty cup deep into an unsightly mountain of stinking fish carcasses, eel spines and broken crab and oyster shells in front of the fish restaurant. As I walked towards the harbour, I turned my attention, reluctantly, to the two recent events that *hadn't* gone so well, intrinsically linked to Jason Jenkins, I was sure.

As I approached the Life Boat Station, I recalled the incident that had left Giles face up, 'having a mud bath'. I knew I hadn't behaved with much integrity. I'd sort of failed to call the emergency services and only remembered at mid-morning the next day, when I woke up with a banging hangover. Fortunately, someone, probably a fisherman, come to check his boat, nets, hut and count his fish, or whatever they do, had come along and found him. To give me credit, out of a keen sense of loyalty, I *had* visited Giles at the hospital though. I was relieved he was alive, but also strangely elated that he was in a coma. It wouldn't have been a good time for this sort of thing to come out. Giles was a mate, but he was also a bit hysterical and knew friends that practiced law. I really didn't need anyone to know about our little stakeout, the dog's ear, the stalker or anything else I'd stupidly let slip that night. As I'd stood over his plump body, his chest raising and falling aided by a tube taped to his mouth, I contemplated that it might even be more helpful if he didn't pull though.

This in turn led me to consider the dog's ear. The man at the harbour had not been Jason Jenkins. He was at least six inches taller and spoke with a better educated, less local, accent.

I had to admit, I was scared. All the success in the world couldn't assuage the feeling of terror the sticky ear, the dog shit on the mirror and the man in the rainbow tinted snowboarding visor had instilled in me.

Then I thought of the one thing that made it all seem better – Pippa. That was why I hadn't obstructed her return, although I didn't really want her back. She would know what to do, if and when she needed to know. She would single handedly take care of this weirdo and deal with Jason too if necessary. I realised I really needed her. It didn't matter that she did my head in, or that she didn't understand my need for freedom, or my beard. She had the balls I needed to be a *real* man.

Just then my phone vibrated pleasingly, near my privates. It was a text from Rachel. 'The situation has changed a bit. Let's have a coffee and talk about it.'

****

As I opened the front door, I could tell, just by the air, or lack of it, that Pippa had arrived early to our fisherman's cottage. There was a stale whiff of her perfume, a reminder of her stifling proximity. Objects had been ordered, lined up, absented from the room. Everything seemed altered, sullied. I already felt marginalised.

I walked into the kitchen and started the long and arduous process of making coffee in the Bezzera coffee maker Pippa had insisted on buying one Christmas.

Her voice boomed from the marital bedroom, down the steep stairs.

'Don't make one for me! No one drinks coffee any more. It's all about Red Bush tea now.'

I considered my options. The machine had already begun its sputtering, hissing progress towards a miniscule amount of over-hyped, expensive caffeine that I didn't really want. At that moment, the object took on all the problems I had. My abject dislike of my own wife, my impotency around my ability to control my daughters, the terrorism I was enduring at the hands of a snowboarding lunatic and finally, the issue that was always there: Jason Jenkins. I unplugged the machine from the wall with a savage tug and took it out to the tiny back yard. I threw it on the small garden table, then I fetched my hammer from the cupboard under the stairs.

I could hear Pippa having a shower. It was now or never. I took the hammer to the coffee machine, marshalling all the venom I could. I put everything into smashing the stupid chrome and black object until it was crushed and crumpled, resembling perhaps, the buckled fender of a 50s American vintage car. I stood, weapon in hand, breathing deeply; sweat dripping from my face and my beard, feeling a rage inside me that was exquisitely satisfying and liberating. At that very moment, I understood the sheer ecstasy I'd witnessed deep in the eyes of Jason Jenkins as he lit up the first beach hut that night. It was a release.

Then I heard the water go off in Pippa's shower. I looked about. We had no shed, no out-house, or cellar. I did the only thing any semi-rational person could under the circumstances. I threw it over the back fence into a neighbour's garden.

I had enough time to compose myself in the living room, when she finally came downstairs in her Boden 'sea-side' clothes. She made a dramatic pretence of looking about the place in confusion, sniffing. She disappeared to the kitchen for thirty seconds then came back.

She was drying her short hair with a small towel. I ignored her and carried on pretending to work on my iPad.

Finally, she said in a sarky voice, 'That's weird, I could have sworn you were making coffee. I can smell it. Where's the Bezzera?'

I deliberately took a long time to answer. 'I haven't got a clue. I had an instant coffee earlier. Thought you'd taken that shit-heap to London with you.' I looked up. She was standing over me with a look of incomprehension. I got up and met her eye. 'We'll catch up later, yah? Got soooo much to do. Soz.' And I slipped past her newly podgy body that had morphed back into its own slouchy comfort zone and climbed the stairs to my safe-haven. I locked her out.

She finally knocked on the door several hours later, having given me ample time to make arrangements with Rachel for a day I knew Pippa would be in London, back at work. I still wasn't prepared to be 'redeemed' or talk honestly about *Burn* and my part in the whole sorry saga, but I missed the thrill of another woman in my life. It seemed worth the risk.

She heaved herself up the last couple of stairs and stood in front of me, hands on hips grinning.

'So! A new beginning for us Con. I hope you don't mind, I've organised a little "welcome home me" evening for us. We've done it darling! We've got there.'

She hadn't really done anything. *I'd* appropriated a dead woman's material and written the screenplay. *I'd* done all the schmoozing with my producer and the director. *I'd* written the essential column, the blog and done the spin off life-style interviews that had created the energy behind the product. *I'd* created, singlehandedly, the synergy across several platforms, dammit, to make the film the success it was! And *I'd* grown the beard!'

I smiled benignly at her.

Her voice took on a strained huskiness. 'I'm cooking a special family dinner, then you and I are going to bed.' She leaned on the doorframe, lifting a chunky leg slightly. 'Miranda will be with us to eat, but after that, we'll be alone.' She frowned. 'I've got no bloody idea where Isobel is. We have to talk about Isobel.'

I just nodded. I slipped past her to take a shower, remembering the snowboarder, remembering Jenkins. I had an unsatisfactory attempt at masturbation, thinking about Rachel, but thoughts of the dead dog's ear kept creeping in. Then, as an additional dampener, the realisation that I would probably have to have sex with Pippa soon. Tonight even.

I got dressed and went up to my office just as Pippa was crawling backwards out of the hole in the wall where I'd created my secret cupboard. She was clutching some low quality porn and the shoe box containing the amputated dog ear and my smashed lens that linked me to the scene that night.

'Sit. *Down*,' she commanded, sounding like Barbara Woodhouse disciplining a wayward Red Setter.

I sat.

'This isn't all I found.'

My face reddened. Had she found my chillum? My DVD copy of Furry Hentai panty number one?

She gave me a long withering look and sat down on my leather swivel chair and wiggled the mouse. My internet history popped up. She started clicking on links to emails and Facebook messages I'd sent to Rachel. Then she opened a document I had very little memory of entitled, 'My Confession – The Truth about *Burn*'. She didn't look at me.

Then, from her back pocket, she pulled out the letter Minnie had written to the local paper. She waved it in the air.

'I haven't read this yet, but I've got a good idea what it is. I thought we could read it together?'

She lined all the objects up on the desk and said, in the sweetest voice, 'We've got ten minutes until dinner. Have a think about what you're going to tell me. And by the way. I checked your phone too.'

****

After necking an entire bottle of wine in fifteen minutes once Pippa had ascended to prepare herself for our lovemaking, I loaded the dishwasher. I heard Pippa chatting to Miranda in her room, so I took the opportunity to sprint upstairs, strip and get into bed before she came in. I huddled down and pretended I was asleep.

I was almost away, when the air went dead. I squinted at her - she was silhouetted in the doorframe. I continued to pretend I was asleep. Then I actually slipped into a sleep of sorts. A dreadful sleep where dead dogs came alive, where one eared people limped about burning buildings. I woke up so hot, I couldn't move. I'd twisted myself back and forth, restlessly resisting the dream.

Then, I realised, I actually couldn't move.

I woke up a little more.

I couldn't move.

She had secured my wrists together and my legs apart to the iron bedstead with cable ties. The more I struggled to get free, the tighter they got.

Pippa stood at the end of the bed with the lighter that Jason Jenkins had sent to me, with Isobel's photograph taped on to it.

'So when were you thinking of telling me about this, *Con*?'

I had no answer. It was never. Why would I?

'Big mistake.'

She swiped back the duvet, knelt between my shins and ignited the lighter. The way she appeared took on a Hammer Horror effect. Her face was ghoulish and long; her features were shadowed unnaturally upwards by the flame.

She swooped the lighter past my balls once and there was a tickle of a flame. She laughed. I tried to tough it out but I heard a sound a bit like a kid goat, escape from my throat.

She swooped again. Something caught. I then remembered that I had applied the gel I'd been using for my beard to my pubes as a little experiment. Sex Wax. It says on the tin: 'Stickier - Easier to apply - More likely to move or rub away at pressure points on your beard'.

Except, upon reflection, I realised it had said *board* not *beard.*

There was an audible whoosh! And up my pubes went. A six-inch flame grew above my groin.

I screamed. She laughed. Then she slammed her All Saints leather jacket down onto my burning cock.

She left and came back with Minnie's letter.

'A story for bedtime, Conrad.'

She unfolded the letter and settled herself in her chair to read. I started to drift, whimpering into sleep, imagining Minnie herself was reading it to me:

'Dear Sir,

If you are reading this, I am already dead. I have left on my own terms and am leaving this letter by way of explanation. Please feel free to use the information and the several dozen letters deposited with my solicitor, Parry's to publish anything you find that might have public interest.

Here is the final, irrefutable truth about what happened to my family the night of the 1953 flood.

On that cold night in February, my husband arrived home in his usual state, soaked with drink. It was my birthday and rather than buy me a gift or take me out, he had done what he did every night since we married, got drunk in The Guinea.

Usually, I would make sure I was in bed, either asleep or feigning it, before he got in. But that night, the storm blew so strong, it kept my dear James awake. He was a sensitive soul and feared most things, especially loud noises. And violence. We stoked the fire and huddled together under some blankets while the gale blew.

As I feared, Robert came crashing into the house after closing time and demanded food. I had prepared nothing but a sandwich for him. He reluctantly ate it, then smashed the plate onto the ground by me, sending sharp ceramic shards into my leg. Before I could react, he swiped my forehead with the back of his hand. All the while, the house rocked in the storm and the wind screamed through the floorboards. He struck me again, sending me backwards. I had blood in my eyes and couldn't see, but what I heard next sent a chill down me. A dull thud, a groan and the sound of Robert's massive body hitting the floor. I wiped the blood away with my pinny and saw my boy James standing over him with the fire poker, breathing hard and looking scared.

I ran to him as he started to cry. He tried to shake his father awake again, too simple to understand what he had done. He began beating his own head with his fists shouting 'bad boy, bad boy'. I held him tight and told him he only imagined he had done it, because he'd thought about it so often. That it had been me, it had been me. I took him up to bed as the storm passed and explained that I had hit him with the poker, that it was Mother. I could tell he knew it wasn't the truth, but was willing to accept it, because he could live with it. He finally fell asleep, my special boy. I kissed his eyelids and each cheek and stroked his hair as I always did. So grateful that he had put a stop to my torment.

When I returned downstairs, a strange thing had happened. Water had started to creep into the house, from the front and from the back. I hastily took a look out into the night. From my back upstairs window, I could see the Saltings were flooded. From my front upstairs window, I could see our road, Nelson Road, was filling up with water.

It was so dark, it was hard to tell how bad it was, but by the time I got back downstairs, Robert was floating several inches from the ground and the fire was out. I hastily buttoned up his huge winter coat and covered his smashed head in his scarf, then drifted him through the kitchen to the back door. The water outside was rising. It was a Godsend. I could never have got rid of him without it.

206

In the pitch dark I did the opposite of everyone else in my street, I let the water in. His body rose by six inches and I got him clear of the back step. The water outside continued to creep up. I put some bricks from the back yard in my coat pockets, then floated his huge body down the yard and out of the back gate. There was no one about. His form was so big, someone might have mistaken it for a boat. It took only light tugs and pushes to guide him out to the Saltings where the water was already thigh deep and rising.

I began to fear for my own life. I took him out as far as I could then I stuffed the bricks into his sleeves, collar and under his thick belt. I pushed him down into the water with all my might, first as far as my arms went, then with my knees, then feet. Slowly, as the water saturated his clothes, he began to sink and take on weight, sending air bubbles to the surface. A great ship going down.

'I'm sorry,' I said to him, 'but you were a bastard'. Then I left to see what I could do to save my home.

They didn't find him until the water subsided, and by then he was in a sorry state. They very quickly decided that he had been done in and they very quickly decided it was me. Apparently, it hadn't been such a secret that he beat me. To my great relief, I was given bail, paid for by my son's Catholic School governors and parishioners' kind donations. They knew James would be taken from me and took pity. Mostly everyone said Robert had it coming, but I kept my mouth shut and maintained it must have been an accident, that I was devoted to Robert, that I could barely live without him. I couldn't risk them finding out the truth. I had but three months to create my case, so I set to work. I began reinventing our story, constructing love letters send back and forth from us starting at 1940, the year we met.

They were easy to write, almost enjoyable. I simply swapped everything about him that was bad for good and created a different man. When Robert deliberately chose to work the land because he did not want to serve in the War, I made him a heroic farmer who kept England's larder full. When Robert didn't come home for three weeks, out on benders with the farms girls, I had him grafting sixteen hour days to pay for a new winter coat for me. When Robert recoiled in disgust when he first saw our baby, knowing he was not alright, I had him take dear James up and smother him with kisses.

And how he loved me! In his letters, he wrote me poetry, he quoted sonnets and told me again and again how wonderful I was. To explain why we still wrote once we were married, he, yes he, wrote that he found it easier to express himself on paper - that speaking emotions out loud was too hard. He said that he missed the letters that naturally stopped when we became man and wife. And he wrote me the most beautiful letter to ask that we strike up our correspondence again.

To convince the judge it had been Robert who wrote them, I got James to re-write them for me. His handwriting was poor, as was Robert's. James was too simple to understand what the content was about. He just copied them out while we listened to the radio in the evening, just as he would his school work.

By the time the case was heard, the diaries were complete right up to that night. I handed them over to my solicitor. They all believed they were authentic. With that and a fairly damning character witness about Robert by the landlady of The Guinea bar, with the fact that he was a chronic drunk, the fact that his body was so decomposed they couldn't tell what had caused the blow to the head that killed him and that my character was held in good regard by the people my solicitor called up from the town, the jury, God bless their souls, ruled that I was innocent and it was death by misadventure.

Except, in a small town like this, mud sticks. I was never fully exonerated by the real judges – the small minded, shallow, two faced people in this town. I managed to find work *at a grocers but was never allowed to work in the shop, just out the back. People ignored me in the street, I was even spat on. Elaborate tales and myths grew about me – I was a witch, a sorceress. No one ever believed that I was innocent. That I, in fact, had been his victim all along. All this had a terrible effect on my beautiful boy who was mercilessly bullied in school.*

As soon as he could, he joined the same fishing fleet his father had worked as a young lad, then again after the war. He was strong and obedient and they were happy to have him.

On the days they joked about his dad, just leg-pulling as working men do, he would come home solemn and brooding. Then, especially if I lit a fire, the tears would come. His conscience preyed on him. His memory played games between the story he remembered and the one I planted in his head. Eventually, Jamie could live with it no longer. He saw his priest and told him everything. The priest told him God would forgive him as long as he said his prayers. He suggested Jamie wrote a letter of confession in case he should die.

Before he set out to catch the tide that night, Jamie insisted I make a promise – I was to do everything I could to make sure my reputation was not sullied by what happened that night. He had an unusual eloquence as he spoke, he seemed more at peace. I had no idea what he was planning. I'd have stopped him from going.

That night, on a rough sea, Jamie slipped off the boat when the others were not looking and was drowned. His body, recovered the next day didn't have a bruise on it. He was just thirty years old. I found his confession on his pillow, written in pencil on a scrap of paper. It simply said, 'I killed Robert Rowden'.

I burned it immediately.

I kept this secret my whole life, to honour him and now, finally I can do as he asked – do all I can to ensure my reputation is properly restored. I have no other children, no known direct relatives left that could be hurt by this, so please help me to put the story straight.

There is just one other matter that I have kept secret these long years. In 1948, Robert's boat dredged up a treasure trove somewhere near the Goodwin Sands. The men divided it between them and swore not to tell another soul.

After Robert died, in a panic, I buried the treasure in his grave at the cemetery up Millstroud Road. I have no idea of the value but it contained many beautiful coins, bracelets, broaches, combs and knives. I'm not certain, but having studied library books over the years, I'm fairly sure they are Viking in origin.

I'd heard that people were speculating about where I might have hidden Robert's cut so I engaged a trusted associate to re-bury the treasure in my own grave straight after my funeral. That's where it will stay, until it can be officially dug up.

If you decide to make this find public and get the antiquities dug up, I would like them to be donated to a museum so they can be seen. I absolutely do not want any individual to personally profit from them. No one but you and my associate know of this.

I have instructed my lawyers that the remainder of my inheritance is given in charity to Mencap.

Thank you for your professionalism,
Minerva Rowden, nee Frend'

****

I was drifting in and out of consciousness as I heard Pippa re-fold the letter.

'Let's start with the least obvious issue first, Conrad. You told me, the press and the public that you had come up with the twist at the end of *Flood* from your own research. That Minnie hadn't killed Robert herself, but that she was covering for her son.'

'Uh-huh.'

'But you couldn't even write that. You kept this letter back because you wanted me and everyone else to think the best bit of that story came from you. But you stole it.'

'I just wanted people to think I could really write! That I was a great researcher, that I had talent.'

'For fuck's sake, Conrad. It's not *talent* that matters, its success! Now onto the more obvious reason you kept this letter hidden. Treasure. Were you ever going to tell me?'

I looked at her. She knew I'd had no plans to tell her anything, ever.

'It doesn't matter. What's important is that I know about it now. I'd like to thank you, Conrad, for actually doing the right thing in this case by holding on to that letter. You may have just guaranteed our future, darling.'

She rose, checked the cable ties and stood over me.

'Night-night, Conrad. Sleep well.'

I passed out again.

****

I awoke the next day in the same position. Trapped, my testes burning, the hair stumpy. Pippa sauntered into the bedroom, freshly showered, towelling her hair. She sat on the edge of our bed.

'Morning, darling.'

'Let me go.'

She put the towel down and folded her hands primly into her lap.

'I've read your confession. Now I want to hear it from your mouth. Tell me about Jason Jenkins, Conrad. Tell me the truth about *Burn*.'

Three days later, I was still massaging myself with camomile, trying to ease the blistering. I had cuts and welts on my ankles and wrists from the cables ties and half a nipple missing that Pippa had snipped off with her nail clippers when I wouldn't tell her where the dog's ear had come from.

She'd kept me tied up for forty-eight hours, going over and over every minute detail of the night I'd followed Jason and every point of the episode of the personal vendetta he had been waging against me since the previous Easter. I came clean about where Rachel fitted in – but only up to a point. And I eventually told her everything about Giles and the mystery snowboarder with one ear.

At first, I'd tried to avoid telling her about what I'd witnessed at the end of that terrible evening with Jason. I'd had the foresight to leave the most damning bit out of my confession. But Pippa was way too blasé.

'For God's sake, Conrad. Jason Jenkins is a psycho. Let's just go to the police! He was probably working up to blackmailing you. God knows why you've kept it so quiet!'

Eventually, my balls burning and itching, after soiling myself several times while she looked on with an amused air of detachment, I broke. I told her what I'd seen Jason Jenkins do to an innocent woman.

She left the room for several hours, visibly shaken. When she came back at the end of the second day of my internment, she was icy. Her face betrayed nothing.

'You are never to see or contact that bitch Rachel again. It's fairly obvious, from what I read, that she wasn't really that into you anyway. If I even hear you've looked at her in the street, I will ruin you.' I nodded. 'I haven't decided what we should do about that little shit Jenkins, but I won't have us rubbished by this, or him. We can't go to the police, it's too risky. I don't want any negative publicity just before Cannes. Your reputation needs to be impeccable. I need some time to think about this lunatic with the dead dog too. In the meantime, I'm going to let you go, but only because I need you to feed the children. I'm back at work tomorrow.' She had stood over me, looking down at my face with a quizzical look.

'Is there anything else you want to tell me while you're getting stuff off your chest?'

I gulped. 'You know Isobel's been seeing someone?' She nodded. 'Well, the boy, Joe, her boyfriend?' She looked impatient. I waited. She squeezed my burning balls, hard. 'He's Jason Jenkins' son!' I yelped.

Once she had calmed down, she sat very still for a further fifteen minutes staring at my face. I couldn't tell what she was thinking. I tried to arrange my features to look as appealing as possible, so she'd warm to me, remember how much she loved her Conrad, the boy she'd been with since college. I actually just wanted to scratch my balls.

She got up and rummaged in a toiletry bag by her dressing table and stood back over me again.

'One last adjustment, Conrad. You clearly think you're a real man with that beard, but we both know you're a spineless girl. That bloody beard is coming off and you are never, *ever* to grow it again. Got it?' She turned her pink electric depilator on and went to work on my pride and joy. I wept as each hair was ripped from its roots. I wept from the sheer agony and also for the loss of my manhood.

I knew, at that moment, that she would always rule me.

And finally, when she pulled the very last hair from my bleeding face, I wept because I knew I would never have it any other way.

****

The next morning, we both rose early. Pippa for her train to St. Pancras and me to get the packed lunches ready for the girls. Isobel had locked herself in her room since the evening before. Pippa had confronted her and banned her from ever seeing Joe again. Isobel had become hysterical, saying that he'd already dumped her anyway because his mum was ill and he needed to concentrate on his daughter. Pippa had attempted to comfort her, with the assertion that all men are total bastards. It didn't work. Our daughter emerged the next day looking very young and pale. A return to her true age, her heartache having stripped her of her attitude.

I finished making the sandwiches and Pippa took them to pack the girls' school bags. I was just mildly fantasising about how I could get hold of Rachel secretly, when I heard Pippa screaming from the front room. We all ran in, the girls looking shocked and worried.

Pippa had dropped the lunches on the floor. She was holding two identical pink satchels, one with purple polka dots, one with orange, up in the air, their buckles unhooked and the innards gaping open.

'Conrad! Look. Wrapped in fleece just like the other one. What the hell are those - *shapes*?'

I inched forwards.

'I think I know what those are. Yes.' I didn't want the children to be alarmed. But Isobel pushed past me.

'Let me get a look at that.' She snatched the satchels from her mother.

There, nestled alongside text books, hair brushes, lipsticks and iPods were two dog parts wrapped in the same smelly Aztec fleece. In one bag, the lower half of the dog's leg, with the just the fluffy paw protruding. In the other, the coil of a long tail with the slightly shaggy flea-bitten tip of fur exposed.

She dropped the bags, started gagging and edged backwards.

'Conrad. I've made my decision about what we need to do. I will tell you tonight. You sort this vile mess out. I'm going to work. Girls, just pretend this didn't happen. Mummy is in charge now.'

214

She snatched up her mac and left without looking back. Her perfume just adequately merging enough with the rancid smell of dead dog to make it tolerable.

****

I peeped around the corner by the Community Arts Centre and did a reconnaissance of the little row of houses behind the pub the celebrity chef ran. It was still very early. No one was about, but I knew Rachel was always in the Centre first. I was desperate to get a message to her. I needed to plead her for help before Pippa put whatever plan she had into action.

I'd written my note on a small strip of paper in capital letters. It said, HELP! WE ARE BEING VICTIMISED BY THE MAN THAT LEFT THE MESSAGE ABOUT THE MISSING EAR. IT'S SERIOUS. CHILDREN IN DANGER. NO TEXT MESSAGES OR EMAILS, CALL ME!

I sprinted down to her house and rammed the note into her door then I didn't stop running until I reached the pub on the beach. When I finally stopped by the tennis courts, my heart felt like it would explode. I sat on the seawall, panting and was just about to walk back the same way, when I heard a familiar voice echoing, amplified, from the public toilet below. I ducked down behind the wall. The man was singing and talking, presumably to someone. He sounded drugged, or demented. The voice changed in timbre and lost its echo as the man moved towards the exit. He continued to rant as he came outside and only when I was convinced he was walking in the opposite direction, did I peep over and take a look.

There was the snowboarding stranger, well over six feet tall and incredibly lean, wearing bright yellow, wrap-around shades. His clothing was ethnic and dated. I imagined he'd been wearing the same clothes since the late 80s. His hair was in ridiculously long dreadlocks, down to the backs of his knees. And there was the smell. I'd not specifically noticed it the night at the harbour as I'd been in the grip of panic. It was the combination of faded Patchouli oil, strong skunk and dog. Dead dog. It smelled just like the fleece blanket I had prized away from the flea bitten ear and that wrapped the tail and the leg. I could identify it even though I was fifteen feet away.

I followed at a distance, down the long road Minerva Rowden had lived in, where tragedy had struck the night of the flood. He took a left and disappeared into a crescent of identical maisonettes. I ducked in behind a garage and watched him. He got half way round and let himself into the front door of a ground floor flat.

At last, I knew where he lived.

****

That evening Pippa and I had dinner alone together for the first time since she'd caught me out. I'd made an effort and laid the table, bought flowers and fish from the harbour. I'd had a pleasant day, despite the continual itchy burning in my pants and the anticipation of a phone call from Rachel. As each hour passed and no call materialised from her, and Pippa's imminent return neared, I became more regretful about the note. I had been rash.

After we ate, Pippa took my hand at the table. I knew what was coming.

'Conrad, do you remember at college, when we met?'

I nodded. This was a story she liked to repeat when I got a little beyond my boundaries.

'You were heading for a Third, going out with that - slut.' She meant Jenny, the girl I'd come up from my home town Harlow, in Essex with. Sweethearts since we were fifteen. 'It was me, Conrad, do you remember, that helped you better yourself?'

I'd had no choice. The moment she'd set eyes on me in the Students' Union, she'd hounded me. I'd found it flattering, then annoying, then I got drunk and slept with her and she let me do things I'd only read about on the walls of public toilets.

This went on for the rest of our time at Uni. The old girlfriend was dispatched. So upset, it turns out, she'd transferred to a different college a hundred miles away without a word. I'd been surprised at the time, but I was so busy and Pippa was making me work so hard, I forgot her.

Pippa squeezed my hand. 'Stay with me, Conrad. Stay with.' I looked at her. She was pointing at her own face, her eyes wide and mouth determined.

She needed to tell the rest of our story.

'Do you remember how we graduated and you got a ridiculous idea in your head that we were finished – over. Remember?'

I nodded.

'Well, just like then, when I made you see sense, when I made you see that it had to be you and me, I'm going to make you see sense now. I made you realise that, in fact, you could only be the man you aspired to be – a successful writer, if you lived with me and made some fundamental changes.'

I nodded again.

My career had not started well. I had ended up with a Third in English, despite the hard work. I had only managed to get a job in Marks and Spencer's café in Tottenham Court Road. I'd lied to her for the brief few months we'd been apart and said I was working as a copywriter and was on an acceptable salary. She'd appeared at the café, nonchalantly eating a scone and reading *Cosmopolitan*, one day. She threatened to tell my parents the truth. So we got back together and I moved into her flat.

'Con!' She shouted, digging her fingernails into my palm. '*Focus!*' I looked at her face as it morphed from stern to dreamy in the candlelight.

'Remember how I helped you become - *you*.' Her eyes drifted away for a moment. 'Colin, do you remember when I created – "Conrad"?'

'Yes,' I said, with genuine gratitude in my voice. 'Yes, I do, my darling.'

'Good.' She said sweetly. 'Well now, I'm going to help Conrad to do the very next big thing he needs to do. I'll get more wine. We're going to need it.'

I stared at the chair where she had just been sitting. It was true. I wouldn't be me without her.

I had been Colin Kevin Blake: Soft rock fan and head banger; Dungeons and Dragons fanatic; lanky haired, un-academic, nine stone be-speckled spod from Essex. Colin was hopeless with women, desperate to be liked. He'd harboured a vague ambition to write a fantasy sci-fi trilogy which Pippa had latched upon like a starved Staffordshire Bull-Terrier savaging a neglected infant. And Colin was still a virgin.

Within a year of living in London, Pippa had re-invented a shining academic past for Colin, writing a fictitious C.V. and creating new convincing degree certificates. She'd given him a makeover and changed his name to one which she deemed reflective of the writerly persona he was to become. She'd forced Colin on a demanding programme of physical metamorphosis, until he was reborn as me – Conrad Klaus Blaine: Chess playing, floppy fringed Britpop fan; a brilliantly talented and intellectual, sporty twelve stone hunk of a real man.

In no time at all I got a job - my dream job, or so I thought, as a copywriter.

But that wasn't enough for Pippa. She wanted so much for me. She had ambitions. I had to write a screenplay. I tried and tried but nothing came. It was after trying for two years with no success that she'd sent me to Whitstable to 'get something on bloody paper', disgusted that I'd let her down.

It was that weekend I found Jason and gave Pippa everything she'd ever wanted.

She returned with the wine and settled back down, holding my hand in her cool, firm grip.

'Conrad.' She pulled my hands forward so they were resting on her ample chest. 'You are going to have to take Jason Jenkins *out*. Kill him.' She released my hands and poured the wine, flaring her nostrils slightly with the adrenalin triggered by her momentous statement.

I felt both sick and elated. It made perfect sense. Pippa had such a good way of seeing the absolute truth of the matter.

He had to go.

She sipped her wine. 'And you know, if he goes, that other weirdo will have to go too.'

I thought of the skeletal man with a slightly juddery walk and a booming voice, talking nonsense. She was right of course. He wasn't going away. Him and Jenkins were linked, I just didn't know how.

'Pippa, you're brilliant - but I just - *can't*. What if I got caught? There must be nothing to link me to this. What about my career – the career I've forged for you! You have to help me out here. *I can't do it.*'

She patted my hand. 'I'm a little disappointed. But I understand. Don't worry. Pippa will sort it out.' I smiled but there was something eating at me. Something I'd forgotten to remind her that might create a problem. 'Drink up, it's your lucky night.' She winked at me and arose. I obediently followed her and forgot the thing, the important potential hiccup in the plan.

That night, I allowed Pippa to have her way with me, even though it hurt. I felt, somehow, I deserved it.

****

The next Saturday morning, Pippa had some errands to run and I got some time alone. I was sipping a cappuccino in the sunshine by the harbour when my phone rang. It was Rachel. I almost dropped it into my beverage as I tried to answer. I wasn't really too sure what to say. I regretted the rash, hysterical note. I'd exposed myself again.

Instead, I thought I'd play it cool. Somewhere in my mind I thought there might still be a fraction of a chance of at least a snog.

'Conrad. I got your note. What's happened? I thought we were meeting for coffee?'

It was in my nature to be honest, but I couldn't afford to be this time. Knowing what Pippa had in mind, knowing she was prepared to carry it out had been a shock but had also given me the first peace of mind I'd had in over a year. Rachel didn't need to know that Pippa knew everything.

'Oh, nothing, you know me. Just paranoid.'

'But it's more than that, isn't it?'

'Er, no.'

She knew something. I thought of the bony shoulders with the long grubby dreads dangling between them.

There was a long silence on the phone before she spoke.

'Conrad, I'm afraid your behaviour has forced us to take action, slightly earlier than planned. We've had to stage, what you might call, an intervention.'

I had no idea what she was saying. She was doing it again. Confusing me with jargon.

'Well, no need to panic on my behalf.' I said, feeling panicky. Who was "we"? The obscure, mystery others who knew all the facts. I went cold. I hadn't told Pippa anything about them, I'd been vague about Rachel beyond our fledgling flirtation.

'Well, you'll be pleased to know that it was me that called the police and ambulance that night for your friend. Giles isn't it? The one that fell into, or rather, was pushed into the harbour. You wrote me an email just after it happened. It was difficult to read but I understood that your friend was likely to drown and you'd run away. I thought you had called the police yourself. I was wrong.'

I had no recollection of this alleged email. I wondered if Pippa had seen it.

'Conrad. That was the last straw. I once asked you if you thought you could be redeemed. That night, I waited for as long as I could, hoping to hear the sirens. Hoping that you'd done the decent, correct thing and found help for your friend. But no one came. If I hadn't phoned the police, that man, *your friend*, would be dead.'

I had no words.

'You would have let him drown. You'd have been an accessory to a murder.'

Just like twenty years before.

And then it came to me. The thing. Like the thing I forgot that night: Giles. He was the road bump in our plan. If he came round from his coma, Pippa's strategy was useless. He knew *everything*. I needed to talk to my wife!

'Rachel. It's been wonderful catching up. There's nothing I like better than a thorough moral chastisement, but I really have to -'

'I think you've been labouring under a misconception. I'm sorry if you like me – sexually - but that was never what I intended. I'm not interested in you that way, *at all*. I told you the first night we went out that I'd found you on purpose – for this. This is all that matters, it's all that's mattered to me for twenty years.'

'Well that's just charming isn't it? Try and protect anyone you like. You can't touch me, or my success. I'm beyond that now. Whatever you *villager oiks* have got going on, it's no longer my concern. You want to talk to me again, do it through my solicitor.'

I hung up.

Stupid patronising bitch. I thought about my first impression of her: a vulnerable, disappointed, but attractive single lady. Seeing her away from her work, in my new exciting guise as 'single man' had given her an aura she didn't really deserve. In reality, she was a cold, unreachable plain-Jane. No wonder she hadn't had a boyfriend for so long. No wonder she didn't have kids. Who was she to reject me again and again! I felt liberated. A renewed loyalty to Pippa swelled my heart.

I put my phone in my inside pocket and looked up. Isobel was standing in front of me, fists on hips, smirking.

'Sweetheart, how long have you been there?' I asked, trying not to sound concerned.

'Long enough to know you're still playing around with the lesbian from the Community Centre. The one you brought to our house when Mum was away.' She stood nodding, with menace shining in her eyes.

'Lesbian? I'm not playing with a lesbian!'

'How come you were on the phone to her, then?'

I had no real answer for this, so I pulled out my trump card.

'These are adult things that you are too young to understand.'

'Bullshit. I hate you. You have ruined my life. It was me that sent Minnie's letters to that editor. Me! I'm not a fucking kid. I'm not too young to understand! You're *pathetic*.'

She started to laugh in a deliberately nasty, maniacal way. So much so that people were watching; conversations were stopping. I jumped up, dragged her down an alley and pushed her against the wall.

'Stop it! I can't believe my own daughter sold me out. You wait 'til your mother hears about this!'

The fake hysterics stopped abruptly.

'Oh yeah? Imagine if she knew you were phoning your "girlfriend"?'

I gulped. The last thing I needed was Pippa knowing – even if I had just sent Rachel packing.

I stomped off to the cottage with Isobel striding behind me with her arms crossed. I felt like an unruly inmate being escorted to solitary by a particularly malicious screw. Once home, I ran upstairs and slammed my office door.

She left me to it.

After an hour waiting for an apology, knowing none would materialise, I decided to write a new blog entry. I checked the BBC website and the lunchtime's news came on.

As I watched, I had the sensation of falling, as though I was in a broken elevator that was hurtling towards the ground at a stomach lurching velocity.

'Giles Purdy, the seventh Earl of Worcester has died in hospital today in Canterbury. He was sixty-four years old. The entrepreneur, philanthropist and wine expert died of heart failure after suffering serious head and spinal injuries earlier in the year. Purdy had been found in Whistable Harbour after an accidental fall, following a day of heavy drinking in the town.'

I sat staring at the screen while other news rolled before my eyes. It just seemed too much like a coincidence. The thing – the potential spoiler had been *eradicated*.

The front door slammed and I heard Pippa come up the stairs. She made straight for the loft and climbed heavily up the steep steps. She crossed the room straight to me and pulled my head towards her belly and held it there, twisting her fingers into my hair, coiling it and tugging it more than was necessary.

'I knew you'd forgotten. Luckily for us, I knew. It's done now. We can get on with our plan. Conrad - the future is *ours*.'

Chapter 16

Dimitri

May 2015

'You've got one week until your father's funeral. Jason, I'd like to help you. Do you remember when we talked in the pub that no one goes in? I told you about a way I may have of giving you an alternative way of seeing things?' Mack spoke quietly. His accent had softened.

Jason was in bed, propped up on one elbow. He wasn't sure how long he'd been there, but once he knew who he was with, he'd surrendered and allowed himself to be cared for. He knew Mack had been sedating him while the alcohol left his system. It was a relief. He slept more deeply and soundly than he had in years. His cut up hand and arm, ripped to shreds on his rampage through several greenhouses, was feeling more comfortable. Mack had been encouraging him to drink gallons of water, eat wholesome, home cooked food and take vitamin injections. This was the first time they'd really spoken since he'd been rescued from the beach just before the police had arrived.

Jason looked at Mack warily. 'What's it about then?'

'I'll come to that in a minute. You're here, being given that chance, because of two people who care about you. The first is Tracy. She got hold of me when she heard your dad had passed away, when you didn't show up at your Joe's place the night he died. She's worried. She knows me better than you do, Jason. She knows what I can do. It's me that helped your son.'

Jason flinched. 'What the fuck?'

'Early in the new year. Tracy came to see me. She knew the methadone was only a sticking plaster on a bigger problem. You and she had fallen out, you weren't talking so she didn't tell you. I think, even then, she knew she wasn't well. She said she needed Joe strong and healthy because she might not be around for ever and she couldn't rely on you.'

Jason hung his head and shut his eyes.

'You were off in your own little world. You hadn't noticed that Joe was slipping. I helped Joe clean up. Now she wants me to help you. It's that simple. This could be a turning point.' Mack folded his arms across his chest. He looked stern, defiant. 'That woman loves you.'

Jason's face twisted, but he was relieved to hear Tracy still cared. He thought about Joe's new physical wellbeing, his new sense of purpose and responsibility.

'Who's the other person?'

'All will become clear soon. Let's just say, you're not just here because Tracy wanted me to help. You're here because someone else has been hurt. The person who wants to help you is worried that more people will get damaged unless we take some drastic action.'

'I never hurt no-one.'

'No. Not directly, but you know who did and you are massively implicated. I'm sorry to say that the gentleman who fell into the harbour passed away.'

Jason thought of Fran, hacking up the dead dog, ranting into the radiator. He thought of the fat man, face up between the fishing boats that he'd heard about in the paper, now dead. Mack was right, it was his fault. Jason slumped back on the bed and stared at the ceiling in despair.

'I want a fucking drink.'

'Sorry. No alcohol, pal. But perhaps I could interest you in a life changing psychedelic experience?'

Jason shot Mack a dark look, thinking he was making light of a terrible situation, but the man's face was open, truthful.

'What? Acid? Is that what you gave my son?'

'No, very much *not* like acid Jason. Ayahuasca. The psychedelic is produced as a brew a bit like tea. Two plants from the Amazon, one contains DMT and one contains something called a MAOI – a monoamine-oxidase inhibitor. To you Jason, that's the stuff that activates the trip.'

Jason sat up with a groan.

'What's DMT? I've never heard of it. Sounds more like an explosive.' The two men laughed.

'You won't be getting your hands on any explosives on my watch, son. It stands for Dimethyltryptamine. Dimitri. I've often said you don't know much about me. I suppose I'm going to have to tell you a bit about myself over the next few days, if you agree to do it.'

'Christ, you make it sound like this won't be fun!'

'What I'm offering isn't like doing shrooms on Duncan Downs with your mates, Jason. This is a fully immersive, shamanistic, divinatory healing experience. It's extremely powerful. And potentially life changing. You need to think about it carefully. You won't come to any harm, but it's quite a commitment.'

Mack had moved to the window of his tiny shack and was staring out across the mud flats. It was a beautiful, clear spring day.

Jason stared at his bandaged hand and thought about his dad. He still felt numb. He thought about how his own son had had the strength to make changes he's never had the will-power to instigate.

'Will it make the bad memories go away?'

'Maybe. Or it might change your perception of them, or of what's important. It tends to open up a gap in your consciousness, to give you a chance to move beyond your physical form, reconnect with the Universe.' Jason looked baffled. 'If we do it, we'll begin tomorrow morning, early. The Aya will probably be an eight to ten-hour experience and I expect to give you two, maybe three doses, depending on your progress. It'll take you another twelve hours of rest before you can really process what you will have experienced.'

'Shit. And you do this with people all the time?' Jason had new found respect for Mack. Mack the Shaman. Who'd have bloody thought it! The song 'Ebeneezer Goode' cheerfully started up in Jason's mind and he remembered a birthday party Tracy had thrown for him at the football club a few years after it came out. He smiled at the memory of himself and his mates dancing about until he remembered that at the same party, some joker had put 'Firestarter' by the Prodigy on. The same nob-head mate of his had made Jason Jenkins masks and everyone had put them on and danced around him with their lighters flaring past. His face fell - another memory he'd rather obliterate.

He needed a drink.

'I work with people all the time. It's illegal of course, so I have to be careful, but I've been practicing for twenty-five years. It doesn't work all the time. As a rule of thumb, like any changes, they will only happen if the person is receptive to the idea. If there's resistance, there's no point. Of course some people have wanted to change for a long time. This might not 'cure' them, but it just gives them a nudge. A glimpse of something better.'

He thought of the little birds by the railway track.

'You mean I have to really believe it could change me, help me?' He thought of his friends in the Jason Jenkins masks, circling him. His own pudgy face replicated dozens of times, leering at him, twisting around him from his drunken pilled-up perspective, like being trapped in a fucked-up kaleidoscope.

'You may well be confronted with some very disturbing stuff, but that's what you must try not to resist. You will also, in all likelihood, experience the nearest thing to God, beauty, joy too.'

'God doesn't exist, Mack.'

'Alright then, you might experience an amazing feeling of being connected to the Universe.' The little birds, the joy he felt when he held Aleisha. He had experienced

227

glimpses but he still wasn't convinced, but he was getting more intrigued.

'What stuff do people see?'

Mack came and sat on the chair beside the bed and opened a laptop on the bedside table. 'There are a few similarities between peoples' experiences. With the Ayahusasca, lots of people see geometric patterns. Weirdly, often these are in the shape of a Benzene ring – a basic organic compound – the building block of life. In layman's terms, that's a hexagon, a six sided shape. People report that they see these shapes everywhere, on everything they look at in sparkling bright acid colours, spiralling, shaking or vibrating in breath-taking beauty. Some people have a sense of nothingness, an ego-less state where they reconnect with the Universe. Some people even report seeing little creatures.'

'Shit! That's fucked up.' He thought of Fran and his radiator people. He suddenly felt wary. He did not want to end up like that.

'Look, here's my laptop. I've loaded up a film about it. Remember what we'll be doing isn't recreational Jason. It's not a bender. You'll be going on a serious journey. This isn't a drug, it is *medicine*. You'll be very sick, for maybe an hour or longer. It may be difficult and distressing at times, but without the intensity, it's unlikely to make any life altering impact.'

Jason pulled himself upright, had a long sip of water and Mack placed the laptop on his legs.

'I'm off out to meet someone from the train. Rachel is here if you need her. Let's eat together tonight and I'll tell you my story.'

Jason wasn't really listening. He was already reading a blog post by some students which detailed their experiences. Could this be it? He couldn't believe that drinking a load of Amazon plant juice could have such a dramatic, positive effect after the decades of problems and abuses that were his life. Then he thought about Tracy, that despite having a serious illness, she was still trying to help him, make his life better and save him from himself.

He pressed play on the film entitled *DMT: The Spiritual Molecule* and sat motionless and gripped. Excitement and hope building the more he watched.

Jason knew, before he'd finished watching the film, that he would do it.

****

Jason tiptoed sheepishly into the kitchen from his bedroom. He was wearing clean clothes; some trackie bottoms and a new t-shirt that someone had brought round for him, or Mack had fetched.

Mack was at his stove and Rachel was just putting her jacket on to leave.

'Jason, sit down,' she said. He sat. He still wasn't sure what was going on. 'Promise me something? You'll take this seriously?' He nodded. 'I'll tell you why you should - we saved you the other day. From yourself this time, but that's not the only person you might need saving from.'

'Who do you mean?' He thought immediately of Fran.

'Let's just say that we've reached a consensus that Blaine is a liability. We've written him off. You haven't got long to wait now, Jason.' She put her hand on his shoulder again like she had in the alleyway all those months before, after he saw the birds. 'You're not the total degenerate you think you are.' She squeezed his shoulder, kissed Mack on both cheeks and left.

Jason still couldn't get his head around the sheer weirdness of the situation. One minute he'd been drunkenly cavorting about causing criminal damage, next he was sober and being nursed like he was in a mental hospital. The truth was, he didn't know how he was feeling. Confused summed it up pretty well.

'Should be a good sunset tonight.' Mack said. They both turned to look out across the calm water at high tide. The sun was still in the sky but already the clouds were frayed with hot pink and citrus colours. 'You'll never look at that the same way again, I can tell you.' Mack smiled at Jason. 'This must all seem very strange to you, son?'

'Strange is better than the same.'

'Come on, sit, we'll eat in here.' Mack set homemade lentil dahl and rice down on the little wooden table for them both. He poured water out of a jug and sat opposite Jason. 'No meat or dairy now and a fast until tomorrow after this. Now, eat.' They ate, the same sombre and moving classical music coming through the open door to the front room. Jason would not normally be comfortable in a situation like this, but he felt oddly at ease. Mack had mellowed somehow. Even his accent had changed.

'Can I ask you something?'

Mack nodded.

'What's up with Rachel? I saw her around for a while after – that night – then she vanished. Then when she came back years later, she was so different. She's not a laugh like she used to be. She's so serious now. I saw her around since she's been back, but we never spoke until you told me I'd get a visit off of someone. I just don't get how she is involved. Why does she know any of it Mack?'

'Ah, Jenkins. All this sea air must be sharpening your senses.' Mack smirked at him.

'She seems so – mardy. So why don't you perform this ritual thing on her? Surely that would help. She seems almost as unhappy as me.'

Mack took several mouthfuls of his curry before answering.

'It's not right for everyone. I know she won't mind me telling you this, but she's struggled with depression since that night. It was traumatic for everyone, but for her, well, let's just say it was a matter of the heart.' Jason thought about *Her*

– how powerful loss could be. About loving someone who didn't know you existed. 'Anyway, that means she has to take a certain medication. The two don't mix. It could be lethal.'

'Shit. My fault too then.'

Mack laughed. 'We can talk about that after. There's a lot of unhappy people out there. That's how come I have so much business.'

Jason watched the older man again. He was still a mystery. Jason could see there was something he had missed before, his level of self-possession, a compassion he hadn't noticed about his green eyes.

'I always thought you hated me.' Mack smiled and carried on eating. 'I mean, you were pretty arsey when you ran the pub, back then. I never did get a lock in.'

Again, Mack smiled and put his fork down. He took a big swig of his water and wiped his face with the back of his hand.

'Well, I was like that to everyone, then. My natural defence system. None of us are perfect, chum. I'm just as messed up as the next man.'

'How come you ended up being into all this hippy stuff then? You are the last person I thought would do this.'

'Which is how I get away with it. I'm not running a business here, this is a calling.' Jason didn't understand. He continued to eat his curry, scowling. 'Time for the biography, maybe.' Mack pushed his plate to one side and started rolling a fag. Jason eyed the tobacco pouch with interest. 'Help yourself, son.'

They left their dishes and sat on the back step, directly on the beach, watching the inevitable sinking of the sun and the developing panoply of acid ribbons the sky.

Jason nodded at the sunset. 'That's lush. The people in the film – they said what they saw was a bit like that.'

'Too true. And once you've done it, done Aya, you'll see nature, the world, in a different way.'

'What's the story then?'

'Are you sitting comfortably?' Mack said in a parody of a childrens' bedtime voice. 'Then I'll begin.'

****

When Mack finished telling his history, how he'd come to practice as a shaman, Jason was speechless. He still wasn't sure if he was in the company of a genius, or an absolute fruitcake.

He also felt exhausted. He said good night to Mack and went to bed, still uncertain how it would help him forget the past. His mind was full of visions of angels and snakes, of crazy strobe lights and chanting. He was terrified, but he was excited. He had his own son as evidence of how Mack could bring about change, no matter how unlikely. He knew this was worth a try.

****

Once Jason was up, just after dawn, the little bedroom was prepared for the ritual. Jason was nervous, but he tried to hide it. Mack spoke little as he finished preparing the brew. It smelled terrible. When it was time to take it, Mack lit up a huge foot long pipe packed with tobacco and stuffed coca leaves into his mouth. He blew the smoke about the room and into Jason's face as he sat on the edge of the bed. The bed had been stripped down to the mattress and a large pail was placed by Jason's feet. It was a bit like his occasional brief visits at Her Majesty's Service. Except the bucket wasn't to shit in this time. Mack pulled the coca leaves out, fetched a large cup of the mixture and crouched down in front of Jason.

'If you need help, ask for it. Call. I will be guiding you through this and protecting you.' Jason just nodded. He wasn't sure why but he knew he totally trusted Mack in a way he never had with any other male in his life.

Jason took the cup and drank it down in one. The liquid was bitter but not foul. Not nearly as bad as the lighter fuel he'd drunk on occasion - this was nectar by comparison. The liquid slid down his gullet and his body convulsed slightly, but he held it down. Then he was gone.

****

'Wanna tell me what you saw?' Mack asked, softly, almost twelve hours and four cups of Aya later.

'Where do I fucking start?' A big smile broke across Jason's face. He laughed and slapped his legs hard. 'Fuck!'

Mack smiled and nodded.

'Plenty of time for recall, Jason. I want you to have some time to contemplate what happened. Get yourself washed up, then come and have some food. You'll be very hungry soon.'

He left Jason grinning. His eyes darting around the room as he tried to piece together what had happened to him and where he had been.

'Mack?' The older man stopped in the doorway. 'Thanks. That was wicked!'

Mack smiled and left.

****

Jason was sitting before a full English breakfast at the tiny kitchen table.

'Well?' asked Mack, placing a piping hot mug of tea in front of him.

'Er, weird bright colours - like Sunny Delight. Er, patterns, like you said. Swirly-wurly patterns like my Nan Gann's curtains. Everything looked fucking - *beautiful*! That was the best trip I have ever had!'

Mack looked at him with a steady gaze.

'Anything more?'

233

Jason didn't want to disappoint him but he was also sick of being stuck inside the pokey house and really wanted a nice cold pint of lager. He felt bloody tip-top. It had definitely lifted his spirits.

He shrugged apologetically. 'Er, can I buy some? Without the bit that makes you sick?' Almost as soon as he said it, he realised this was the wrong thing to say, especially to a Shaman he was still a bit scared of. He knew he'd failed. There's been no mind shattering revelations, no spiritual awakening. No little alien angel people 'entering' him. He remembered Rachel's warning, that the truth would come out. He now felt apprehensive.

Mack stood up, knocked on the door that led to the small living room and sat back opposite Jason.

'Plan B, pal.' he chuckled. 'I thought this might happen. You have the constitution of a Prehistoric Bison. If you had any idea just the sheer dosage you consumed, you would not be sitting here asking me if you could buy some. That would have had a whole village of Amazonian natives tripping for a week.'

Jason sniggered. Yet he could see in Mack's face that there was concern.

'What's Plan B?' said Jason, stuffing bacon into his mouth.

Tracy walked into the room alone. He stopped chewing. She looked well. She had put some weight back onto her face, which no longer sagged on one side. She looked so pretty, but she also looked so serious and disappointed.

Jason could hear voices and knew there were other people in the living room. He assumed it was Rachel, but he didn't know who else. He felt caged in, the kitchen turned from cosy to claustrophobic.

Jason stood up and went to his ex-wife. She was still in her jacket. He tried to help her out of it but she waved him away. Before, he'd have felt chastened, offended. Today he felt nothing except respect. She managed her coat and hung it on the hook on the back of the door. Tracy brushed past him and leaned against the Aga.

'Sit down, Jace. There's something we need to talk about.'

Her eyes were bright and less distant. She looked strong, alert. She had been recovering while he had been breaking apart. He sat.

'I need you to tell me what really happened that night, Jason. I want you to try and remember, in your own words, the night Conrad Blaine followed you.'

'Um, the pub that everyone has a fight in was a bit sketchy. After that, all I remember is that I set fire to stuff. I know I hurt her, but I can't remember. That bloody film didn't help. You know – *Burn*. I was mullered that night. Then I watched the film too much. Over and over, looking for clues. It sort of replaced my memories then I sort of thought of that as real. I'm sorry.'

She smiled. 'That's ok. I thought you might say that.' She rubbed her eyes and sighed. 'Do you still have memories about – other sad things?'

Jason knew she did not mean his mum. She meant *Her*.

He saw Sacha, a little more distant perhaps, but she was still there. Dancing. Beautiful. Unreachable.

He nodded at her but wouldn't meet her eyes.

'Mack, what's this?' Tracy picked up a strange, ethnic looking object from a shelf on the dresser. The wood was carved and it had two long brightly coloured feathers dangling from short leather straps.

'Ah, that's my shaman's stick.' he said with a lopsided grin, Mack gestured for her to take it.

She turned it over in her hand, slapped it a couple of times in her palm like a Bobby with a truncheon and then thwacked Jason - hard, around the back of the head, thrice.

'Perhaps this voodoo stick might jog your memory and sort your head out your utter prat!' She hit him again. Mack leaned back and folded his arms. He watched calmly as Jason flinched and took the beating he knew he'd had coming for decades.

'Strongest mind-bending drugs on the planet and they don't even touch the sides! *Pathetic!*' Thwack. 'Jason Jenkins, you are a bloody nimrod.' Thwack. 'Two decades, a son and a grandchild.' Thwack. 'And you're still taking us all for granted!' Double thwack!

Tracy replaced the stick on the shelf with its two feathers now looking distinctly shredded. She was panting hard. 'Get yer arse in there.' She took a fist full of t-shirt and dragged Jason up by his shoulder and pulled him into the front room. She appeared to have recovered all her strength, at least on her right side.

Jason tensed. For a sick moment, for a nano-second, his paranoid mind thought Blaine would be in there. Instead, a tiny, very composed woman was sitting at the end of the Chesterfield with Rachel positioned closely next to her.

'Hello Jason.'

Noelle smiled kindly at Jason. She took Rachel's hand.

'You're alive.' Jason said. He stumbled into the room and fell to his knees in front of her.

'I am.' Noelle bit her lip. 'And think I owe you a bit of an apology.'

****

The day of John Jenkins funeral was one of sunshine and showers. Jason wore his new pressed suit. He took his family to the graveside of his troubled father and he wept. He shook the hands of every one of his scheming, flawed, two-faced, snide, crook relatives along with all the decent, sound folk he valued and loved. He left a handsome lump behind the bar of the pub that no one goes in, to kick start the mammoth drinking session they were all about to embark upon. And then he took his immediate family home where they broke bread, ate and reminisced about John, about Jason's mum and grandparents, until it was time for the little one to go to bed.

After dinner, Tracy nodded to Joe then took Aleisha upstairs for a bath. Jason tensed, sensing a confrontation. He began washing pots up to give him the excuse to turn his back to his son.

'Leave that. Do it later. Sit down, Dad.'

Jason stiffened. Joe had never spoken to him with such assertion. He slowly wiped the soap suds from his hands, set the tea towel down and sat opposite his son.

'I realised something when Granddad died – when you lost him.' said Joe, quietly. 'I realised that I'd lost my dad too, but a long while ago. I hadn't even known until that moment. Maybe I've never really had a dad at all.'

Joe wasn't looking at Jason. He was rolling one of Aleisha's crayons between finger and thumb, his head to one side, slouched slightly.

'And I realised I don't know you. I don't know who you are.'

He looked up and Jason found that once he locked eyes with Joe, he couldn't look away. He was surprised to notice that Joe's eyes were exactly the same colour as his own, a tawny brown, with flecks of gold at the centre. It was as though he saw his son's eyes for the first time. Jason, once again, had the very same sensation he'd had witnessing the little birds by the tracks. He understood that life goes on, it is fleeting, that he should take notice, wake up, see it, enjoy it, then let it go. Let the fear of all that was bad pass, just as the birds had, the moment the train had vanished. It was as though time had stopped, as though he and Joe were in a capsule where nothing else mattered.

'And I'd like to get to know you, now, if that's alright?'

Joe smiled, touched his dad's hand and stood up. Jason could feel his lip trembling. He wasn't sure what had just happened, but he knew something fundamental had shifted. Images from Joe's childhood flashed past in a blur. Traces of important moments, milestones which Jason had witnessed but had never really participated in. Fragments of a childhood that he had done his best to avoid. Jason looked at his son who stood before him, now, as a man, and nodded solemnly.

Jason realised, what had just happened was that he had finally become a parent.

****

Joe put Aleisha to bed then went to his own room. Tracy joined Jason, drying the plates as he washed them, her left hand so much stronger than it was.

'Jace, there's something I want to show you.' They dried their hands and Tracy got her iPad out. 'I got it free with my iPhone. I can't use it properly yet.' she said apologetically. 'Look - you need to see.'

First, Tracy went on Facebook and showed him the profile picture of a really strange looking woman who she was 'friends' with. Her name was Sach von Gash. Jason's face began to burn while she flicked back through the profile pictures as the clock chronologically ticked backwards over the last five or six years.

It was *Her*, but the most nightmarish, vulgar, terrifying version of *Her* he could have imagined.

'Want to see more?'

'Yes – No! Yes.'

She Googled Sash von Gash and clicked on Images. Jason was saddened, shocked and revolted. Tracy found the latest news story about her most recent divorce, this time from a fitness instructor ten years younger than her. She was now on her own with five children. She looked old, bloated and warped by her fillers and Botox injections.

'I knew she'd done modelling, but not – *this*. That's why you didn't stay friends?'

'She dropped me. She dropped all of us. You weren't the only one who lost her.' Jason finally fully realised what an utter cunt he had been. 'Sacha Reeves doesn't exist anymore, Jace. Not the one in your head, the one who was my friend that we knew in real life. She's gone. So, now you know that,' she turned the iPad off and put it in her bag. 'It's time to *get the fuck over it*.'

His ex-wife stood and kissed him on the head, then left without looking back.

Chapter 17

Beacon

May 2015

I'd been on stake-out duty for a fortnight. My wife had created a complex log book for me to jot down my observations about both the mystery hippy and Jason's whereabouts and interactions. I was finally closing in.

The Snowboarder had been easy. He didn't do anything. He shuffled to the pub every other afternoon. Almost always sat by himself, or with someone who looked as unhinged as him, then he went home. Through binoculars, I observed him from behind a garage in the evenings. He didn't seem to sleep and his curtains were so threadbare, it was easy to spy on him.

When I'd thought it was safe, just once, I had sprinted across the grass in the middle of the crescent and peeped into his living room. He was naked, in a headstand, facing the radiator. His dirty dreadlocks were splayed all around him and his savaged ear was clear to see. The top half entirely absent, the rest of it in a strange, crimped hook. He had the smallest bottom I'd ever seen outside of a TV famine appeal and it reminded me a bit of the eccentric, emaciated Indian Sadhus I'd seen in a documentary.

Pippa had decided that she was not going to give away too much about how she would do it - commit murder. Her argument was that I was too stupid to lie convincingly if questioned. I thought this was a bit harsh, but really, I wanted nothing to do with it. I did have my reputation to preserve.

Jason proved harder to track down. He seemed to have vanished for a protracted period of time. Then he was back at the house. I was able to observe him at what must have been his dad's funeral. There he stood, looking considerably more together than I had seen him for months. He appeared to be getting on with his ex-wife quite well too.

I used the opportunity at the same graveyard to locate the exact whereabouts of the grave of Robert Rowden and that most slippery of mischiefs, of Minnie herself, which I then plotted onto an OS map extract Pippa had downloaded.

I watched Jenkins for a fortnight. He seemed to be working again, not going to the pub quite so much. It looked like he was decorating his house, which seemed pointless really.

On the day Pippa planned to strike her victims down, she had arranged for me to be up in London by early evening. I was to see people. I was to be *seen*, seeing people and prepare for *Flood* to go to the Cannes Film Festival.

Our tickets were booked for France, and we were planning to leave the girls with a family friend in London while we stayed out there for a week. The film wasn't likely to be selected for any prizes, but it was a good opportunity to schmooze, get further distribution deals in place and get seen on the red carpet.

Now the day had come, I had an increasingly bad feeling about what Pippa was planning. Not especially in a *moral* way - I'd thought about murdering Jason Jenkins often enough myself. It was more a dragging, heavy sense that I would be shackled to her forever. At least someone else had pushed Giles into the harbour. This would be *all her doing*.

****

The day I was due to go to London, I was trying to distract myself from my wife's murderous intentions, so I wandered into town, then all the way to Minnic's long road.

I walked slowly to the beach and picked up a take away coffee from the corner café. I couldn't resist one last look at the snowboarder's house. I wanted one last glimpse of the freak.

I'd always suspected there was a connection with Jenkins, I just couldn't work out how. A few days before, my superior sleuthing had paid off and I was finally proved right. I'd followed Mr. One Ear to the pub on the beach, where Jason had approached him. It was a brief meeting and most peculiar: Jason had stood over him, emphatically muttering close to his remaining ear. The hippy sat rocking back and forth on the bench. Jason had stalked off leaving the snowboarder grimacing and hugging himself. There'd been no chumminess, back slapping or loud jokey shouting, which was Jason's usual performance when he met people he knew. I was no clearer about their relationship, but I knew there was a link and it proved Pippa's plan was entirely justifiable.

That last day, I adopted my normal reconnaissance position, crouching down by the garages about to check on the dreadlocked man through my binoculars, when a knackered old Ford Orion pulled up just behind me on the waste ground. A small, vaguely familiar woman was driving. She left the engine running. As I raised my binoculars to search for him, convinced I'd gone unnoticed by the driver, I felt a sharp scratch on my upper arm and the last thing I remember was falling backwards.

****

I came round, curled up on a small sofa in a familiar house, overlooking The Street – the spit of shingle where two tides meet, in Tankerton. I'd been there the summer before for my photo shoot - Beacon House. It looked no different, yet the circumstances made the place seem less Arts and Crafts and more Gothic Horror. My head was throbbing and my vision was blurred. It took me a long time to focus on anything, but when I did, I realised that I was not alone.

Sitting rather stiffly in a chair opposite me, was Rachel. She was holding some sort of tribal stick decorated with bird engravings, with a ratty feather hanging off it.

'Sorry Conrad, couldn't afford a solicitor's fees. I thought it made more sense to meet face to face,' she said, enmity emanating from her eyes. I could hear other people – her accomplices – moving about in the kitchen.

'You drugged me! Let me go! I'm going to call the police!' I squawked.

She held up my phone. I sat up awkwardly.

'You are not permitted to speak. You are not holding the stick.' She waved the tribal object.

'What?'

My foggy head was beginning slowly to clear and register the danger I was in.

'This is the talking stick. You can only speak if you are holding it. Just sit and wait.'

I sat, incredulous.

A steely haired man and the tiny woman that had been driving the car entered the room and joined her on two other chairs set opposite. They didn't speak. There was a tap at the back door and I heard some heavy footsteps thudding through the kitchen. Even before he entered the room, I knew who it would be.

Jason Jenkins shuffled in, looking sheepish, apologetic. He shot me a malevolent glance.

The man motioned for the stick and Rachel passed it to him.

'Mr. Blaine,' the dark haired man said in a gruff Scottish accent. 'Would you be so kind as to move your *arse* along, so our pal Jason here can sit beside you on the sofa? Thank you.' I unfolded my stiff legs and squashed myself as far to the right of the sofa as possible. I realised I had no idea how long I'd been unconscious, or of what the time was.

'I demand to know what this fiasco is all about!' I said in a squealing plead, at least an octave higher than I'd intended.

'Shh! You do not have the stick.' Rachel reprimanded. After retrieving the talking stick back from her accomplice.

'Conrad, Jason – that night twenty years ago, there were two other witnesses, besides you two and the victim.'

I looked at the small woman in front of me and felt a wave of shame, like a convulsion, rippled right through my body.

'Conrad, you never met Noelle, but you saw her. You followed her and Jason. She was his victim.'

The small woman nodded at me. She had a stony look on her face.

'You're alive.' As I whispered the words, I was overwhelmed by a sense that I'd just set down something burdensome that I'd been shouldering for decades. I felt an incredible lightness. I laughed. She continued to stare.

'Stick!' Rachel snapped.

I turned to Jenkins – the 'murderer', still looking as culpable as ever. Exasperated, I pointed at the talking stick and Rachel threw it across the room to me.

'But don't you see?' I said to Jenkins. 'If she's not dead, you're not guilty! And neither am I!' I laughed again.

They continued to stare.

I realised then, that whether she was dead or alive, they knew I'd *thought* I'd witnessed a murder, then deliberately walked away. And worse, used it for my own profit. *That* was my crime. *That* was what made me guilty.

I forced myself to look at Noelle.

'Um – sorry?' My thin, reedy voice trailed off.

Rachel marched across the blue painted wooden floor and snatched the stick from my hand and sat opposite again.

'Conrad, another piece in the puzzle – this is Mack. He was there too. You didn't see him, but he saw everything. You have him to thank that your cowardice that night was not exposed.'

The man opposite was giving me the evil eye. I felt Jason turn and look in my direction. I gulped and continued to stare at Rachel, at her clear blue eyes and youthful freckles. She'd set me up for this from the start, the slag.

'I need to call my wife.' I squeaked.

'Stick.' Jason mumbled.

I scowled at him. I desperately needed to stop Pippa carrying out her ambush on the one eared menace. The bad feeling was now a gut wrenching conviction that it *would not end well*.

Mack took the talking stick.

'Blaine – you're not calling anyone or leaving until you've told Jason everything you saw him do. He's known about Noelle for a couple of weeks, all that's missing now is what you saw. He needs to hear it if he's ever going to move forward.'

The Scottish man carried the stick across the room to Jason then sat with his fists clenched, resting on his knees. I realised he must have been the one that drugged me. My heartbeat quickened.

Jason looked at me and spoke in an inarticulate mumble.

'I remember you there, but I don't remember us talking. You legged it just before Fran came and found me.'

'Sorry – who the hell is *Fran*?'

'Stick!' Mack boomed.

I needn't have asked. I knew. *That* was the connection. The creep was the other witness. But where did the missing ear fit in?

I nodded at him to continue.

'He told me to run, before the Pigs turned up. He said he'd cover it all up - that if I kept my mouth shut about what he'd done to her, he'd protect me. So I ran away too. I left him there to get rid of her body, all by himself.' He stared at Noelle, then hung his head.

Jason Jenkins put his face in his hands and wept. It was far more disturbing than anything that had happened that night. The sight of this potato of a man crying like a girl sickened me.

I'd had enough of all this bullshit now. I still couldn't see why the bloody hell it all had to come out or what anyone would gain from it. After all, no one had *died*.

I grabbed the stick from Jason.

'Why, actually, do we need to hear any of this? I'm struggling a little to see the point. I am a very important man and I have people I need to see immediately. Please let me go now!'

Rachel marched across the room in three strides and swiped the stick away.

'Conrad, you're not going anywhere,' she stated flatly, standing over me.

I snatched the stick back.

'Well, you know what, I don't care. And besides, Jenkins here still caused criminal damage that night. Yes, he did! He set fire to a *lot of things*. He screamed a confession at me. See, you didn't know that, did you? I know he killed his own mother the same way! He told me he did. Let me go, or I will go to the police with this and tell them that you all drugged and kidnapped me!'

Jason started laughing and lunged for the stick. 'You cunt. I didn't kill my old mum. I felt like it was my responsibility. But I didn't burn her alive in her own home.'

'Who did then?' I snapped.

'Stick!!' They all bellowed.

'She was very ill. With MS. I didn't want to go out, but she made me. Told me to go and have fun. Our old granddad was living with us then. He was meant to stay in with her, but he was losing his marbles. He must have gone into my room and nicked some fags, lit one in there, dropped it or not put it out properly, then went to the pub to find my dad. They'd both got wrecked. Fire brigade said it had started on my bed. She died of smoke inhalation. God rest her soul. My dad and my granddad always blamed me for going out that night. Easier than taking the blame themselves, I suppose. But it wasn't me.'

Jenkins looked small and tired. He wiped his eyes again. My insurance policy was blown.

Then, he looked at me with expectation. 'I want your story. You must have followed me the whole night. I've seen your film over and over but it just seems – I don't know – too *tame*. I need to know what really happened.'

Mack nodded at me. The women were staring at me with mealy-mouthed hostility. All I could think about was Pippa making her way to Fran's house by herself. She really didn't know what she was dealing with. If I was ever going to get out of here, I had to tell the stupid plebeian once and for all. Jenkins pushed the stick towards me on the sofa. I reluctantly picked it up, momentarily fantasising about beating them all with it and escaping.

'It seems 'tame', *Jenkins*, because the film missed out quite a lot of things that you did. Some of the worst things in fact - largely because the producer really didn't believe that anyone could be that depraved. Where can you remember up to? I'll tell you, but after that, can I please, *please* leave?'

They nodded in consent. This was the world's most pointless kidnapping ever. It was more like a group therapy session at a hippy commune in1974. I threw the stick onto Jason's lap.

Jason blew his cheeks out. 'Fuck - hard putting it into words. Ok - I was working in the pub with the crap pool table, flipping burgers. I was already a bit hyper - I'd been sucking on a biro full of whizz for most of my shift. I was psyching myself up for a proper pukka night out. I'd distracted myself by giving Mandy one from behind over the chest freezers when she was on her fag break. She was the Landlord's daughter.'

Rachel and Noelle tutted. Jason sniggered. 'She was a bit of a fish mitten, but alright, if you know what I mean?'

I really didn't, but I nodded for him to go on.

'I was naturally paranoid and feeling shifty from the speed. Even then, I thought someone was following me.'

247

He shot me a sideward glance.

'I got back to my flat in Oxford Mansions. I loved it - it was a *palace*. I was the only one of my friends who had a flat and I was right at the top. Sea views, easy for the pubs. Wicked.

'A lot was riding on that night – I had big expectations, so I made sure I looked boss. Clean jeans, Nike Air Max 90s, white Hollister polo shirt with my best Adidas zipped all the way up. I gelled my hair back - it used to be long then - into a nice, tight ponytail. Generous slap of Tommy Hilfiger cologne on my face and a wee sprinkle down the front of me cacks for good measure. I was looking *fly*.

'The night was important because of *Her* – Sacha Reeves. This girl - I just couldn't get out of my head. I'd been mad about her, well, since forever. I was so nervous about seeing her, I had a big spliff and a Stella to calm myself down.

'It was my first chance in three years to ask her out, try and get off with her. She'd just split up with my cousin. I was so desperate I was prepared take anything she gave me - even a smile would have cheered me up a bit.'

Jason stared at his hand covered in broad white scars and burns from that night. There was a fresh bandage on his right hand from some other rampage or altercation he'd been in which I hadn't noticed at his dad's funeral. I was close enough for the first time to read the blurry tattoos across his unbandaged limb and struggled to suppress an incredulous laugh. He had FISH 'N' tattooed in letters as long as his entire fingers in a gothic font across the digits of his left hand. I guessed the word CHIPS was on his right one. The tool.

'What a dickhead I was,' he said. 'She didn't even know I existed.'

Jason rubbed his hands hard over his bald, cropped head and sniffed.

'There were a few parties on that night. Summer solstice and all. I knew I'd see her because Tracy was her best mate and she'd told me they were out. I wasn't sure *where* I'd see her though.'

He turned to me again, 'You got my Nan's birthday at the pub that no one goes in about right. I can't believe I didn't spot you in there, or that you weren't lynched. You must have stuck out like a sore thumb. Um, three pints and a line of billy in there - lovely.'

I thought back. What an unpleasant place. The thick gaudy carpeting, low ceilings - and the people! I'd settled in a corner in the over-heated garish boozer and started feeling drowsy. I knew I wouldn't make it past midnight, so I'd snuck off the gents shortly after Jenkins went in there and chopped myself the biggest line of charlie I could and snorted the whole lot, just as he was hoovering up what I'd assumed was rough speed in the next cubicle. Five minutes later, I was fired up and ready to rumble. Senses primed, sharp as a tack, I'd followed Jenkins over the road.

'Then your film *did* go to the pub that everyone has their receptions in, for my cousin Shelly's wedding disco. But you missed stuff out in that scene too.'

I interrupted, taking the stick. 'Oh what, bridesmaids glassing each other? The bride giving her new husband's brother a blow job in the gents? The best man's father urinating over his estranged brother while he slept, passed out on a sofa? No, wasn't allowed to put any of that in either.' I threw the stick back.

'Yeah, I love my family, but they can be a bit lively.' Jason conceded, smiling. 'So, four pints and two shorts in there.'

Then smile faded.

'The next place I - we, went was the Assembly Rooms. It was full of hippies all swaying in their floaty, smelly clothes, listening to dub so bassy, I could feel my insides melting. She wasn't in there. Of course she wouldn't have been. Wasn't her thing. Then, I was over the road and straight into the big pub in the middle of town. Used to have a wicked night club

249

at the back. It was pitch black. They were playing 'Loops of Infinity' by Cosmic Baby as I came in. As the disco lights swivelled, there she was - all *illuminated*.'

Jason's eyes drifted upwards as he thought back, his voice became dreamy. 'She was tall, skinny. Her hair was long - light brown and wavy, and her face – the face of an *angel*. She had her eyes shut and she was holding a bottle of Two Dogs. My Sacha Reeves.'

Everyone in the room fidgeted uncomfortably. It was so cringe-worthy, but not half as embarrassing as it had been to witness that night. I wasn't sure 'angelic' was how I'd have described his intended. Mediocre perhaps. A bit of a trollop, maybe. But what I do remember was the moment I knew this story had potential.

Jason continued in his pathetic whisper. 'My face was aching just looking at her and I realised, then, that all around the edges of the place, were many, many more blokes, like me, staring at her. I felt sick. Then her chubby mate she was dancing with, Tracy Shilling, *my* Tracy, waved.   I hoped no one saw. Back then, I didn't really think she was my type. I thought I could do better.

'She was drunk and all 'sexy' dancing over to me. You could literally hear everyone sigh with relief that Sacha Reeves was still alone and that Tracy, who everyone thought was a bit of a mushmalt, was targeting me - again.'

What a way to talk about the woman that was to become his wife! Then Pippa's face presented itself. Her cropped hair. Her lack of waist. Her slightly humped shoulders. I wasn't really sure what 'mushmalt' meant, but I was pretty sure Pippa was one.

'A track by Dance to Trance started. There were more people on the dance floor, even some blokes. I temporarily lost sight of *Her* and felt panicky, but then the crowds parted and there she was again, swaying with her arms in the air.

'Tracy was trying to find out which party I was going to. We all knew there was a massive road protesters' party at the tall house on the beach, but I'd proper upset Fran the previous New Years and I didn't really fancy seeing the mardy git that night. Tracy went to the bar and while she was gone, my whole world just fell apart.

'Sacha was swaying and getting really into the music. She looked blissed out and I realised she's done a tab or four. Then, as I watched her, I became aware of someone nearby her.

'I'd been so focused on her I hadn't noticed this *male*. He was everything that I feared - taller than her, slightly older, good looking in an out-of-town kind of way and dressed in really pukka clothes. She had begun to dance close to the bastard. It made me feel sick, physically sick.

'I stood helpless, watching the one chance I'd waited three years for, just disappear. I felt betrayed, even though Sacha never promised nothing. I'd imagined this night so many times and how it should end up, never once did I think I might fail - that she might prefer someone else.

'Soon they were necking on the dance floor and there were thirty broken-hearted mugs like me crying into their lagers all around the edges of the room.

'Tracy came back and asked me if I fancied a jump – I said yes, drained my pint and left for the door. I could feel the rage building. It was the same way it went after my mum died. I was out of control, but high on it. Life no longer had meaning. I no longer cared about anyone or anything including himself. Least of all my stupid self.

'We reached the bouncers, who told us we wouldn't be let back in. I didn't care. I'd seen enough.

'I turned back to take one last look at *Her,* before I left. There they were, the beautiful couple. I felt utter, pure white hot hatred for them. I wanted them to burn in Hell. I wanted *everything* to burn.'

Jenkins' eyes were out on stalks as he stared, unblinking at the floor. He was back there, I could see. The same ferocity rumbling under his flushed skin. He swallowed hard. Then his gaze softened. He rubbed the thumb of his injured hand over a tiny letter T tattooed on the inside of his other wrist and sighed.

'I pulled Tracy down the lane by the Indian that does cheap buffets, until we were away of the street light. I tried to - you know – but nothing was happening. It was embarrassing. I'd had too much whizz. She just said, "It doesn't matter – come home, we can *cuddle*". I told her I'd see her around. Then I just left her there and headed off to the party at the squat in the posh house by the beach. "If I can't have Sacha," I'd thought, "what I can have is a *seriously fucked up* night right on it."

'I found my mate Gary loading up a huge chillum in the kitchen. Had a right lush smoke which calmed me down a bit, then I bought two purple microdots, a bag of speed and five Doves. I decided to candyflip and took a microdot and a Dove at the same time. With hindsight, on top of how much speed and booze I'd had, that was *probably* where I went wrong.' Jason sat nodding, looking at the scars on his unbandaged hand before looking apologetically at Noelle.

I didn't really understand the terms he was using, but he'd got one thing right. It did all go very, very wrong.

I could never forget the look on Jason's stupid face when the object of his affection started eating some man's face on the dancefloor. That was the moment I started translating what I was seeing into a film. I had him framed in medium shot, scores of other disappointed *chumps* in the shadows, slightly out of focus, all looking at Sacha Reeves.

Then my eyes panned across the dance floor, following his eye-line, then cut! – medium close-up from Jason's point of view, of the couple vigorously snogging and cut! – back to a close up of Jenkins' face, frozen in horror, eyes stinging with tears as his heart was torn apart.

That was the moment something had changed in him and he gave up caring. *That* was the moment when *I* became curious about what he would do next.

Jason perked up at bit then.

'I came up on the E first, which is probably just as well because by then, I wanted to murder someone. I popped into the pub where everyone has a fight and there was already a punch-up going on. Last thing I remember was trying to break the fight up, then having a really good dance to the happy house in the middle of the scrum, while everyone around me was covered in blood. After that – blank – until I saw you by the burning hut. Before you ran away and *stole my life*!'

Jason narrowed his stoaty eyes, wanting some answers. Mack gave an authoritative nod and I begrudgingly took the stupid talking stick.

'Alright. I'm not spending hours on this. This is what I saw.'

I fidgeted and cast my mind back to the pub where everyone has a fight.

I had visualised the fight scene being shot in a jerky, hand-held style. Jump cuts to signify the chaos and violence of the customers, the camera whip-panning, following Jason cavorting from one antic to another.

He had brazenly ducked under the flap in the bar and unhooked a bottle of vodka right off the optic and taken several theatrical swigs. The staff were too drunk, stupid or distracted to notice. He'd tucked it into his inside pocket (extreme close-up cut-away shot), then danced between the sweaty men who continued shouting and wrestling. He'd tried to kiss and embrace them all, to spread whatever Ecstasy-induced love he was feeling, until he got lost in the music, pumping his arms maniacally in the air.

I witnessed this in a montage of him gurning, getting physical with a pillar, grinding up against it and licking it. The images were dissolving, blending, creating a sense that his behaviour was out of control, all the while the fighting continued around him, regardless. He tried to dance with some of the men on the side-lines and got hit hard in the face a couple of times, but he didn't seem to care.

253

He'd just wandered out into the warm night with an elated smile on his face, swigging the vodka.

Then he'd gone utterly blank - through my film-vision, this was a crossfade to a long shot of him sitting on the iron railings in front of a powerboat shop, swinging his legs like a child, waving at his pikey mates roaring past in their pimped Golf GTs, beeping their horns at him.

'Hmm. Microdot.' Jason interrupted. 'I must have come up. They're *fucking* strong.'

'Stick.' Mack growled. Jason bit his lip.

Jenkins had then broken into the vending machine that dispensed worms for fishermen and skipped – literally skipped, like a seven-year old girl - to the Life Boat Station. I imagined this from his point of view, through a distorting fish-eye lens to mimic his obvious disorientation.

He'd sat in the Life Boat tractor for about an hour, drinking the vodka, talking to the worms, then eating them, the whole time the camera switching back and forth from a hand held pan, circling the vehicle, to extreme close-ups of the worms as he chatted to them before gobbling them up.

I'd started to feel sleepy again and did a mental tot up of how much beer I'd consumed before I'd even seen Jason all those hours ago for the first time. I sheltered under a dinghy and cut myself another fat line of charlie, which kicked in just as he fell out of the tractor, giggling.

Feeling the strong stimulant coursing through my veins, my senses were super sharp. I followed him as he lurched off towards the Gorrell Tank where I witnessed this scene as a static long shot. As his tiny figure moved further away across the vast car park, the echoey sound of a party wafted across in the night air. His figure shrank, became more vulnerable and small to signify that he was entering a new more disturbing phase of his intoxication. Finally, in the distance, he disappeared into a house with coloured lights flashing behind the curtains.

Cut! - Party sequence: music blaring and back into hand held camera-work and point of view shots as Jason staggered through the dense, sweaty throng of people.

I'd slipped in unnoticed. It was pitch black, save for the occasional flash of disco lights and everyone was wasted. It took very little time to locate Jenkins because he'd suddenly become extrovert, shouting jovial greetings and chest bumping men who were in a similar condition. He seemed to know everyone there. Lots of people in the same gurning state - dancing, taking their clothes off, humping the air and perving. The scene, again, was a montage of faces and bodies, dissolving, of time ellipsing and passing in slow motion, some wafty visuals, some blurring and distortion.

There was a D.J., with decks set up in the bay window of the front room. Jenkins was dancing like a lunatic in the middle. He'd taken his jacket and shirt off and stuffed them in his giant back pockets and started really giving it some to the terrible, monotonous dance music. Dripping with sweat, eyes shut, a chemical grimace twisting his mouth, he was really touching himself up like a bad parody of a rubbish lap dancer. No one seemed to take any notice.

A couple of friends handed something to him. They were all guffawing in a little huddle. My imaginary camera circled them, tilting in as though trying to get a glimpse of whatever was causing such mirth. When the camera tracked back, Jason had bunched his trousers and boxers around his ankles. He took the object, which looked like a baton and shoved it up his butt and his friend lit it.

It was a roman candle.

Jenkins shuffled from one end of the house to the other, laughing like a jackal, with a screaming shower of white fire coming out of his backside. I saw the scene unfold with alternating shots from Jason's point of view, to close ups of the streaming white sparkles and horrified reaction shots from stunned party-goers.

When it stopped, he just whipped it out, pulled his trousers back up and carried on dancing.

'That's a relief.' interjected Jenkins again. 'I always wondered about the, you know, anal scorching.' he said, smirking.

'Stick.' Rachel and Noelle droned. Jason smiled apologetically.

Cut to the exterior and someone had made a bonfire in the back garden, but they were running out of things to burn. Cut to interior shots of Jenkins - a choppy montage of jump-cuts - him rushing about, acquiring a crowbar then gleefully dismantling the staircase, carrying planks that used to be steps and banister railings and throwing them on the burning pile. Other people joined in and by the time he got bored, the bonfire was six feet high and only half the staircase was left. People had to stand on each other's shoulders to get from the ground to the first floor toilet. No one seemed to mind.

To signify a change in mood and the onset of pre-dawn party-chill, the scene before me faded to black, then up again to focus on Jenkins - the only one still awake.

Jenkins was about to do something I'd been at pains to un-remember for years. Something so base, so *primordial*, it convinced me I was in the company of someone capable of *anything*.

Around him, bodies were strewn everywhere - sleeping, monged out, mouths lolling open. He was dancing, but the decks had been abandoned and it was the same intro looping over and over again. The hand held shot I visualised the scene through, began to edit to the same rhythmic repetition of the intro, creating a kinetic escalation, a forewarning of the vile act Jenkins was to perform.

He had staggered to the decks frowning and twiddled a few knobs, grumbling to himself as the rhythm stirred and pulsed. While the edits punctured and paced.

He dragged the needle off the turntable, got a chair and stood on it then yanked his trousers and boxers down. As my imaginary editing sped up to a terrifying velocity, Jenkins curled out a giant turd right onto the vinyl.

There it sat, in close up, going round and round and round. In my mind, the camera performed a Hitchcock dolly-zoom made famous in *Vertigo* – tracking back and zooming in on the giant poop in one long, slow take. The log appeared to grow in size as the perspective distorted, shrinking the background, transforming it into the menacing mega-turd before me.

There it stayed, rotating, lit from above by a single red spotlight.

Jenkins yanked up his giant trousers, got off the chair and stood back with his hands on his hips like a hillbilly admiring a lynching.

That's when the smell hit. The distinct stench of one seriously poor diet.

I'd dragged my top over my face. It was so offensive, people started to come-to. Jenkins seemed to realise that other people might not appreciate his work of art and hastily put his shirt and jacket on then made a bolt for the door. On his way out, he stole a massive Puffa that came down to his knees that made him look like a giant glow worm.

The next sequence took on a hurried pace, my vision camera swinging wildly as Jenkins was pursued by a giant fella with dreads, presumably the owner of the decks who'd realised what Jenkins had done. He easily caught him and head butted his face, bursting the bridge of his nose open and instantly bloodying the whites of his eyes - revealed in a harrowing extreme close up, blood splattering on my imaginary lens. Jason stumbled away clutching the coat about himself and ran across the car park to the harbour.

He was visibly shaken, in pain, and spent half an hour tip toeing around the edge, looking into the inky water. I observed him again as though through a long shot, occasional point of view shots from his perspective to show how perilously near the side he was.

I considered intervening, but realised my true purpose that night wasn't to interfere in any wrongdoing, but just to observe it – like a war reporter. Like the Prime Directive in Star Trek – *don't meddle*.

He took off up the piles of dusty stones and aggregate with a flattened cardboard box which he used like a sledge. For half an hour he merrily sledged the steep piles of rubble, seemingly unaware of any continued pain in his smashed nose and bulging, blackened eyes.

He clambered aboard a massive commercial boat that was moored by the quayside and ran around the deck, loudly shouting songs by the Charlatons. He'd climbed all over the cabin, swinging like a monkey from the ropes and cables, until a big man came on board, shouted something in Flemish and punched him in the mouth. Then literally threw him, like he was casting a net, back onto dry land.

Jenkins then sprinted off up to the end of the quay where there was an old warehouse. He kept himself busy by throwing everything he could get his hands on, off the edge. Lobster pots, big polystyrene crates, planks of wood, a bicycle, plastic chairs, anything. Then he was back at the top of the piles of pebbles, waving his fists about and beating his chest like Tarzan and screaming, '*I love you Sacha!*'

That's when we saw Noelle. He'd stood staring, his swollen mouth gaping open, his arms hung at his sides like an ape, squinting through the congealing blood. She was really messed up – a blood apron spread from her face and down to her waist. She was stumbling along, looking exhausted and scared, keeping watch over her shoulder every ten paces or so.

Jenkins ran down the pile of stones and followed her back to the old warehouse where she made her way along the beach. He jogged along behind her, keeping low. I couldn't understand why he was following – I wondered if he knew her. All sorts of mad scenarios started presenting themselves in my mind. I knew I had to continue to monitor him – he was now my protagonist, my *lead man*. While I knew it should have been fear for the woman's safety that was building, it wasn't. It was excitement. I wanted something bad to happen, I knew he was on the brink of something depraved, I just needed to bear witness. I needed to evaluate its *cinematic potential*.

I had no idea what time it was but there was a glimmer of light in the sky by then. Jenkins jumped down behind the wall and overtook the scared girl by running past the bowling alley. He ran until he reached a dodgy looking nightclub that still had its doors shut. I was trailing behind Noelle, crouching, convinced someone would see her, the state she was in, but the bouncers were too busy breaking up a fight between two pissed women. She kept on the beach and she was so small she passed by unnoticed. I lost sight of Jenkins then, I wasn't sure what he was up to, but I suspected he planned to attack her.

I followed her until she reached The Street, where my vision cut to an extreme close up. She violently spat something gristly out of her mouth. She was so blood-soaked I hadn't noticed she'd had it gripped between her teeth.

Remembering now, I realise it was an ear. Fran's ear.

Hearing a shout, my vision whip-panned wildly away, scouring the huts, the slopes, seeking Jenkins out, worried my real story - my villain - would disappear if I didn't keep close.

Then my perspective re-framed to a medium shot of him vanishing behind a hut, maniacal grin across his face, racing between the wooden structures. My view jump-cut again and again of snippets, glimpses, suggestions, of the little man hard at work, doing what he loved. Subtle enigmas in the shots – indexical signifiers that pointed the finger: A spark here, a wisp of smoke there. Clues he was doing the only thing he was any good at - setting fire to stuff.

As I broke from my re-telling of the story and for a few seconds in the dimming light of Beacon House, Jason Jenkins met my gaze. There was no animosity, no edge. Just a strange acknowledgement that we had shared such a pivotal night. He nodded for me to go on.

Jenkins had ignited the first hut and the next thing I had heard was a *whoosh*! Suddenly, I was transported in my 'mind cinema' to the beach scene in *Apocalypse Now* - cinema-verite camera shots - the Huey Cobras swooping towards the shoreline with the 'Ride of the Valkyries' blaring in my head. Multi-coloured missiles *ka-boomed* into the little wooden huts as Jenkins launched an arsenal of stolen French fireworks concealed in the Puffa, under and into the buildings.

He had run between the first and second row of huts, discarding the Puffa and unleashing a rainbow coloured Hell. We both heard a woman scream. My imaginary camera-work became blurred, distorted, the editing disjointed and erratic.

Jenkins disappeared, then reappeared dragging a bin up the slopes behind him. He ignited one of the fireworks and shoved it into the greasy rubbish, waited for the bright explosions to fizz to life, then let it roll down the slopes. He'd jumped up and down, whooping and swinging his arms in huge circles as the hissing projectile tore towards the prom below.

The girl flashed into focus. She ran to a rickety old hut and wriggled through a low gap where a plank had come loose, to hide. Jenkins was on her tail, his laughter unhinged, echoing around the blazing structures. He packed her hut with all the fireworks he had, then ignited it.

And that's when he finally noticed me. A direct eye-line match of malice. He stopped laughing and approached me, just as the hut behind him erupted into a starburst of colours.

I was no longer seeing him through a camera, on a big screen. He was there, in front of me - and he was *real*.

He'd stood panting, took a deep breath and screamed, 'I killed her! It's my fault my mum was burned alive!' As the roof and sides blew right off the hut.

I turned and ran. I knew it would be moments before police arrived. I was in a montage, a chase scene with an imaginary assailant in pursuit. My life depended on me getting as far away from that little weasel-like murderer, as fast as I could.

I didn't even bother to return to the bed and breakfast. I headed straight for the station. That morning, I returned to civilisation with a rare and precious sea-side souvenir.

My unique story.

I crossed my arms to indicate I'd finished. Noelle and Rachel also had their arms crossed and were shaking their heads in judgement. I smiled at them, warmly.

Mack sauntered across the room and picked up the stick from my lap and sat back down.

He cleared his throat. 'I dragged Noelle out while Jason was ranting and shouting at you,' said Mack, his accent hard, his eyes harder. 'Jason didn't know she was under there. It wasn't deliberate. Then Fran arrived, covered in blood. We clocked each other. He knew I'd make sure Noelle was safe. If she hadn't made me promise to keep her secret, I might have killed him myself with my bare hands, but a promise is a promise. She just wanted to disappear.'

Then the patronising bastard looked at me and said, 'I think there's something else you should say to Jason, eh Conrad?'

Jason's eyes were cast down. He didn't look relieved to know the missing pieces. He looked sad. I looked at Mack who had his thick eyebrows raised in an aggressively expectant way and I realised he wanted me to say sorry. I laughed, inappropriately.

'You want me to apologise!'

'STICK!' Mack roared.

They were now all staring at me, Jason sniffing, shoulders hunched over. I looked into his baggy eyes.

Mack rolled the stick across the floor.

'I can't say sorry, because I'm not.'

It just came right out. Jenkins' mouth fell open and he blinked a couple of times. Mack jumped up and Noelle pulled him back down.

In that moment, I knew and he knew, that even if I had never met him, Jason Jenkins would still turn out to be the ruined, useless waster who'd achieved nothing with his life.

I laughed again. A confident laugh.

'That's probably the only honest thing you've ever said.' Jason mumbled. Then he went back to looking at his hands, his scars, the bandages.

'Um, stick? Well - whatever. Now, are we *ever* going to find out why we're here? Hmm?' I wondered if Pippa found Fran yet. It was twilight outside now. The time she'd chosen to attack.

Noelle ran her hands through her short, boyish hair as she collected the stick from me. She seemed nervous.

'Well, alright.' She cleared her throat and began. 'I came down to Whistable as a leader of the Dragon Environmental Group. We were a grassroots organisation dedicated as an ecological protest movement.'

Jason and I shuffled in our seats. I was now worried I was going to be put under some pagan spell. Jenkins and I exchanged a glance. The only moment we both had something we shared – a dislike of new age *do-gooders*.

'We'd been contacted by Fran and some other locals we'd met at similar action across the country, demonstrating against the Criminal Justice Bill, other stuff. They invited down to join them protest against the building of the new Thanet Way, the A299.'

And that's when I zoned out. While I half listened to her story, her long, boring story that had no relevance to my life at all, I thought about Cannes. Of drinking fizz in the sun dressed cooly in white linen, looking out over the azure sea, watching beautiful, topless women on the beach.

I was aware of snatches of her dialogue, abruptly intruding on my daydream. Something about a birthday, summer solstice. Then, 'Fran had put something in my lemonade.' Another respite, where my fantasy overpowered her monotonous drone, then I was back in the room hearing, 'Fran had said to the four men "After me, she's all yours".'

I refocused and thought about the press photos of the cast of *Flood* on the red carpet, how I'd have an opportunity to pitch any *new ideas* I had to producers, finance people. I felt a pinch, which became a clench, which morphed into a gut clanging sense of gnawing inadequacy.

I had no new ideas.

Noelle's annoying victim-mumble encroached again. 'I saw the Devil himself,' she said. Then, 'He hated me. My type', and - 'I grabbed a fistful of his hair, pulled his head down. I bit, *hard*. He twisted away, then realised that the more he moved, the more of his ear would come off. Then my teeth met through the gristle.'

I shook my head to unscramble it, but instead there was something that refused to shift. It wasn't an idea *per se*, more of an embryonic *ideation*.

I was back in Cannes, walking along the promenade, depressed. Every café and restaurant packed with writers younger than me, heavily bearded, excitedly pitching brilliant ideas to keen executives. My paranoia and sense of failure was building with every step.

Noelle bleated on, her voice raised, impassioned. 'I yanked my head back and ripped off the top half off his ear, I pushed him off, fought to get away and out of the door before the others could hurt me. Then I ran.'

Back in France, in my fantasy-turned-nightmare, I was on the flight back. Hemmed in by a terse, silent Pippa on one side - perfectly aware that the trip had been pointless; and on the other side, young hipsters - high from a productive few days making contacts and getting positive feedback on their *original new ideas.*

I felt utterly despondent. Noelle continued to rant her version of our dreadful night. I realised some horrible violation had happened to her, which was only made worse by Jason's pyromania and my lack of morals. I rubbed my brow, and yet still this nugget of something held on, a little tickle of something that stopped me wanting to give it all up and just – oh I don't know – become an F.E. teacher or something.

'Seconds before the hut went up, someone grabbed my arms and pulled me out, hid me behind the next hut along. After that, the shouting continued for a while and I passed out again. When I woke up, I was somewhere safe, with a kind stranger.'

Noelle smiled at Mack. The kind stranger. The one who knew everything.

Then, I had the strangest feeling of discombobulation. An out-of-body experience. Here were these perfectly mad people all talking rubbish and I was floating above them, not really present. Maybe it was how Terry Waite survived. Or Nelson Mandela. I was one step removed from their *torture*.

'He got me some clothes an ex-girlfriend had left behind and put me on the first train out of Whitstable. I knew then that I needed to stop saving trees and find my birth mother.'

Bosh! I was back in my body, listening intently.

'I knew how to find her, the woman who they said should never have had me, too simple to even look after herself. I knew which unit she was looked after in. I had been afraid before, of her uniqueness. She was more like a child than me, my adoptive parents had said, but I needed to find out for myself.'

Wallop! The ideation blossomed, took shape. Just like that night twenty years before, my ears pricked up. *This* was my new idea! I stifled a laugh.

'I'd discovered I was adopted by accident when I went through my adopted father's desk looking for documents to apply for a passport. I was eighteen. I confronted them and they came clean and told me everything. I never went back after that and my family became my friends in the protest movement.

'I found her and visited her once before the press put my face on every front cover. I don't think she even knew who I was, really. Then, when I was all over the news, missing, serious concerns about my physical wellbeing, I let people think I was dead and I have done ever since. I created a completely new identity for myself and managed to live a good life, under the radar.

'My mum had been in continual institutional care since she was very small and had attended a special boarding school for the mentally disabled as a teenager. That's where she got pregnant.

'The pregnancy was discovered so late on, she was allowed to go to full term. Then she had me. They weren't expecting a "normal" baby. To prevent a scandal, I was adopted and she was put in a facility for adults. I dug around and found out who her parents – my grandparents, were. Turns out they were rich, owned some pile up in Gloucestershire. Generations of the family had run a big estate up there and had since retired. My mum, Kathy, had one brother, Gordon, many years her senior, who had no children.

'So, why am I here? Well, my adoptive parents got their solicitor to push for Declaration of Death in Absentia because they needed closure. It was granted. I was officially dead, which also meant my birth family needn't worry about me reappearing. They were free to forget me.

'Last year my mother became very ill and this year she died. I'd kept in touch with a nurse at the home who kept me abreast of her condition and kept my identity a secret. She has since told me she has a suspicion who my father is. My mother used to say the name Michael over and over. He was another student at the special school. He might not even know I exist. If I can find him, I could have a whole other family out there. After the nurse called me, I did some research and found out my grandparents had died too. Then I found out Gordon is seriously ill with terminal cancer.

'You know my politics - I'm not into personal wealth, but this is a substantial amount of money. I knew it was destined to some right wing cause if I didn't divert it somehow. So now I need my identity back.

'I was named Noelle by my adoptive parents because they took me in at Christmas, but it's not who I really am. Kathy had called me Sandy when I was born. Apparently, she was obsessed with the musical *Grease*. The nurse told me she used to watch it all the time right up til she died. Now she's gone, I'm going to change my name back and I am going to make a claim for Kathy's inheritance.'

If I could have kissed her I would have. Why ever bother coming up with your own stories if you can just 'borrow' someone else's?

'I have two main motivations. First, I want to set up a charity to continue the environmental work I'm passionate about. Second, and most importantly, I - we - are planning to adopt a baby.'

Rachel put her arm around Noelle. Jason looked up and said 'Nice one.' No one reprimanded him about the stick. Noelle was laughing through her tears. This was beginning to feel like I was trapped in a low budget, 1980's South American soap opera.

'I intend to walk into a police station on my birthday, summer solstice, to declare myself alive. I know the papers will pick it up, especially because of my family connections. That's why the secrecy - everything that happened that night will come out. I'd like you two - Jason, Conrad - to promise me you won't resist this, react badly or seek revenge?'

She'd lost me again. It didn't matter much. I'd already cast Jennifer Lawrence as Noelle.

'Sorry - what was the middle bit? About your mum in the home?' Noelle frowned and shook the stick. Ah well, I thought. I'll just wait for the inevitable tabloid coverage to get the details, then dump the whole story over the pond and add some bling. 'Never mind. Yeah, er, cool. I'm good to go, right?'

'Conrad, you realise, you won't come out of this looking too good?' said Noelle.

I weighed it up for, maybe *five* seconds. Then, remembering the way Pippa had manipulated the Minnie story, I said, 'I'll take my chances. And enough with *the stick*.'

I turned to Jason Jenkins who had sunk into his seat and looked every bit the burnt out tosspot he was. 'Jenkins, I'd like to say it was nice meeting you again, but I can't, because it wasn't. I sincerely hope I never lay eyes on you again.'

'Likewise,' Jason growled, making eye contact with Mack, who smiled at him.

I walked across the room to Rachel. She handed me my phone. I wanted to say something *devastating*. She looked up at me expectantly.

I whispered, 'We could have been *so good* - shame.'

She and Noelle laughed awkwardly - too late, I remembered what Isobel had called her – 'that lesbian from the arts centre'; I remembered Rachel's arm around Noelle and the baby. It wasn't that she wasn't into *me*, she just wasn't into *men*! I laughed. My ego remained resolutely intact.

As Noelle was unlocking the front door, I stopped next to her. I had a rare moment of empathy. This woman had a name and identity forced onto her just as I had, but there was one crucial difference. She was now free.

'What will you do about Fran? I mean, he hurt you. None of this would have happened if he hadn't attacked you.'

She smiled at me. 'Oh Conrad, I forgave him years ago. I let go of it. But, anyway, we *are* helping him-' She looked at her watch, 'right about now actually.'

Leaving, I felt a sudden desperate need to get back to one of my kind - Pippa. I couldn't risk her getting tied up in whatever these mentalists were doing. I ran to the Gorrell Tank and got in the van then flew round to Fran's place. I parked by the garages and looked over through my binoculars. An ambulance and a police car were outside. The light in the sky was all but gone, but the streetlamps hadn't yet clicked on.

Much to my relief, Fran was carried from the building secured to a stretcher, with a crowd of neighbours watching. He was writhing about, howling like a wolf and had shaved all his hair off. His wrists were attached by cable ties to a ripped out radiator. With him were two paramedics, a doctor and two policemen. They flew off in convoy, to a special hospital, presumably. This was the 'help' Noelle was talking about. It wouldn't have taken a doctor long to realise he was a danger to himself and others. I felt immense relief and thought of poor Giles. Then thought of Pippa.

I got a text. 'Gone treasure hunting. Hope you're ok in London.'

I jumped in the V-Dub and drove to the graveyard. It was now dark and the temperature had dropped considerably.

I parked some way from Robert and Minnie Rowden's adjacent graves right next to her husband, Robert's and crept up. If I ever needed proof that my wife was a terrifying mixture of focused and stubborn, this was it. There she was, in her Boden wellies with a shovel, following the instructions in Minnie's letter, digging up her grave – looking for buried treasure.

I'd never loved her more.

I was just about to join her, when I noticed Jenkins' wife coming at her from behind - fast. The small woman kicked my wife very hard on the backside so she fell into the shallow, newly dug trench. She picked up the shovel.

I edged closer and hid behind a family tomb.

'Caught you!' the Jenkins woman hissed at Pippa.

'Huh?' said Pippa in rather a disappointingly pathetic whine.

Pippa was trying to get out of the hole but Jenkins' ex kept brandishing the spade and growling.

'I followed you from Fran's. I saw you. I bet you got a shock when the police turned up to have him sectioned, eh?'

Pippa's face was a mask of contradictions. She was struggling to assert her normal 'in control' demeanour. It was obvious that she was totally out of her depth and really quite intimidated by this bolshie harpy.

'Look, I can explain -'

'I know exactly what you're doing, you twat.'

'What? How?'

'Because it's a Whitstable *thing*.'

'*Thing*?'

'You're here digging up Robert Rowden's buried treasure, right? Well you're digging up the wrong grave for a start, but please don't let me stop you. We all know your husband stole Minnie's story – not hard to put two and two together. Everybody, *every single person in the town* knows the story of Robert Rowden's buried treasure. It's a *thing*. And it's *cursed*.'

'I don't get it.'

'No. You really, really don't get it. Minnie Rowden wasn't a "victim"! She was the one victimising her poor simple husband and son. Everyone knows what she did. She murdered him. There are old ladies in a dozen nursing homes in town that could tell you what a horrible old bullying cow that woman was. She killed Robert that night for sure. And then she made her son's life a misery afterwards. She *told* him he'd done it. On and on at him, trying to convince him he'd done it until he threw himself off his fishing boat to get away from the old witch.'

'Oh.'

'Yeah. Oh.'

'So, there *is* treasure in there then?'

Jenkins wife moved closer with the spade.

'Blaine got those letters from Joanne Kemp right?'

Pippa gulped and shrugged her shoulders.

'She's my second cousin. The moment she heard your slimy husband had turned it into a film, she told everyone. She shouldn't have given him the letters, but you know - she's a bit thick. She told everyone there was another letter in there too - one she didn't read. We could all guess what was in that one. The old bat was constantly spreading rumours about herself and Robert - his treasure trove. She just loved the attention. The whole town know where C.K. Blaine got his story from - and the whole town know he got his facts all wrong. Minnie used you.'

Pippa looked about her wildly as Tracy edged closer with the shovel.

'Now, unless you want to end up in that grave with that evil old witch, I suggest you get the fuck out of it and fill it in, you disrespectful bint. Your sort has taken enough from this town, you're not having whatever is in there.' Pippa's face went white. 'Then, I suggest you take that tosser of a husband of yours, and your family, and you *fuck off back to London*!'

Pippa clambered out and Jenkins' wife handed her the spade. Pippa started shovelling fast. Then stopped.

'Hang on a minute. If we got the story all wrong and she *did* kill her husband, why did she write the letter saying it was her son and do herself in?'

'A state of mind I should think you're all too familiar with. Denial. The old battle-axe knew it was her fault - knew she had two men's blood on her hands. She wanted to remain innocent, even beyond her own death. She just wanted to get away with it. So, well done Mr. and Mrs. Blaine. All that film *Flood* served to do was cover the truth up even more. Now *shovel.*'

Pippa finished the job. Jenkins' wife grabbed the spade from her. She stared at Pippa, then simply gave her head a firm nod to one side and said, 'Jog on.'

Pippa scurried away. I could hear her sobbing with fear. It was so unlike her it was almost distressing. I caught up with her, grabbed her and bundled her into the van.

'Christ! Did you hear all of that? Who the hell was she?' she said in a shrill voice, clearly surprised to see me. Then in a much more forceful, deeper growl, 'Why aren't you in London?'

I gave her a reassuring glance, then drove home as fast as I could.

'Pippa - we are getting out of here with the girls first thing tomorrow. We can stay in London until it's time to go to Cannes. That woman was Jason Jenkin's ex-wife.'

She was so shaken, she didn't argue. I left her to pack and I slipped out of the house under the pretence of getting the van ready. Instead, I went back up to the cemetery.

I used a long-handled beach shovel the girls had played with a few summers ago, knowing the soil had already been well dug over and would be loose. I only had to go down about three feet and my spade made a dull *thunk* on the top of something solid. I pulled it out and put the box in my inside pocket, then hurriedly re-filled Minnie's grave.

I decided not to tell Pippa until a later date. When I got home she was in bed snoring loudly and had left me a note.

'Sorry. I let you down. Left unfinished business.'

She meant Jenkins. There were two very good reasons why I couldn't care less and besides, in two days' time, we'd all be in the South of France.

****

Pippa had the window seat and stretched her solid legs out before her, kicking off her mules. We were in the Business Class on our British Airways flight to Cannes and Miranda was in Economy, right at the back. Isobel had refused to come. She had become so hysterical, Pippa had slapped her, hard. For once I could see my daughter's point. She had her exams. They were important. After much tense debate, Pippa capitulated and let her stay. She was not to answer the door or speak to anyone until I arrived back after the festival. She agreed.

Pippa lifted her flute of champagne and I lifted mine. We chinked glasses.

She sighed and looked at me with affection. 'We got out.'

We got away with it, more like, I thought.

'Only because of you!' I beamed.

'Why didn't you go to London that day like we arranged? What were you up to?'

'It doesn't matter now.' I said lazily, patting her hand. I was never going to tell her about the revelations at Beacon House. 'I'm so glad the police got to Fran's before you did anything. Who'd want that on their conscience?'

Pippa's mouth puckered slightly. '*Did* they though?'

'What do you mean?'

'Who do you think tied him to the radiator? Who do you think shaved that revolting hair off?'

I looked at her with incredulity. She sipped her bubbly and stared out of the window.

'What else did you do, Pippa?'

'Like I said, its better you don't know. It's been taken care of.' She squeezed my leg.

I thought about the box in my inside pocket – reason number one. Then, I thought about the other reason I had for not caring.

'Oh, guess what? I might have an idea for my next screenplay.'

She sat upright. 'Really? Please tell me this is all your own material.'

'Absolutely.'

'Well, what is it?'

'It a story about the protest movement, concentrating on a new age traveller who ends up as the leader of an elite group. She has a tragic past, mother mentally disabled, lost inheritance - regained. She survives, triumphs. I'm thinking of setting it in the U.S.'

'Why?'

Why? So I am a few thousand miles from the real Noelle.

'I'm thinking,' I leaned in close and whispered in her ear, 'we should move to L.A.'

Pippa squealed and put her arms around my neck.

'Colin, sorry, I mean *Conrad* - you are a *genius* and I love you.' She kissed my face all over, like an excited puppy.

I waited until she had nodded off after lunch and I squeezed myself into the cramped toilet. I took the box out of my inside pocket, feeling excitement rising. I held the object over the sink and licked my lips as I unravelled the cloth it was wrapped in, knocking the dried mud off.

The object inside was an old cigar box, presumably from the 40s or 50s from the era the treasure was found. I prized the box open. It smelled wonderfully musty. I poked about, feeling for metal, looking for a glint of gold, but all that lay inside was an off-white shell, a white feather and a folded piece of paper.

I felt my insides plummet with disappointment.

I opened it.

It said: 'Until you understand the meaning of the objects within this box, you will never be free of the curse of Robert Rowden.'

Shit, I thought. Stupid me! *Real* treasure would never have got through airport security. And now, on top of everything, I was cursed! I felt a wave of self-pity and hopelessness wash over me and I sat down heavily on the tiny loo. Minnie, the manipulative old harridan had done a right number on me. Joanne had warned that the letters were 'dirty'.

I stared at the two white objects. The shell looked familiar in type. Maybe it was the champagne, the altitude, or the vista of hot, Mediterranean beaches, but to me, the shell looked like an exotic conch, albeit a much smaller, grubbier

273

version. I tugged my phone awkwardly from my pocket in the cramped toilet and hurriedly Googled 'symbolism of conch shell'. I scanned the various hippy and Buddhist websites, picking out phrases, gaining a vague impression: 'signifies truthful speech…a prosperous journey…the spiral motif – signifies infinity…the human journey of life…the beginning of existence…strength.'

I turned the cool spikey object over in my hand and remembered where I'd seen representations of a conch shell before: a small lino cut of a similar shell on the wall at Beacon House, hung just above the very place Noelle was sitting when she told her sad tale.

Then I imagined Jennifer Lawrence playing young Noelle in the dramatized version. She was tied to a tree with baling twine, her tongue pierced, her hair bleached by the sun, her chest was heaving as she shouted slogans while the U.S. police came to handcuff her. But something wasn't right. The other object seemed to suggest something else. Something more negative.

A white feather.

It could only mean one thing: I was a coward. The big question was how did the two objects relate to each other? Until I worked that out, I was under Robert Rowden's curse.

I slipped back into my seat and I looked at Pippa's saggy profile. Her nostrils were gently flaring as she snored and I thought - if I'm cursed, and if I manage to get us the fuck out of Whitstable, there's one thing this bitch is going to have to give me. The one thing she took that really *hurt*.

My beard.

I felt the hard edge of the box deep in my pocket. I thought of Whitstable. Not so much a quaint fishing village in my imagination. More like a bizarre, nightmare theme park. A Las Vegas version of its real, unknowable self.

I realised then, fully, just how much I bitterly regretted the day I'd moved down from London.

Chapter 18

Home

June 2015

Jason Jenkins

It was a beautiful summer solstice. Jason Jenkins liked to end up at The Street at about 11.30am to meet his Tracy while she was on a shift break from the old people's home.

It was a magical morning. The tide was right out, as far as it could go. The light was luminous; the sea and the cloudless sky merged in a thick azure belt. Mercifully, the Isle of Sheppey, Jason thought with amusement, had almost disappeared in the mist and ozone. He sniggered when he remembered over-hearing some D.F.L.s confidently identifying the tiny island as 'the Danish Peninsula', and continued along the Tankerton prom.

Jason wandered along, pushing his Serco rubbish cart plugged into his iPod with a grabber in his hand, attempting to pick up all the litter in time with the beat to 'Outer Space' by The Prodigy. It was a challenge. He knew he was getting looks from the D.F.L.s but he didn't care. It was *his* beach.

Tracy was sitting on the sea wall eating her lunch. She'd been on a shift since 5am at the care home. He approached her just as the tune dropped, so he treated her to a bit of old skool rave dancing around his beach cleaning cart. She started laughing so much she rolled onto her back and held her hand over her mouth so her sandwich stayed put.

He parked the cart, ran up the steps and sat on the wall next to her, aware again of how much history, how many former versions of himself had been in this place before. He glanced at three lads sparking up a huge doobie a few beach huts away, laughed and nodded at them. He knew all their mums.

'Gis' a kiss, beautiful.' He grabbed her and gave her a squeeze and a kiss on the lips, catching a bit of tuna mayo. 'Right fucking mess on the beach this morning. They've burnt right through three breakwaters now with their barbeques. Fucking D.F.L.s. I mean, don't they have bins in that London?'

Tracy gave him a hug.

'Jace – look! You work *here*!' She spread her arms wide. 'Not on a building site with your bad back. Not in a shit office somewhere in a shirt and tie. *Here*. Stop moaning.'

'It's just the D.F-'

'Jason Jenkins, where do you think your great grandmother was from?'

'Er. Here?'

'Bermondsey. South East London. She came down here to work in service in one of the big houses around about, Doddington, somewhere like that.'

'Yeah, but, that's on my mum's side, isn't it? I'm proper Whissaple on me dad's side.'

'Yeah? Where do you think your dad's great, great, great, well a lot of greats, grandma comes from, Jace?'

Jason laughed. She always was cleverer than him.

'Outer Space?'

'No. From France or Belgium. Something like that. Huguenots. Came over to get away from a big war or something. Refugees. *Asylum* seekers. Said last week in the papers, most people in this bit of England are 48% French.'

'I'm not bloody *French*! How do you know this shit?'

Tracy shrugged. She was always on the internet looking up this and that. Family trees, local history. All that crap. She jumped off the wall and started walking backwards up the prom.

'Of course *my* family have been here loads longer than *yours*!'

'Right! That's it!'

Jason abandoned his cart and started chasing Tracy up The Street trying to smack her bottom. She was a lot fitter than him, having now fully recovered. She slowed down as the water petered out. They were both breathing hard.

'That's the point, Jace.' said Tracy, once she'd recovered her breath. 'No one is really from anywhere, not if you go back far enough. People here, they pick the side of the family that's been here longest and they stick to it. I do it too. We're all just trying to make an identity for ourselves, I reckon. But it's not real, and actually, it just doesn't matter. People are just people.'

She put her arms around his neck and they kissed. Jason held Tracy tight and looked out over the horizon to where Sheppey was almost visible.

'Shame about Fran, really.' Tracy said, pulling away slightly. 'I suppose they had to assume he'd done it himself, but really, who would honestly believe he'd been injecting himself with Botox? He was hardly known for his youthful looks. It would be like Keith Richards having a chemical peel - what would be the point?' Jason smiled sadly at her. 'You know they say he'd injected so much, his face was too paralysed, by the time he got to hospital, to tell them either way. That Blaine woman did it. I'm sure.'

Jason knew the truth. Mack had found him at the pub on the beach, the day after Fran died of pneumonia, following several days of paralysis and breathing problems. He had bought Jason a drink and had fixed him with a serious, but fatherly look.

'Do you remember that story about the bomber blowing up his own legs – and how friends and foe came together to craft a unique punishment?' Jason nodded. 'Well let's just say Fran has had his comeuppance. There's no need for this to go any further. Do we understand each other?' Jason nodded that they did.

And that had been that.

Jason wrapped his arms a little tighter around Tracy.

She said, 'Jace, Noelle called to say she'll be telling the police it was Fran that Blaine followed. That it was him that torched those huts, not you. You're in the clear now. The way I see it Jace, if that cow did finish him off, she's done you a favour.'

Jason chewed his lip looking pensive, then nodded. He already knew he'd been let off the hook. Mack had told him, but it was on the agreement that he would never, ever set fire to anything more dangerous than a barbecue, so long as he lived. He'd reluctantly agreed.

'My mum always did say "It'll all come out in the wash". Trace, I'm really glad Rachel finally realised who she was and who she should be with. She's made too much of a sacrifice staying apart from Noelle just to protect her, if you ask me. I hope they get their baby.' said Jason.

'It worked out alright, didn't it?'

Jason kissed his ex-wife again, then took her hand, leading her slowly back to shore.

'Listen, I never told you this before. Remember I told Blaine's wife Robert Rowden's treasure was a Whistable "thing", so she'd think it was in the grave? Well, I didn't mention to her that it was also a massive wind-up. That Minnie had spread the rumour it was in poor Robert's grave since the 60s. I failed to comment that over the years it just turned into an elaborate laugh that parents played on their children to shit them up. Your Dad got you good when you dug the grave up, didn't he?'

'Yeah, I was eight. Got a good hiding too, for being so disrespectful.' Jason chuckled.

'What did you get in the box?'

'A rusty padlock and a rosary bead. I honestly thought the message was that I'd get locked up for bunking Sunday school. I never found out it was a wind up until years later. You think they took it, then?'

'I *know* they did. Weird Bob the grave digger watched Blaine take the box. Remember I said Blaine's wife was digging up Minnie's grave, not Robert's? There must have been something in that other letter Joanne didn't read. They, or at least, *he* thinks they are *cursed*.'

'Nice one.' Jason laughed as he inhaled on his e-cigarette.

'Minnie had Bob on a backhander since she started the whole treasure thing, all those years ago. She lost interest, but kept paying him. He told me she still got a sick pleasure from knowing her poor husband's grave was being disturbed. Bob told me, to start with, she always decided what should go in the box. She liked religious stuff - like your rosary bead, that sort of thing. When she got too old to bother, Bob chose what went in.

'His wife had just died and left every surface of their house decorated with tiny glass ornaments - little animals, insects - cheap crap. He'd always hated them, so rather than chuck them out, he used them as Robert's "cursed objects". Every time the box got dug up, he replaced it with a completely random pair of meaningless glass creatures stuffed in a new box for the next gullible mugs to uncover. He took great pleasure in scaring the crap out of the little shits that vandalised his graveyard. He said it was the only thing that made grave digging worthwhile.'

Jason laughed. 'I'd love to have seen Blaine's face when he opened the box. Do you know what Weird Bob put in it?'

Tracy snorted. 'That's the best bit. Bob had run out of glass tat. He's retiring soon, but after seeing me and Blaine's wife having words at Minnie's grave, he thought he'd do the curse thing one more time. He found a tatty old seagull feather by his runner beans and a whelk shell in his compost. He used an old cigar box his wife had kept her needles and thread in and buried it before Blaine came back. Bob loved a whelk.'

Jason laughed hard and hugged Tracy. 'A smelly old whelk!' he said. 'Trace, do you think Robert did ever find actual treasure?'

'Christ knows, but I'd be interested to find out how come Bob can afford a brand new static home in Seasalter.'

They both laughed.

Jason sighed and stopped, turning his wife to look at the town.

'Trace, it might be a bit shit round the edges, Whitstable, but it's ours.' They both looked at the massive funnel of the aggregate processing plant, churning a great plume of smog into the otherwise perfect sky, and smiled.

'It is,' she said, wrapping her arms tight around his middle.

Jason pulled away from her. Something moving had snared his attention, flickering in his peripheral vision. The stoners had nicked his Serco cart and were running away along the prom with one of them urban surfing unsteadily on the top.

'Little shits. I'm going to kill them!' Jason started to run after them but Tracy soon caught up and stood in front of him.

'Oit! You'd have done the exact same thing, or worse, at that age.'

He leaned forward, put his hands on his knees and breathed hard.

'Yeah. You're probably right.' He wiped the sweat from his brow.

'Just call it in. We can have a full hour together then. Besides, have you decided what hobby we should take up?'

'Er, crown green bowls?' Jason thought of the cheap bar.

Tracy shook her head. 'I'm not prepared to keep your trousers that white.'

He knew this was the massive compromise he would have to make for twenty years of acting like a cock. He had no choice. This time, he was actually prepared to do anything to keep her. She leaned in close, hooking her arm through his as they sauntered back to the beach.

'Ballroom dancing,' she stated. She leaned in to his ear and whispered, 'You're a lovely mover, Jason Jenkins.' He stopped dead. 'And besides, I'd love to see you in spandex.' Jason laughed and they walked on.

'Jason, look.'

They stopped right in front of the beach huts where it had all happened that night.

'What do you feel now it's all out in the open? It's all in the past?'

The memories were elusive, distant, and mercifully irrelevant. He looked at Beacon House and smiled.

'Nothing. Nothing bad anyway. I don't even want to kill C.K. Blaine anymore.' Tracy looked up at him, frowning. 'I know. I'm surprised myself. It was something Mack said.' Tracy nodded for him to go on. 'He told me he never did believe in revenge. He reckons it just means you're still obsessing about the person that wronged you. He told me about some old writer and said "the best revenge is to live well". It just made sense. I *am* living well now. I have you.'

Tracy kissed him. 'I'm all yours.'

'Trace? Where do you think Blaine is now? C.K. Blaine, the tosser that stole my life.'

Tracy tipped her head to one side, then smiled at him with a wicked glint in her eye.

'Oh, I know where they are, darlin'. They're on their way to *Hell*.'

****

C.K. Blaine

I was drunk on champagne, trying to push down the feelings of dread as Pippa gripped my arm, leaning on me to get a better view of the Atlantic Ocean beneath. We'd realised our ultimate dream - flying off to a new life in L.A. Yet I couldn't ignore the intense, suffocating pain in my chest that made me want to jump out of the window.

The shell and the feather were all I had thought of in Cannes. Every time I heard the cawing of a gull or the beat of a wing in the air, I felt a choking sense of doom. I snatched every moment to research conch shells; their meaning, their significance. I learnt about the sound a conch shell makes when blown: the atavistic 'om', meant to mimic man's first utterances. I shuddered whenever I heard trumpets or horns. Ambient lift music wafting in hotel lobbies or emanating from pavement jazz cafés freaked me out. It was as though the conch was calling me. But the more I tried to see the link between the two things the further it eluded me. How one object, juxtaposed to the next could influence its meaning, I could not fathom. Until I did, it felt as though the giant form of Robert was shadowing me in every waking moment.

I was convinced the curse had worked and had specifically shape-shifted into the bulky form squashed claustrophobically near me - the ambitious, murderous Pippa. I would always be trapped, pushed by her determination to be better, richer and more successful. Forced to rely on stealing countless life-stories for my ideas again and again and I knew I would never be strong enough to break away. She had single handedly crafted my identity and now I didn't even know who I really was - I would forever just be her helpless puppet.

My feeble grasp of my own identity and, in fact, my plans for the future of my DNA, had taken a further knock when I'd stealthily returned to the cottage after returning from Cannes. Pippa had point-blank refused to go back to Whitstable. I was to go, pack, get Isobel and return to London, without being seen.

****

Isobel had let me in without uttering a word then let me cook for her. She withdrew silently and ate in front of the television, alone. After dinner, I felt tense, anticipating a confrontation. I began washing up our plates with my back turned to her, as she leaned on the kitchen counter.

'Leave that,' she had said, 'I'll do it later. Turn around Dad.'

I froze. There was a calm assertiveness about the way she addressed me which lent her the upper hand. I slowly wiped the suds from my hands and turned to look at her.

'When Mum moved to London,' said Isobel, quietly. 'I realised that wasn't when she really left me. She left me a long time ago and I hadn't even noticed. Maybe I've never really had a mother at all. Not the sort I needed, anyway.'

Isobel wasn't looking at me. She was curling a long strand of hair around her finger checking for split ends. She was slouched against the worktop, her other hand deep in the front pocket of an enormous hoodie. A man's hoodie. Joe Jenkins' hoodie.

'Once she had gone and I was alone here with you, I also realised that I didn't know you at all. I still don't know who you are.'

She looked up and I found that once my eyes met hers, I could only hold her gaze for a matter of seconds. I didn't want to be reminded that we had the same blue-green irises, the same intense rather serious gaze at a resting level. I realised she was trying to really talk to me, to open up a longstanding problem - our lack of intimacy, communication and kinship. A gaping hole in our relationship that I was aware of, but resistant to doing anything about. Instead of waking up, facing the uncomfortable truths and letting her get under my skin, I shrugged. How could I possibly tell her that I didn't know who I was either?

'Right up until your friend fell in the harbour, I thought I'd give you a chance. I thought I wanted to finally get to know you. Then she moved back. You let her move back.'

Isobel smiled and straightened to her full height. I tried to feel involved but I just felt detached. To change her opinion

283

of me was an insurmountable challenge. I wasn't sure what was happening, but I knew the outcome of the conversation would be negative - for me, at least. Isobel's young life flashed through my muddled mind, fast forwarding to this moment; the very instant she had decided to break away. It was happening here and now, and yet I was powerless to stop her. I just couldn't find the words.

'I'm not coming to L.A. I have exams until July. You two seem to have forgotten that. I'm staying here and I'm going to advertise for foreign student housemates.'

'You're too young.'

'I'm sixteen. I'll be out by August. You can do what the hell you want with this damp hell-hole after that.'

'I command you as your father and the adult with parental responsibility to come with me to London, then to L.A. and *no more arguments*!' Even as I shouted it, I knew it sounded feeble. The thought of Pippa's reaction when I arrived at the London flat without Isobel had spurred me into a false show of dominance.

Isobel smiled at me and slowly lifted the pocket of the oversized hoodie to her shoulder to reveal a swollen expanse of midriff protruding beneath her cropped vest. My first thought was simply that sadly, yet inevitably, she shared her mother's endomorph body shape. She'd apparently reached that critical age when she was going to naturally balloon, never again to enjoy the toned, svelte body she'd had the luxury of inhabiting for the first sixteen years. I smiled back sympathetically, baffled as to where the conversation was going and why being fat would help her side of the argument.

I shrugged, quizzically.

Isobel rolled her eyes and let out a mean laugh.

'I'm pregnant, *dickwad*!'

I stared at the bump. My mouth fell slack. Instantly the vision of Joe Jenkins' weasily face erupted, laughing before my eyes.

She nodded, slowly. Lowering the hoodie back down. Understanding the fresh horror on my face.

'That's right. It's his. I'm keeping it. He doesn't know yet, but he will. I'm not sure when. After my exams, maybe.' Her face betrayed no emotion whatsoever. 'From August, I'm going to live with Grandma and Granddad in Essex. Your parents. Remember them?'

She stopped to let this information sink in, her eyebrows arched, maybe expecting a reaction of shock, an objection. She was right about something: I could barely remember them. My parents. I struggled to take all the information in, put it into an order of what I should be more alarmed about.

'Why, Isobel? That's all I want to know.' I wasn't even sure if I did.

'I love him.'

I put both hands to my face and dragged them upwards, hard, combing my fingers through my hair.

'When is it due?'

'He. When is *he* due? November. Your parents know everything. They want to support me. Have you got anything to say?' Her voice reminded me of Rachel. It was clipped, efficient. Completely devoid of compassion.

'Your mother is going to fucking murder me.'

'Don't tell her then.'

'What?'

'Simply don't tell her. It's not like you've got a problem with blurring the truth is it *Colin*? And yes, I know all about that too.'

I felt a rush of nostalgia. I missed Colin. I felt jealous Isobel was able to go back, to inhabit what had been my house, with my parents. I thought of the beautifully wrapped Christmas and birthday gifts for the girls that arrived, without fail, every year. The card, albeit brief but nethertheless sincere, which I received every year on my birthday. I felt queasy and I realised I was homesick. But however much I missed me – the real me – or them, reconciliation was out of the question. Pippa forbade it.

'But – what do I say?'

'Tell her a partial truth. I'm living with them. Then I'm going to Art College in Essex in September. Just miss the whole baby bit out of it. She won't care and she'll never visit me while I'm with them. I'll be safe enough.' She walked forward and put a firm hand on my shoulder. Less a gesture of affection, more a demonstration of power. 'I'll stay in touch with Miranda - she's my sister. But as for us, for the foreseeable future, we're finished.'

'Why?'

'Because you are crap. You had a chance to get away from her, to be yourself and do something - real. Then you let her control you again. Being part of Joe's family made me realise what I'd been missing. I've had it with the both of you. Now, I suggest you do one and leave me to live my own life.'

She had flicked her long hair over her shoulder, flared her nostrils and pointed at the front door.

I shrugged again, and left, attempting to appear more nonchalant than I was really feeling. In reality, my heart burned with a new impassioned hatred that made my body shake with adrenaline. Jason Jenkins. My blood relative.

It was unthinkable.

I'd thought Pippa would go mental when I told her our fabricated version of the truth, but instead she barely looked up from her phone and said, 'Probably for the best. Let her get on with it. She'll be running back when she realises a crap degree in Art doesn't get her a job she can live on.'

****

As the plane soared, I stretched my legs and gulped my bubbly. I'd barely slept since seeing my pregnant daughter and I couldn't eat.

286

My daughter: An innocent vessel; a host being sucked dry by an evil parasite!

My plan was to get as wasted as possible and sleep, just to put Isobel and the fact that she was growing Satan's baby in her womb, out of my thoughts. I gulped down another glass full of champagne.

As the alcohol began to relax me, I turned my attention to my new project - the story of the adopted girl who took on the mighty force of the U.S. military to save the planet. I imagined Lawrence again, in cut-off jeans, an ankle bracelet and a nose ring, tied to a tree with bicycle chains, waving her fist at the U.S. Marshalls as they came to arrest her. Then I thought of the ultimate prize - an Oscar.

As I imagined just how I'd write the scenes, a theory I had long forgotten emerged in my mind: The Kuleshov Effect.

Of course! The meaning of the conch and the feather wasn't about connection; it was about sequencing! Russian filmmaker Kuleshov proved he could control the way his audience interpreted a sequence, depending how he ordered the images. When he screened a shot of a smiling man followed by a shot of a bowl of soup, the audience believed the man looked hungry. But when Kuleshov swapped that bowl of soup for a lady in a bikini, the audience agreed he looked like lecherous old creep, despite using the exact same smiling shot of the man.

I thought back to all I had read about the conch and its meaning - man's journey, courage, truth. Now, side by side with the conch, the feather's meaning was miraculously transformed. No longer did the message mean I was a coward. No! It meant I had to be brave. A feather that symbolised freedom, flight, liberty. The lino cut of the conch, above Noelle's head in Beacon House resonated. It was a sign. *Beacon* House! This had to mean I was to be a beacon of courage and truth and go on my journey to tell the world Noelle's story. Yes!

Not only would I go ahead and act out what I would now call The Prophecy of the Conch, I would make it my emblem. Jennifer Lawrence as Noelle would have a conch tattoo on her ankle, or maybe somewhere more revealing. It would become my motif. Always appearing fleetingly in every film. An enigmatic indicator of the struggle I had overcome at the hands of the lunatic people of Whitstable. The struggle, thanks to the virulent pikey seed of Joe Jenkins that I would have to continue to fight for all eternity, as long as my blood line continued.

I looked at my wife and she pouted, wrinkled her nose then snuggled down for a sleep. A private smile spread across my face. I had invaluable information about our daughter and I had no intention of telling her for as long as was humanly possible. I enjoyed the temporary sense of power I had over Pippa, even if it only masked the underlying misery at my daughter's condition.

While Pippa slept, I opened my wallet and thumbed out an old photo of me, Colin, aged about nine with Pete and Shirley, my parents, in our back garden. I swallowed the lump in my throat and resolved to contact them in secret. I wasn't prepared to 'do one' and leave Isobel to live her own life, however sickened I was that she was forever linked to that Neanderthal. She was my daughter and I had a grandfatherly right to assert. A genetic legacy to protect. And besides, there was always the miniscule chance that Isobel might actually need her old dad in the coming months. Even if she did think I was a dickwad.

What did give me deep joy was the other matter: I had managed to negotiate on an issue that was important to me, in exchange for achieving the move to America - my facial hair.

I relaxed back in my seat. As I took another gulp of my champagne, finally beginning to feel drowsy, I wondered, optimistically, if Hollywood was ready for a man with a really big beard.

Batting away visions of burning beach huts at dawn, wrestling with my abhorrence to my own wife and compromising with the truth that I was a talentless fraud, I began to feel optimism. The spectre of Robert vanished and the power of the conch gave my ambitions a satisfying validation.

Whilst I knew I would never be free of Jason Jenkins, I'd succeeded in gleefully deserting and transcending Whitstable, with its small town back-stabbing and abysmal jolliness.

Here was I, C.K. Blaine, emigrating to the movie capital of the world – to live by palm trees, bask in constant sunshine and be surrounded by very hot women. And all the while, as my career took off to new heights like an Exocet missile, I would exercise my re-claimed masculine right to do the only thing that genuinely articulated the true me.

I got to grow back my magnificent beard.

Boom! Shake the room! I had arrived.

6913446R00171

Printed in Germany
by Amazon Distribution
GmbH, Leipzig